Crochet
Private Collection™

the Needlecraft Shop™

Editorial Director ~ Donna Robertson
Design Director ~ Fran Rohus
Production/Photography Director ~ Ange Van Arman

❧ *Editorial* ☙

Senior Editor ~ Jennifer Christiansen McClain
Editor ~ Sharon Lothrop
Associate Editors ~ Lyne Pickens, Jana Robertson, Trudy Atteberry

❧ *Production* ☙

Production Manager ~ Joanne Gonzalez
Book Design/Production Assistant ~ Diane Simpson
Color Specialist ~ Betty Radla
Production Coordinator ~ Glenda Chamberlain

❧ *Photography* ☙

Photography Manager ~ Scott Campbell
Photographers ~ Russell Chaffin, Keith Godfrey
Photography Coordinator/Stylist ~ Ruth Whitaker
Assistant Photo Stylist ~ Beth Augustine

❧ *Product Design* ☙

Design Coordinator ~ Tonya Flynn

❧ *Business* ☙

CEO ~ John Robinson
Vice President/Marketing ~ Greg Deily

❧ *Credits* ☙

Sincerest thanks to all the designers, manufacturers and other
professionals whose dedication has made this book possible.

Library of Congress Cataloging-in-Publication Data
ISBN: 1-57367-106-1
First Printing 1999
Library of Congress Catalog Card Number: 98-66977
Published and Distributed by:
The Needlecraft Shop, LLC, Big Sandy, Texas 75755
Printed in the United States of America.

Cover clockwise from top left:
Poinsettia Garden, pattern begins on page 119;
Forever Friends, pattern begins on page 104;
Berry Ripples, pattern begins on page 50;
Simply Sarah, pattern begins on page 139.

Dear Friends,

Surrounding ourselves with the things we like most is what collecting is all about. Whether it be an assortment of trinkets or a houseful of antiques, we enjoy having those items around us that warm our hearts and homes. For lovers of needlecraft, collecting patterns is a common trait, as we love having that well-stocked library to pull from whenever we get the urge to create something new. That's why this special book is one you'll treasure.

Created for the needlecraft connoisseur, Crochet Private Collection is a one-of-a-kind find. Filled with a hand-picked selection of our most requested projects, it is sure to be a volume you'll turn to time and time again. You'll have everyone asking where you get your wonderfully inspiring designs, but you won't have to tell them your secret.

Start collecting compliments today when you choose your next project from this incredible collection of crochet for your private enjoyment.

Happy Stitching,

Jennifer

Table of Contents

Sun-Kissed Gardens

Playful Pets

Christmas Splendor

Gifts & Goodies

Kitchen Charm

The kitchen is the heart of the home, so it's only fitting that you decorate it with a fresh batch of crochet delicacies made straight from your heart. Family and friends alike will appreciate the chance to savor your culinary expertise enhanced by the warmth of hand-made kitchen accessories. Whatever your taste, these projects are a sure recipe for success.

Sunshine Set

Designed by *Jocelyn Sass*

JAR COVER

Rnd 1: With G hook and white, ch 2, 6 sc in 2nd ch from hook (6 sc).

Rnd 2: 2 sc in each st around (12).

Rnd 3: (Sc in next st, 2 sc in next st) around (18).

Rnd 4: (Sc in each of next 2 sts, 2 sc in next st) around (24).

Rnd 5: (Sc in each of next 3 sts, 2 sc in next st) around (30).

Rnd 6: (Sc in next 4 sts, 2 sc in next st) around (36).

Rnd 7: Working this rnd in **back lps** only, ch 2, hdc in each st around, join with sl st in top of ch-2.

Rnds 8-17: Ch 2, hdc in each st around, join.

Rnd 18: Ch 3, skip next st, (hdc in next st, ch 1, skip next st) around, join with sl st in 2nd ch of ch-3 (18 hdc, 18 ch sps).

Rnd 19: Ch 3, 4 dc in same hdc, skip next ch sp, sl st in next hdc, skip next ch sp, (5 dc in next hdc, skip next ch sp, sl st in next hdc, skip next ch sp) around, join with sl st in top of ch-3, fasten off.

BASKET TRIM

Rnd 1: With G hook and white, ch 121, 3 sc in 2nd ch from hook, sc in each ch across with 6 sc in last ch; working on opposite side of ch, sc in each ch across with 3 sc in last ch, join with sl st in first sc (248 dc).

Rnd 2: Ch 3, 4 dc in same st, skip next st, sl st in next st, skip next st, (5 dc in next st, skip next st, sl st in next st, skip next st) around, join with sl st in top of ch-3, fasten off.

TOWEL TOPPER

NOTE: Cut towel in half crosswise; if desired, zigzag raw edges to secure.

Row 1: With C hook and white, place lp on hook; with right side of towel facing you, starting at **right corner,** push hook through towel, yo, draw lp through, complete as sc; evenly space 37 more sc across, turn (38 sc).

Rows 2-4: With G hook, ch 1, sc in each st across, turn.

Row 5: Ch 1, sc first 2 sts tog, (sc next 2 sts tog) across, turn (19).

Rows 6-9: Ch 1, sc in each st across, turn.

Rows 10-13: Ch 1, sc first 2 sts tog, sc in each st across to last 2 sts, sc last 2 sts tog, turn, ending with 11 sts in last row.

Rows 14-18: Ch 1, sc in each st across, turn.

Rows 19-20: Ch 1, sc first 2 sts tog, sc in each st across to last 2 sts, sc last 2 sts tog, turn (9, 7).

Rows 21-42: Ch 1, sc in each st across, turn.

Rows 43-44: Ch 1, sc first 2 sts tog, sc in each st across to last 2 sts, sc last 2 sts tog, turn (5, 3). At end of last row, fasten off.

continued on page 11

Pumpkin Caddy

Designed by *Kathy Wigington*

Size: 6" tall.

Materials: Worsted-weight yarn — 3½ oz. orange and small amount brown; polyester fiberfill; tapestry needle; G crochet hook or size needed to obtain gauge.

Gauge: Rnd 1 of Pumpkin Outside is 1" across.

Note: Use orange unless otherwise stated.

Skill Level: ☆ Easy

PUMPKIN
Outside

Rnd 1: Ch 5, sl st in first ch to form ring, ch 3, 11 dc in ring, join with sl st in top of ch-3 (12 dc).

Rnd 2: Ch 3, dc in same st, 2 dc in each st around, join (24).

Rnd 3: Ch 3, 2 dc in next st, (dc in next st, 2 dc in next st) around, join (36).

Rnd 4: Ch 3, dc in next st, 2 dc in next st, (dc in

each of next 2 sts, 2 dc in next st) around, join (48).

Rnd 5: Ch 3, dc in each of next 2 sts, 2 dc in next st, (dc in each of next 3 sts, 2 dc in next st) around, join (60).

Rnd 6: Ch 3, dc in each of next 3 sts, 2 dc in next st, (dc in next 4 sts, 2 dc in next st) around, join (72).

Rnds 7-12: Ch 3, dc in each st around, join.

Rnd 13: Ch 3, dc in each of next 3 sts, dc next 2 sts tog, (dc in next 4 sts, dc next 2 sts tog) around, join, fasten off (60).

Liner

Rnds 1-5: Repeat same rnds of Pumpkin Outside.

Rnds 6-11: Ch 3, dc in each st around, join.

Rnd 12: Ch 3, dc in each of next 2 sts, dc next 2 sts tog, (dc in each of next 3 sts, dc next 2 sts tog) around, join, fasten off (48).

Assembly

Lightly stuff sides and bottom of Pumpkin Outside, place Liner inside. To **join,** working through both thicknesses in sts of rnd 13 on Outside and rnd 12 on Liner, join with sc in any st, easing to fit, sc in each st around, join with sl st in first sc, fasten off.

For **shaping,** working through both thicknesses, using Backstitch (see page 159), embroider a line from rnd 1 to top, secure, fasten off. Repeat 7 more times evenly spaced around Pumpkin.

LID
Outside

Rnd 1: Starting at **stem,** with brown, ch 2, 7 sc in 2nd ch from hook, join with sl st in first sc (7 sc).

Rnd 2: Working this rnd in **back lps** only, ch 3, dc in each st around, join with sl st in top of ch-3.

Rnd 3: Working this rnd in **both lps,** ch 3, dc in each st around, join.

Rnd 4: Working this rnd in **back lps** only, ch 3, dc in same st, 2 dc in each st around, join, fasten off (14).

Rnd 5: Join orange with sl st in any st, ch 3, dc in same st, 2 dc in each st around, join (28).

Rnd 6: Ch 3, 2 dc in next st, (dc in next st, 2 dc in next st) around, join (42).

Rnd 7: Ch 3, dc in next st, 2 dc in next st, (dc in each of next 2 sts, 2 dc in next st) around, join (56).

Rnd 8: Ch 3, dc in each of next 2 sts, 2 dc in next st, (dc in each of next 3 sts, 2 dc in next st) around, join, fasten off (70).

Liner

Rnds 1-5: Repeat same rnds of Pumpkin Outside. At end of last rnd, fasten off.

Assembly

To **join,** working through both thicknesses in sts of rnd 8 on Lid Outside and rnd 5 of Lid Liner, with Lid Outside facing you, join with sc in any st, easing to fit, sc in each st around stuffing lightly before closing, join with sl st in first sc, fasten off.

For **shaping,** working through all thicknesses, using Backstitch, embroider a line from rnd 5 to rnd 8, secure, fasten off. Repeat 7 more times evenly spaced around Lid. ✄

Sunshine Set

continued from page 9

Row 45: Working across outer edge of Towel Holder; for **edging,** with right side of towel facing you, starting at beginning of row 1, join white with sc in end of row 1, sc in end of each row and in each st around to opposite end of row 1, fasten off.

Row 46: With No. 6 steel hook and yellow, join with sc in first st, (ch 4, sc in next st) across, fasten off.

FLOWER (make 3)

Rnd 1: With No. 6 steel hook and yellow, ch 4, sl st in first ch to form ring, ch 1, 6 sc in ring, join with sl st in first sc (6 sc).

Rnd 2: Ch 1, sc in first st, 2 sc in next st, (sc in next st, 2 sc in next st) around, join (9).

Rnd 3: Ch 1, sc in first st, ch 6, (sc in next st, ch 6) around, join (9 ch-6 sps).

Rnd 4: Ch 1, sl st in first sc, 6 sc in next ch sp, (sl st in next sc, 6 sc in next ch sp) around, join with sl st in first sl st, fasten off.

FINISHING

1: Cut 24" piece of ribbon, weave through rnd 18 of Jar Cover. Place jar in Cover; tie ribbon into a bow to secure. Tack one Flower over bow.

2: Cut 66" piece of ribbon, weave through every 3rd or 4th st of rnd 1 on Basket Trim. Glue Trim around rim of basket, let dry; tie ribbon into a bow to secure. Tack one Flower over bow.

3: Tie remaining ribbon into a bow; sew to back of Towel Topper over rows 43 and 44. Tack one Flower over bow. Sew Velcro™ bottom over rows 19-20 and sew Velcro™ top over rows 43 and 44 on front of Topper. ✄

Happy Hot Mats

Designed by *June Hardy*

Oval Mat

Size: 10½" x 20".

Materials: Chunky yarn — 4 oz. main color (MC), 1 oz. contrasting color (CC) and small amount green; tapestry needle; I crochet hook or size needed to obtain gauge.

Gauge: 3 dc = 1"; 3 dc rows = 2".

Skill Level: ☆☆ Average

MAT

Rnd 1: With MC, ch 22, 3 dc in 4th ch from hook, dc in each ch across with 7 dc in last ch; working on opposite side of ch, dc in each ch across with 3 dc in last ch, join with sl st in top of ch-3 (48 dc).

Rnd 2: Ch 3, dc in same st, 2 dc in each of next 2 sts, dc in next 19 sts, 2 dc in each of next 5 sts, dc in next 19 sts, 2 dc in each of last 2 sts, join (58).

Rnd 3: Ch 3, dc in same st, 2 dc in each of next 3 sts, dc in next 23 sts, 2 dc in each of next 6 sts, dc in next 23 sts, 2 dc in each of last 2 sts, join (70).

Rnd 4: Ch 3, dc in same st, 2 dc in each of next 5 sts, dc in next 27 sts, 2 dc in each of next 8 sts, dc in next 27 sts, 2 dc in each of last 2 sts, join (86).

Rnd 5: Ch 3, dc in same st, 2 dc in each of next 7 sts, dc in next 35 sts, 2 dc in each of next 8 sts, dc in last 35 sts, join (102).

Rnd 6: Ch 3, dc in each of next 3 sts, 2 dc in each of next 9 sts, dc in next 42 sts, 2 dc in each of next 9 sts, dc in last 38 sts, join, **turn** (120).

Rnd 7: Ch 14, skip next 7 sts, (sl st in next st, ch 14, skip next 7 sts) around, join with sl st in bottom of first ch-14, **do not** turn (15 ch lps).

Rnd 8: Sl st in next ch, ch 2, hdc in each ch and sl st in each sl st around, join with sl st in top of ch-2, fasten off. Front of rnd 8 is right side of work.

Trim

Rnd 1: Working in unworked sts of rnd 6, behind ch lps of rnd 7, join CC with sl st in center dc between sl sts, ch 12, (sl st in center dc between sl sts, ch 12) around, join with sl st in first sl st (15 ch lps).

Rnd 2: Sl st in next ch, ch 1, sc in each ch and sl st in each sl st around, join with sl st in first sc, fasten off.

With green, using Lazy Daisy Stitch (see page 159) embroider 3 sts at base of each MC ch lp as shown in photo. With pink, using French Knot (see page 159) embroider one st in center of each Lazy Daisy group as shown.

Square & Round Mats

Sizes: Square Mat is 10½" square. Round Mat is 11" across.

Materials: Chunky yarn — 3 oz. main color (MC), small amount each contrasting color (CC) and green; tapestry needle; I crochet hook or size needed to obtain gauge.

Gauge: 3 dc = 1"; 3 dc rows = 2".

Skill Level: ☆☆ Average

SQUARE MAT

Rnd 1: With MC, ch 4, sl st in first ch to form ring, ch 3, 2 dc in ring, ch 2, (3 dc in ring, ch 2) 3 times, join with sl st in top of ch-3 (12 dc).

Rnd 2: Ch 3, dc in each of next 2 dc, (2 dc, ch 2, 2 dc) in next ch-2 sp; *dc in each of next 3 dc, (2 dc, ch 2, 2 dc) in next ch-2 sp; repeat from * around, join (28 dc, 4 corner ch sps).

Rnds 3-5: Ch 3, dc in each dc around with (2 dc, ch 2, 2 dc) in each corner ch-2 sp, join, ending with 72 dc and 4 corner ch sps.

Rnd 6: Sl st in next 4 sts, **turn,** *ch 12, skip next 6 sts, sl st in next st, ch 12, skip next 5 sts, sl st in next ch-2 sp, ch 12, skip next 5 sts*, sl st in next st; repeat between **, sl st in next st; repeat between ** around, join with sl st in first sl st (12 ch lps).

Rnd 7: Sl st in next ch, ch 2, hdc in each ch and sl st in each sl st around, join with sl st in top of ch-2, fasten off. Front of rnd 7 is right side of work.

Trim

Rnd 1: Working in unworked sts of rnd 5, behind ch lps of rnd 6, join CC with sl st in center dc

between sl sts, ch 10, (sl st in center dc between sl sts, ch 10) around, join with sl st in first sl st (12 ch lps).

Rnd 2: Sl st in next ch, ch 1, sc in each ch and sl st in each sl st around, join with sl st in first sc, fasten off. Embroider same as Oval Mat.

ROUND MAT

Rnd 1: With MC, ch 6, sl st in first ch to form ring, ch 3, dc in same ch, 2 dc in each ch around, join with sl st in top of ch-3 (12 dc).

Rnds 2-3: Ch 3, dc in same st, 2 dc in each st around, join, ending with 48 sts in last rnd.

Rnd 4: Ch 3, dc in same st, dc in each of next 2 sts, (2 dc in next st, dc in each of next 2 sts) around, join (64).

Rnd 5: Ch 3, dc in same st, dc in each of next 3 sts, (2 dc in next st, dc in each of next 3 sts) around, join, **turn** (80).

Rnd 6: Ch 12, skip next 6 sts, sl st in next st, ch 12, skip next 6 sts, (sl st in next st, ch 12, skip next 5 sts) around, join with sl st in first ch of first ch-12 (13 ch lps).

Rnd 7: Sl st in next ch, ch 2, hdc in each ch and sl st in each sl st around, join with sl st in top of ch-2, fasten off. Front of rnd 7 is right side of work.

Trim

Work same as Square Mat Trim. ✂

Apple Medley

Designed by _Michele Wilcox_

Sizes: Pot Holder is 7" square. Wall Hanging is 14½" x 20".

Materials For Both: Worsted-weight yarn — 3½ oz. each off-white, dk. green and lt. green, 2 oz. red; sport-weight yarn — small amount brown; four plastic 1" rings; polyester fiberfill; tapestry needle; F crochet hook or size needed to obtain gauge.

Gauge: 9 sc = 2"; 9 sc rows = 2".

Skill Level: ☆☆ Average

POT HOLDER

Front

Row 1: With off-white, ch 21, sc in 2nd ch from hook, sc in each ch across, turn (20 sc).

Rows 2-21: Ch 1, sc in each st across, turn. At end of last row, fasten off.

Apple

Row 1: With red, ch 10, sc in 2nd ch from hook, sc in each ch across, turn (9 sc).

Row 2: Ch 1, 2 sc in first st, sc in each st across with 2 sc in last st, turn (11).

Row 3: Ch 1, sc in each st across, turn.

Rows 4-6: Repeat rows 2 and 3, ending with row 2 and 15 sts in last row.

Rows 7-11: Ch 1, sc in each st across, turn.

Rows 12-13: Ch 1, sc first 2 sts tog, sc in each st across to last 2 sts, sc last 2 sts tog, turn (13, 11). At end of last row, leaving long end for sewing, fasten off.

Sew to Front diagonally, stuffing lightly.

For **stem,** with brown sport yarn, ch 6, sc in 2nd ch from hook, sc in each ch across, leaving long end for sewing, fasten off.

Curve slightly and sew to Front centered over top of Apple as shown in photo.

Leaf

Row 1: With dk. green, ch 7, sc in 2nd ch from hook, sc in next 4 chs, 3 sc in last ch; working on opposite side of ch, sc in last 5 chs, turn (13 sc).

Rnd 2: Working in rnds, ch 1, sc in first st, hdc in each of next 3 sts, sc in next st, 2 sc in next st, (sc, ch 2, sc) in next st, 2 sc in next st, sc in next st, hdc in each of next 3 sts, sc in last st, join with sl st in first sc, leaving long end for sewing, fasten off.

Sew to Front over top of Apple at a slight angle.

Horizontal End (make 2)

Row 1: With lt. green, ch 21, sc in 2nd ch from hook, sc in each ch across, turn (20 sc).

Rows 2-4: Ch 1, sc in each st across, turn. At end of last row, leaving long end for sewing, fasten off.

Sew one long edge of one End across top edge of Front. Sew one long edge of second End across bottom edge of Front.

Vertical Side (make 2)

Row 1: With lt. green, ch 5, sc in 2nd ch from hook, sc in each ch across, turn (4 sc).

Rows 2-21: Ch 1, sc in each st across, turn. At end of last row, leaving long end for sewing, fasten off.

Sew one long edge of one Side to end of rows on side of Front. Sew one long edge of second Side to opposite side of Front.

Corner (make 4)

Row 1: With dk. green, ch 5, sc in 2nd ch from hook, sc in each ch across, turn (4 sc).

Rows 2-4: Ch 1, sc in each st across, turn. At end of last row, leaving long end for sewing, fasten off.

Sew each Corner in place as shown.

Back

Row 1: With dk. green, ch 29, sc in 2nd ch from hook, sc in each ch across, turn (28 sc).

Rows 2-29: Ch 1, sc in each st across, turn.

Rnd 30: To **join,** holding Front and Back wrong sides together, matching sts, working around outer edge through both thicknesses, ch 1, sc in end of each row and in each st around with 3 sc in each corner, join with sl st in first sc, fasten off.

Rnd 31: Join dk. green with sc in center st of 3-sc corner directly above stem, (ch 2, skip next st, sc in next st) around; for **hanging loop,** ch 10; join with sl st in first sc, fasten off.

WALL HANGING

Square (make 6 each off-white and lt. green)

Work same as Pot Holder Front.

continued on page 21

Watermelon Trio

Designed by *Jocelyn Sass*

Sizes: Basket is 5¾" tall not including handle. Tissue Cover fits boutique-style tissue box. Sachet is 3" x 6".

Materials For All Three: Worsted-weight yarn — 9 oz. green, 5 oz. red, 2 oz. off-white and small amount black; 2 pieces 12" x 18" stiff plastic canvas; ⅓ cup potpourri; tapestry needle; F crochet hook or size needed to obtain gauge.

Gauge: 9 sc = 2"; 9 sc rows = 2".

Skill Level: ☆☆ Average

BASKET

Outer Side (make 2)

Row 1: Starting at **top,** with red, ch 34, sc in 2nd ch from hook, sc in each ch across, turn (33 sc).

Row 2: Ch 1, sc first 2 sts tog, sc in each st across to last 2 sts, sc last 2 sts tog, turn (31).

Row 3: Ch 1, sc in each st across, turn.

Rows 4-16: Repeat rows 2 and 3 alternately, ending with row 2 and 17 sts in last row. At end of last row, **do not** turn.

Rnd 17: Working around outer edge, ch 1, sc in end of each row and in each st around with 3 sc in each top corner, join with sl st in first sc, fasten off.

Outer Rind

Row 1: Working across curved edge, with right side of rnd 17 facing you, join off-white with sc in first corner, sc in each st across to opposite corner leaving sts across straight edge unworked, turn.

Row 2: Ch 1, sc in each st across with 3 sc in each lower corner, turn, fasten off.

Row 3: Join green with sc in first st, sc in each st across, turn.

Row 4: Repeat row 2.

Rnd 5: Working around entire outer edge, matching colors, join green with sc in end of row 3, sc in end of each row and in each st around with 3 sc in each top corner, join with sl st in first sc, fasten off.

Cut two pieces from plastic canvas ¼" smaller than crocheted piece.

Inner Side (make 2)

Rows 1-16: With green, repeat same rows of Outer Side.

Rnd 17: Repeat same rnd of Outer Side.

Inner Rind

Rows 1-2: With green, repeat same rows of Outer Rind. At end of last row, **do not** fasten off.

Row 3: Ch 1, sc in each st across, turn.

Row 4: Ch 1, sc in each st across with 3 sc in each lower corner, turn.

Rnd 5: Working around entire outer edge, ch 1, sc in each st and in end of each row around with 3 sc in each top corner, join with sl st in first sc, fasten off.

To **join,** holding one Outer Side and one Inner Side wrong sides together with one piece plastic canvas between, working through both thicknesses in **back lps,** join green with sl st in any st, sl st in each st around, join with sl st in first sl st, fasten off. Repeat on other Outer Side and Inner Side pieces.

With black, using French Knot (see page 159), embroider 9 seeds over each Outer Side as shown in photo.

Gusset (make 2)

Row 1: With green, ch 23, sc in 2nd ch from hook, sc in each ch across, turn (22 sc).

Rows 2-72: Ch 1, sc in each st across, turn. At end of last row, **do not** turn.

Rnd 73: Working around outer edge, ch 1, sc in end of each row and in each st around with 3 sc in each corner, join with sl st in first sc, fasten off.

Cut one piece from plastic canvas ¼" smaller than crocheted piece.

To **join,** holding Gusset pieces wrong sides together, join same as Inner Side and Outer Side pieces.

To **form basket,** with green, sew curved edge of one Side to each long edge of Gusset.

For **trim,** working in **front lps** around top of Basket, join green with sc in any st, ch 3, (sc in next st, ch 3) around, join with sl st in first sc, fasten off.

Handle

Rnd 1: With green, ch 2, 6 sc in 2nd ch from hook, join with sl st in first sc, **turn** (6 sc).

Rnd 2: Ch 1, 2 sc in each st around, join, **turn** (12).

Rnds 3-59: Ch 1, sc in each st around, join, **turn.** Cut one piece plastic canvas 1¼" x 12½". Flatten handle, insert plastic canvas inside.

continued on page 21

Floral Jar Covers

Designed by *Patricia Hall*

Sizes: Off-white Cover is 6" across. Lt. Yellow Cover is 6" across. White Cover is 6¾" across.

Materials: Worsted-weight yarn — 1 oz. each off-white, lt. yellow and white; size-10 bedspread cotton — 42 yds. avocado, 20½ yds. purple, 16 yds. red, 10 yds. orange and 3 yds. yellow; 24" each off-white, orange and white ⅝" satin ribbon; tapestry needle; No. 4 steel crochet hook and G crochet hook or sizes needed to obtain gauges.

Gauges: With **G hook,** rnds 1-3 of Top is 3½" across. With **No. 4 hook,** Red Flower is 1¾" across; Orange Flower is 1½" across; Purple Flower is 1¼" across.

Skill Level: ☆☆ Average

OFF-WHITE COVER
Top

Rnd 1: With G hook and off-white, ch 4, 11 dc in 4th ch from hook, join with sl st in top of ch-3 (12 dc).

Rnds 2-3: Ch 3, dc in same st, 2 dc in each st around, join (24, 48).

Rnd 4: Working this rnd in **back lps** only, ch 4, skip next st, (dc in next st, ch 1, skip next st) around, join with sl st in 3rd ch of ch-4 (24 dc, 24 ch-1 sps).

Rnd 5: Ch 1, sc in each st and in each ch around, join with sl st in first sc (48 sc).

*NOTES: For **beginning treble cluster (beg-tr-cl),** ch 3, *yo 2 times, insert hook in same st, yo, draw lp through, (yo, draw through 2 lps on hook) 2 times; repeat from *, yo, draw through all 3 lps on hook.*

*For **treble cluster (tr-cl),** yo 2 times, *insert hook in next st, yo, draw lp through, (yo, draw through 2 lps on hook) 2 times; repeat from * 2 more times in same st, yo, draw through all 4 lps on hook.*

Rnd 6: Beg-cl, ch 9, tr-cl in next st, skip next 2 sts, (tr-cl in next st, ch 9, tr-cl in next st, skip next 2 sts) around, join with sl st in top of beg-tr-cl, fasten off (24 tr-cls, 12 ch sps).

*NOTE: For **picot,** ch 4, sl st in top of st just made.*

Rnd 7: For **edging,** with No. 4 hook and red, join with sc in sp between last and first tr-cls, ch 7, (sc, hdc, dc, tr, picot, tr, dc, hdc, sc) in next ch sp, ch 7, *sc in sp between next 2 tr-cls, ch 7, (sc, hdc, dc, tr, picot, tr, dc,

hdc, sc) in next ch sp, ch 7; repeat from * around, join with sl st in first sc, fasten off.

Leaves

Rnd 1: With No. 4 hook and avocado, ch 12, sl st in first ch to form ring, ch 3, 23 dc in ring, join with sl st in top of ch-3 (24 dc).

Rnd 2: Ch 1, sc in first st, (ch 5, skip next st, sc in next st) around; to **join,** ch 2, skip last st, dc in first sc (12 sc, 12 ch lps).

Rnd 3: Ch 1, sc around joining dc, (ch 5, sc in next ch lp) around; to **join,** ch 2, dc in first sc.

Rnd 4: Ch 1, sc around joining dc, ch 5, (sc in next ch lp, ch 5) around, join with sl st in first sc.

*NOTES: For **beginning double treble cluster (beg-dtr-cl),** ch 4, *yo 3 times, insert hook in same st, yo, draw lp through, (yo, draw through 2 lps on hook) 3 times; repeat from * 2 more times, yo, draw through all 4 lps on hook.*

*For **double treble cluster (dtr-cl),** yo 3 times, *insert hook in next st, yo, draw lp through, (yo, draw through 2 lps on hook) 3 times; repeat from * 3 more times in same st, yo, draw through all 5 lps on hook.*

Rnd 5: Beg-dtr-cl, ch 6, sc in next ch sp, ch 6, (dtr-cl in next sc, ch 6, sc in next ch sp, ch 6) around, join with sl st in top of beg-dtr-cl, fasten off.

Tack over rnds 1-3 of Top.

Red Flower

Rnd 1: With No. 4 hook and red, ch 6, sl st in first ch to form ring, ch 3, 23 dc in ring, join with sl st in top of ch-3 (24 dc).

Rnd 2: Ch 6, skip next 7 sts, (sl st in next st, ch 6, skip next 7 sts) around, join with sl st in first ch of first ch-6 (3 ch sps).

Rnd 3: Sl st in first ch sp, ch 1, (sc, hdc, dc, 5 tr, dc, hdc, sc) in same sp and in each ch sp around, join with sl st in first sc, fasten off.

Rnd 4: Fold petals forward, join with sl st in 4th dc of any skipped 7-dc group on rnd 1, ch 6, (sl st in 4th dc on next skipped 7-dc group, ch 6) around, join with sl st in first sl st (3 ch sps).

Rnd 5: Repeat rnd 3.

Rnd 6: Fold petals forward, join with sl st in 2nd dc of any skipped 3-dc group on rnd 1, ch 6, skip next 3-dc

group, (sl st in 2nd dc of next skipped 3-dc group, ch 6, skip next 3-dc group) around, join with sl st in first sl st.

NOTE: *For **double treble crochet** (**dtr**—see page 158), yo 3 times, insert hook in next st, yo, draw lp through, (yo, draw through 2 lps on hook) 4 times.*

Rnd 7: Sl st in first ch sp, (sc, ch 2, 2 tr, 10 dtr, 2 tr, ch 2, sc) in each ch sp around, join with sl st in first sl st, fasten off.

For **center of flower,** with No. 4 hook and yellow, ch 3, (2 dc, sl st) in 3rd ch from hook, fasten off. Tack to center of flower.

Tack Red Flower to center of Leaves.

Weave off-white ribbon through ch sps of rnd 4 on Top. Tie ends into a bow.

LT. YELLOW COVER
Top

Rnds 1-5: With G hook and lt. yellow, repeat same rnds of Off-White Cover Top.

Rnd 6: Ch 1, sc in first st, ch 6, skip next st, tr-cl in next st, ch 8, tr-cl in next st, ch 6, skip next 2 sts, *sc in

continued on page 20

next st, ch 6, skip next 2 sts, tr-cl in next st, ch 8, tr-cl in next st, ch 6, skip next 2 sts; repeat from * around, join with sl st in first sc, fasten off (14 tr-cls, 14 ch-6 sps, 7 sc, 7 ch-8 sps).

Rnd 7: With No. 4 hook and orange, join with sc in first sc, ch 10, 2 sc in next tr-cl, ch 14, 2 sc in next tr-cl, ch 10, *sc in next sc, ch 10, 2 sc in next tr-cl, ch 14, 2 sc in next tr-cl, ch 10; repeat from * around, join, fasten off.

Leaves

Rnd 1: With No. 4 hook and avocado, ch 12, sl st in first ch to form ring, ch 3, 23 dc in ring, join with sl st in top of ch-3 (24 dc).

Rnd 2: Ch 1, sc in first st, (ch 5, skip next st, sc in next st) around; to **join,** ch 2, skip last st, dc in first sc (12 sc, 12 ch lps).

Rnd 3: Ch 1, sc around joining dc, ch 11, (sc in next ch lp, ch 11) around, join with sl st in first sc.

Rnd 4: Ch 1, *sc in next st, ch 6, (sc, ch 4, sc) in next ch lp, ch 6; repeat from * around, join, fasten off.

Tack Leaves over rnds 1-3 on Top.

Orange Flower

Rnd 1: With No. 4 hook and orange, ch 5, sl st in first ch to form ring, ch 2, 13 hdc in ring, join with sl st in top of ch-2 (14 hdc).

Rnd 2: Ch 3, skip next st, (sl st in next st, ch 3, skip next st) around, join with sl st in first ch of first ch-3 (7 ch sps).

Rnd 3: (Sl st, ch 2, 2 dc, ch 2, sl st) in each ch sp around, join with sl st in first sl st, fasten off.

Rnd 4: Fold petal forward, join with sl st in any skipped st on rnd 1, ch 4, (sl st in next skipped st, ch 4) around, join with sl st in first sl st.

Rnd 5: Sl st in first ch sp, ch 1 (sc, ch 1, dc, 3 tr, dc, ch 1, sc) in same ch sp and in each ch sp around, join with sl st in first sc, fasten off.

For **center of flower,** with No. 4 hook and yellow, ch 3, (2 dc, sl st) in 3rd ch from hook, fasten off. Tack to center of flower.

Tack Orange Flower to center of Leaves.

Weave orange ribbon through ch sps of rnd 4 on Top. Tie ends into a bow.

WHITE COVER

Rnds 1-5: With G hook and white, repeat same rnds of Off-White Cover Top on page 18.

Rnd 6: Ch 1, sc in first st, ch 9, skip next 3 sts, (sc in next st, ch 9, skip next 3 sts) around, join with sl st in first sc (12 sc, 12 ch-9 sps).

Rnd 7: Ch 1, sc in first st, (5 dc, ch 2, sc, ch 2, 5 dc) in next ch sp, *sc in next sc, (5 dc, ch 2, sc, ch 2, 5 dc) in next ch sp; repeat from * around, join, fasten off (120 dc, 24 ch-2 sps, 24 sc).

Rnd 8: With No. 4 hook and purple, join with sc in first sc, *[ch 9, skip next 4 dc, sc in next dc, ch 5, (sc, ch 4, sc) in next sc, ch 5, sc in next dc, ch 9, skip next 4 dc], [sc in next sc; repeat from * 10 more times; repeat between [ ], join, fasten off.

Leaves

Rnd 1: With No. 4 hook and avocado, ch 12, sl st in first ch to form ring, ch 3, 23 dc in ring, join with sl st in top of ch-3 (24 dc).

Rnd 2: Ch 1, sc in first st, (ch 4, skip next st, sc in next st) around; to **join,** ch 2, skip last st, dc in first sc (12 sc, 12 ch sps).

Rnd 3: Ch 1, sc around joining dc, (ch 5, sc in next ch lp) around; to **join,** ch 2, dc in first sc.

Rnd 4: Ch 1, sc around joining dc, ch 7, (sc in next ch lp, ch 7) around, join with sl st in first sc.

Rnd 5: Sl st in first ch sp, ch 1, (sc, hdc, dc, 2 tr, picot, tr, dc, hdc, sc) in same ch sp and in each ch sp around, join, fasten off.

Tack over rnds 1-3 of Top.

Purple Flower (make 3)

Rnd 1: With No. 4 hook and purple, ch 5, sl st in first ch to form ring, ch 2, 9 hdc in ring, join with sl st in top of ch-2 (10 hdc).

Rnd 2: ◊Ch 4, *yo 2 times, insert hook in same st, yo, draw lp through, (yo, draw through 2 lps on hook) 2 times*; repeat between **, yo 2 times, insert hook in next st, yo, draw lp through, (yo, draw through 2 lps on hook) 2 times; repeat between **, yo, draw through all 5 lps on hook, ch 4, sl st in same st◊, [sl st in next st; repeat between ◊◊]; repeat between [ ] around, join with sl st in first sl st, fasten off.

For **center of flower** (make 3), with No. 4 hook and yellow, ch 3, (2 dc, sl st) in 3rd ch from hook, fasten off. Tack to center of each flower.

Tack flowers to rnds 1-3 of Leaves.

Weave white ribbon through ch sps of rnd 4 on Top. Tie ends into a bow.✄

Apple Medley

continued from page 15

Apple (make 6)

Work same as Pot Holder Apple on page 15. Sew one Apple to each off-white Square centered over rows 3-15, stuffing lightly.

For **stem** (make 6), work same as Pot Holder Apple Stem on page 15.

Leaf (make 6)

Work same as Pot Holder Leaf on page 15.

Alternating colors, sew Squares together in 3 rows of 4 Squares each.

Border

Rnd 1: Working around entire outer edge, join dk. green with sc in any corner, 2 sc in same sp, sc in each st and in end of each row around with 3 sc in each corner, join with sl st in first sc (292 sc).

Rnd 2: Ch 1, sc in first st, ch 2, skip next st, (sc in next st, ch 2, skip next st) around, join, fasten off.

Sew rings evenly spaced to top back edge.✂

Watermelon Trio

continued from page 17

Rnd 60: Ch 1, (sc next 2 sts tog) around, join, leaving long end for sewing, fasten off.

Sew opening closed. With green, sew each end of Handle over top 3 rows on insides of Basket as shown.

TISSUE COVER

NOTE: Row 1 is wrong side of work.

Row 1: Starting at **top,** with red, ch 19, sc in 2nd ch from hook, sc in each ch across, turn (18 sc).

Rows 2-9: Ch 1, sc in each st across, turn.

Row 10: Ch 1, sc in first 5 sts; for **opening,** ch 8, skip next 8 sts; sc in last 5 sts, turn (10 sc, 8 chs).

Row 11: Ch 1, sc in each sc and in each ch across, turn (18).

Rows 12-19: Ch 1, sc in each st across, turn.

Rnd 20: Working around outer edge, ch 1, sc in each st and in end of each row around with 3 sc in each corner, join with sl st in first sc, **do not** turn.

Rnd 21: Working this rnd in **back lps** only, ch 1, sc in each st around, join, **turn.**

Rnds 22-37: Working in **both lps,** ch 1, sc in each st around, join, **turn.** At end of last rnd, fasten off.

Rnd 38: Join off-white with sc in any st, sc in each st around, join, **turn.**

Rnds 39-40: Ch 1, sc in each st around, join, **turn.** At end of last rnd, fasten off.

Rnd 41: With green, repeat rnd 38.

Rnds 42-46: Ch 1, sc in each st around, join, **turn.**

Rnd 47: Ch 1, sc in first st, ch 3, (sc in next st, ch 3) around, join with sl st in first sc, fasten off.

With black, using French Knot (see page 159), embroider 10 seeds on each side of Tissue Cover as shown in photo.

SACHET

Front

NOTE: Row 1 is wrong side of work.

Row 1: With red, ch 16, sc in 2nd ch from hook, sc in each ch across, turn (15 sc).

Row 2: Ch 1, sc first 2 sts tog, sc in each st across to last 2 sts, sc last 2 sts tog, turn (13).

Row 3: Ch 1, sc in each st across, turn.

Rows 4-6: Repeat rows 2 and 3 alternately, ending with row 2.

Rnd 7: Working around outer edge, ch 1, sc in end of each row and in each st around with 3 sc in each end of row 1, join with sl st in first sc, fasten off.

Rind

Row 1: Working across curved edge, with right side of rnd 7 facing you, join off-white with sc in first corner, sc in each st across to opposite corner leaving sts across straight edge unworked, turn, fasten off.

Row 2: Join green with sc in first st, sc in each st across with 3 sc in each lower corner, turn.

Row 3: Ch 1, sc in each st across, turn.

Row 4: Working in this row in **back lps** only, ch 1, sc in first st, (ch 3, sc in next st) across, fasten off.

With black, using French Knot (see page 159), embroider 3 seeds across Front as shown in photo.

For **back,** work same as Front and Rind omitting row 4 of Rind.

To **join,** holding wrong sides together, sew Front and Back together stuffing with potpourri before closing.✂

Farm Friends

Designed by *Michele Wilcox*

Rise 'n' Shine

Size: Rooster is 13" tall.

Materials: Worsted-weight yarn — 6 oz. white, 1 oz. gold, small amounts each rust and black; polyester fiberfill; tapestry needle; F crochet hook or size needed to obtain gauge.

Gauge: 9 sc = 2"; 9 sc rows = 2".

Skill Level: ☆☆ Average

HEAD & BODY SIDE (make 2)

Row 1: With white, ch 20, sc in 2nd ch from hook, sc in each ch across, turn (19 sc).

Rows 2-3: Ch 1, 2 sc in first st, sc in each st across to last st, 2 sc in last st, turn (21, 23).

Row 4: Ch 1, sc in each st across, turn.

Rows 5-13: Repeat rows 2-4 consecutively, ending with 35 sts in last row.

Rows 14-19: Ch 1, sc in each st across, turn.

Row 20: For **middle tail feather,** ch 1, sc in first 5 sts leaving remaining sts unworked, turn (5).

Row 21: Ch 1, sc first 2 sts tog, sc in each st across to last st, 2 sc in last st, turn.

Row 22: Ch 1, 2 sc in first st, sc in each st across to last 2 sts, sc last 2 sts tog, turn.

Rows 23-25: Repeat rows 21 and 22 alternately, ending with row 21. At end of last row, fasten off.

Row 20: For **2nd tail feather,** skip next unworked st on row 19, join white with sc in next st, sc in next 4 sts leaving remaining sts unworked, turn (5).

Rows 21-29: Repeat rows 21 and 22 alternately, ending with row 21. At end of last row, fasten off.

Row 20: For **3rd tail feather,** working in ends of rows 14-18 under middle tail feather, join white with sc in first row, sc in next 4 rows, turn (5).

Rows 21-25: Repeat rows 21 and 22 of middle tail feather alternately, ending with row 22. At end of last row, fasten off.

Row 20: For **neck,** join white with sl st in next unworked st on row 19, sc first 2 sts tog, sc in each st across, turn (23).

Row 21: Ch 1, sc in each st across to last 2 sts, sc last 2 sts tog, turn (22).

Row 22: Ch 1, sc first 2 sts tog, sc in each st across, turn (21).

Rows 23-26: Repeat rows 21 and 22 of neck alternately, ending with 17 sts in last row.

Rows 27-30: Ch 1, sc first 2 sts tog, sc in each st across to last 2 sts, sc last 2 sts tog, turn, ending with 9 sts in last row.

Row 31: Ch 1, sc in each st across, turn.

Row 32: Ch 1, 2 sc in first st, sc in each st across to last st, 2 sc in last st, turn (11).

Rows 33-39: Ch 1, sc in each st across, turn.

Rows 40-42: For **first side,** ch 1, sc first 2 sts tog, sc in each st across to last 2 sts, sc last 2 sts tog, turn.

Rnd 43: Working around outer edge, ch 1, sc in end of each row and in each st around with 3 sc in tip of each tail feather, join with sl st in first sc, fasten off.

Rows 40-42: For **2nd side,** ch 1, sc first 2 sts tog, sc in each st across to last 2 sts, sc last 2 sts tog, **do not** turn.

Rnd 43: Working around outer edge, ch 1, sc in end of each row and in each st around with 3 sc in tip of each tail feather, join with sl st in first sc, fasten off.

Holding Head & Body Sides wrong sides together, matching sts, working in **back lps** only, with white, sew together stuffing before closing.

WING (make 2)
Side (make 2)

Row 1: With white, ch 9, sc in 2nd ch from hook, sc in each ch across, turn (8 sc).

Rows 2-4: Ch 1, 2 sc in first st, sc in each st across to last st, 2 sc in last st, turn (10, 12, 14).

Row 5: Ch 1, sc in each st across to last st, 2 sc in last st, turn (15).

Row 6: Ch 1, 2 sc in first st, sc in each st across, turn (16).

Row 7: Repeat row 5 (17).

Row 8: Ch 1, sc in each st across to last 2 sts, sc last 2 sts tog, turn (15).

Row 9: Ch 1, sc first 2 sts tog, sc in next 7 sts, sc next 2 sts tog leaving remaining sts unworked, turn (9).

Rows 10-11: For **first and 4th sides,** ch 1, sc first 2 sts tog, sc in each st across to last 2 sts, sc last 2 sts tog, turn (5).

Rnd 12: Working around outer edge, ch 1, sc in end of each row and in each st around with 3 sc in tip of each Wing, join with sl st in first sc, fasten off.

Rows 10-11: For **2nd and 3rd sides,** ch 1, sc first 2 sts tog, sc in each st across to last 2 sts, sc last 2 sts tog, turn. At end of last row, **do not** turn (5).

Rnd 12: Working around outer edge, ch 1, sc in end of each row and in each st around with 3 sc in tip of each Wing, join with sl st in first sc, fasten off.

Holding first and 2nd Wing Sides wrong sides together, matching sts, working in **back lps** only, with white, sew together stuffing before closing. Repeat with 3rd and 4th Sides. Slanting slightly, sew one Wing over rows 13-21 on each Side of Body.

continued on page 24

LEG (make 2)
Side (make 2)

Row 1: Starting at **top,** with white, ch 7, sc in 2nd ch from hook, sc in each ch across, turn (6 sc).

Rows 2-3: Ch 1, 2 sc in first st, sc in each st across to last st, 2 sc in last st, turn (8, 10).

Rows 4-7: Ch 1, sc in each st across, turn.

Rows 8-9: Ch 1, sc first 2 sts tog, sc in each st across to last 2 sts, sc last 2 sts tog, turn. At end of last row, fasten off (8, 6).

Row 10: Join gold with sc in first st, sc in each st across, turn.

Row 11: Ch 1, sc in each of first 2 sts, sc next 2 sts tog, sc in each of last 2 sts, turn (5).

Rows 12-14: Ch 1, sc in each st across, turn.

Rnd 15: Working around outer edge, changing colors as needed, ch 1, sc in end of each row and in each st around with 3 sc in each gold corner, join with sl st in first sc, fasten off.

Holding 2 Leg Sides wrong sides together, matching sts, working in **back lps** only, with white, sew together leaving bottom of Leg open. Stuff.

FOOT (make 2)
Side (make 2)

Row 1: With gold, ch 4, sc in 2nd ch from hook, sc in each ch across, turn (3 sc).

Row 2: Ch 1, 2 sc in first st, sc in next st, 2 sc in last st, turn (5).

Row 3: Ch 1, sc in each of first 2 sts, 2 sc in next st, sc in each of last 2 sts, turn (6).

Rows 4-5: Ch 1, sc in each st across, turn.

Row 6: For **first toe,** ch 1, sc in each of first 2 sts leaving remaining sts unworked, turn (2).

Rows 7-8: Ch 1, sc in each st across, turn. At end of last row, fasten off.

Row 6: For **2nd toe,** join gold with sc in next unworked st on row 5, sc in next st, turn (2).

Rows 7-8: Ch 1, sc in each st across, turn. At end of last row, fasten off.

Rows 6-8: For **3rd toe,** repeat same rows of 2nd toe.

Holding Foot Sides wrong sides together, matching sts, working in **back lps** only, with gold, sew together stuffing before closing. Sew Foot to bottom of each Leg.

Sew rows 2-7 on one side of Leg to rows 3-8 on each side of Body.

COMB
Side (make 2)

Row 1: With rust, ch 10, sc in 2nd ch from hook, sc in each ch across, turn (9 sc).

Row 2: (Sc, hdc) in first st, 2 dc in next st, ch 1, sl st in next st, *(sc, hdc) in next st, 2 dc in next st, ch 1, sl st in next st; repeat from *, fasten off.

Holding Comb Sides wrong sides together, matching sts, working in **back lps** only, with rust, sew together, **do not** stuff before closing. Sew Comb to top back of Head over seam.

BEAK
Top

NOTE: *Do not* *join rnds unless otherwise stated. Mark first st of each rnd.*

Rnd 1: With gold, ch 2, 6 sc in 2nd ch from hook (6 sc).

Rnd 2: Sc in each st around.

Rnd 3: (Sc in each of next 2 sts, 2 sc in next st) around (8).

Rnd 4: Sc in each st around, join with sl st in first sc, fasten off.

Stuff. Sew Beak Top in front of Comb.

Bottom

Rnds 1-3: Repeat same rnds of Beak Top. At end of last rnd, join with sl st in first sc, fasten off.

Stuff. Sew Beak Bottom under Beak Top.

WATTLE (make 2)

Rnd 1: With rust, ch 2, 6 sc in 2nd ch from hook (6 sc).

Rnd 2: (Sc in next st, 2 sc in next st) around (9).

Rnds 3-4: Sc in each st around.

Rnd 5: (Sc next 2 sts tog) 4 times, sc in last st, join with sl st in first sc, fasten off.

Tack top of Wattles together. Tack under Beak Bottom.

With black, using Satin Stitch (see page 159), embroider **eyes** over row 40 on each side of Head as shown in photo.

Handy Holstein

Size: Potholder is 9" x 10".

Materials: Worsted-weight yarn — 3½ oz. white, small amount each black, peach and beige; tapestry needle; F crochet hook or size needed to obtain gauge.

Gauge: 9 sc = 2"; 5 sc rows = 1".

NOTE: Do not join rnds unless otherwise stated. Mark first st of each rnd.

Skill Level: ☆ Easy

BODY SIDE (make 2)

Row 1: With white, ch 17, sc in 2nd ch from hook, sc in each ch across, turn (16 sc).

Rows 2-6: Ch 1, 2 sc in first st, sc in each st across to last st, 2 sc in last st, turn, ending with 26 sts in last row.

Rows 7-18: Ch 1, sc in each st across, turn.

Row 19: Ch 1, sc first 2 sts tog, sc in each st across to last 2 sts, sc last 2 sts tog, turn (24).

Row 20: Ch 1, sc in each st across, turn.

Rows 21-24: Repeat rows 19 and 20 alternately, ending with 20 sts in last row.

Rows 25-30: Repeat row 19, ending with 8 sts in last row.

Rows 31-33: Ch 1, sc in each st across, turn.

Rows 34-35: Repeat row 19, ending with 4 sts in last row. At end of last row, fasten off.

MUZZLE

Rnd 1: With peach, ch 6, sc in 2nd ch from hook, sc in each of next 3 chs, 3 sc in last ch; working on opposite side of ch, sc in each of next 3 chs, 2 sc in last ch (12 sc).

Rnd 2: 2 sc in first st, sc in each of next 3 sts, 2 sc in each of next 3 sts, sc in each of next 3 sts, 2 sc in each of last 2 sts, join with sl st in first sc, fasten off.

Sew Muzzle to one Body Side centered over rows 25-31.

LARGE SPOT

Rnd 1: With black, ch 2, 6 sc in 2nd ch from hook (6 sc).

Rnd 2: 2 sc in each st around (12).

Rnd 3: (Sc in next st, 2 sc in next st) around (18).

Rnd 4: (Sc in each of next 2 sts, 2 sc in next st) around, join with sl st in first sc, fasten off.

MEDIUM SPOT

Rnds 1-3: Repeat same rnds of Large Spot. At end of last rnd, join with sl st in first sc, fasten off.

SMALL SPOT (make 3)

Rnds 1-2: Repeat same rnds of Large Spot. At end of last rnd, join with sl st in first sc, fasten off.

Sew Large, Medium and 2 Small Spots to front of Body Side leaving remaining Small Spot for Leg.

FINISHING

1: With black, using Satin Stitch (see page 159), embroider **eyes** above Muzzle over row 33 of Body Side spaced ½" apart.

2: With black, using French Knots (see page 159), embroider **nostrils** between rnds 2 and 3 on top half of Muzzle spaced ¼" apart.

3: With black, using Straight Stitch (see page 159), embroider **mouth lines** on Muzzle as shown in photo.

EDGING

Holding Body Sides wrong sides together, matching sts, with front facing you, working through both thicknesses, join white with sc in first st, sc in each st and in end of each row around with 3 sc in each corner, join with sl st in first sc, fasten off.

LEG (make 4)

Side (make 2)

Row 1: With white, ch 9, sc in 2nd ch from hook, sc in each ch across, turn (8 sc).

Rows 2-7: Ch 1, sc in each st across, turn. At end of last row, fasten off.

Sew Small Spot over one Leg Side.

For **edging**, holding Leg Sides wrong sides together, matching sts, working through both thicknesses, join white with sc in any st, sc in each st and in end of each row around with 3 sc in each corner, join with sl st in first sc, fasten off.

Sew one Leg to each slanted edge on Body Side.

EAR (make 2)

Rnd 1: With white, ch 2, 6 sc in 2nd ch from hook (6 sc).

Rnd 2: 2 sc in each st around (12).

Rnds 3-7: Sc in each st around.

Rnd 8: (Sc next 2 sts tog) around, join with sl st in first sc, leaving long end for sewing, fasten off.

Flatten last rnd and sew Ears to each side of Head on Body Side as shown in photo.

HORN (make 2)

Rnd 1: With beige, ch 2, 6 sc in 2nd ch from hook (6 sc).

Rnds 2-4: Sc in each st around. At end of last rnd, join with sl st in first sc, leaving long end for sewing, fasten off.

Sew Horns to each corner above Ears on Head.

For **hanging loop**, working in center 2 sts of edging on top of Head, join white with sl st in first st, ch 18, sl st in next st on edging, fasten off. ✂

Family Comforts

Whether a grand mansion or a cozy cottage, any home says "Welcome" better when filled with handmade pleasures that invite everyone to stay just a little longer. Loved-ones from near or far will appreciate journey's end when they're able to relax amid a haven of crocheted trappings designed to please and pamper. Treat them to the love and luxury they deserve when you stitch-up loving comforts that will strengthen the tie that binds.

World Friendship

Designed by *Alma Shields*

Size: 37" x 46".

Materials: Worsted-weight yarn — 16 oz. med. blue, 9 oz. lt. blue, 3 oz. each dk. blue, tan and med. brown, 1½ oz. each dk. green, lt. green, reddish-brown and peach, small amount white; tapestry needle; F and H crochet hooks or sizes needed to obtain gauges.

Gauges: With **H hook,** 7 sc = 2"; 4 sc rows = 1". With **F hook,** 9 sc = 2"; 9 sc rows = 2".

Skill Level: ☆☆ Average

AFGHAN

NOTES: When changing colors (see page 158), always drop yarn to wrong side of work. **Do not** *carry yarn across to next section of same color for more than 2 or 3 sts. Use a separate ball of yarn for each color section.*

Each square on graph equals one sc.

Row 1: With H hook and med. blue, ch 119, sc in 2nd ch from hook, sc in each ch across, turn (118 sc). Front of row 1 is right side of work.

Rows 2-36: Ch 1, sc in each st across, turn.

Rows 37-112: Ch 1, sc first 25 sts, sc in next 68 sts changing colors according to graph on page 37, sc in last 25 sts, turn. At end of last row, fasten off all colors except med. blue.

Rows 113-148: Ch 1, sc in each st across, turn. At end of last row, **do not** fasten off.

BORDER

Rnd 1: With H hook, ch 1, 3 sc in first st, sc in each st across with 3 sc in last st; *working in ends of rows, skip first row, sc in next 7 rows, (skip next row, sc in next 7 rows) across to last 4 rows, skip next row, sc in each of last 3 rows*; working in starting ch on opposite side of row 1, 3 sc in first ch, sc in each ch across with 3 sc in last ch; repeat between **, join with sl st in first sc, fasten off.

Rnd 2: Working this rnd in **back lps** only, join dk. blue with sc in any st, sc in each st around with 3 sc in each center corner st, join, **turn.**

Rnd 3: Ch 1, sc in each st around with 3 sc in each center corner st, join, **turn,** fasten off.

Rnd 4: With right side facing you, using lt. blue, repeat rnd 2, **do not** turn.

Rnds 5-8: Ch 1, sc in each st around with 3 sc in each center corner st, join. At end of last rnd, fasten off.

HAND (make 3 each peach and med. brown, make 2 each tan and reddish-brown)

Row 1: With F hook, ch 7, sc in 2nd ch from hook, sc in each ch across, turn (6 sc).

Rows 2-4: Ch 1, sc in each st across, turn.

Row 5: Ch 1, 3 sc in first st, sc in each st across to last st, 3 sc in last st, turn (10).

Row 6: Repeat row 2.

Row 7: Ch 1, 2 sc in first st, sc in each st across to last st, 2 sc in last st, turn (12).

Rows 8-11: Repeat row 2.

Row 12: For **first finger,** ch 8, hdc in 3rd ch from hook, hdc in next 5 chs, skip first st on row 11, sl st in each of next 2 sts; for **2nd finger,** ch 10, hdc in 3rd ch from hook, hdc in next 7 chs, skip next st on row 11, sl st in each of next 2 sts; for **3rd finger,** ch 12, hdc in 3rd ch from hook, hdc in next 9 chs, skip next st on row 11, sl st in each of next 2 sts; for **4th finger,** ch 11, hdc in 3rd ch from hook, hdc in next 8 chs, skip next st on row 11, sl st in each of last 2 sts; working in ends of rows, sl st in each of next 2 rows; for **thumb,** ch 8, hdc in 3rd ch from hook, hdc in next 5 chs, skip next row, sc in next row, **do not** turn.

Row 13: Working around outer edge of Hand and fingers, spacing sts so piece lays flat, sc in end of each row and in each st around, join with sl st in first sc, fasten off.

Sew Hands around world as shown in photo. ✂

graph on page 37

Trio of Pillows
Designed by *Dorris Brooks*

Green Cables

Size: 17" square.

Materials: Worsted-weight yarn — 8 oz. green; 15" square pillow form; 16" x 32" piece of matching fabric; sewing thread; sewing and tapestry needles; I crochet hook or size needed to obtain gauge.

Gauge: 3 dc = 1"; rows 1-5 = 2".

Skill Level: ☆☆ Average

PILLOW SIDE (make 2)

NOTES: *For **cable**, skip next 2 sts, tr in each of next 2 sts; working in back of sts just made, tr in last 2 skipped sts, skip next 2 sts, tr in each of next 2 sts; working in front of sts just made, tr in last 2 skipped sts.*

*For **popcorn stitch (pc)**, 4 dc in next st, drop lp from hook, insert hook in first st of 4-dc group, pick up dropped lp, draw through st.*

Front of row 2 is right side of work.

Row 1: Ch 46, sc in 2nd ch from hook, sc in each ch across, turn (45 sc).

Row 5: Repeat row 3.

Row 6: Ch 3, dc in each of next 3 sts, ch 1, skip next st, cable, ch 1, skip next st, dc in next 4 sts, pc, dc in next 7 sts, pc, dc in next 4 sts, ch 1, skip next st, cable, ch 1, skip next st, dc in last 4 sts, turn.

Rows 7-9: Repeat rows 3 and 4 alternately, ending with row 3.

Rows 10-35: Repeat rows 2-9 consecutively, ending with row 3.

Rnd 36: Working around outer edge, ch 1, 2 sc in first st, (sc in each st across with 3 sc in last st; working in ends of rows, evenly space 49 sc across), 3 sc in next st; repeat between ( ), sc in same st as first st, join with sl st in first sc, fasten off (196).

For **pillow form cover,** from fabric, cut 2 pieces each 16" square. Allowing ½" for seams, sew right sides together leaving one side open. Clip and trim edges, turn, stuff with pillow form. Sew opening closed.

Edging

Rnd 1: Holding Pillow Sides wrong sides together with pillow form between; working through both thicknesses, join with sc in first center corner st, sc in same st, sc in each st around with 3 sc in each corner st, sc in same st as first st, join with sl st in first sc (204 sc).

NOTES: For **corner shell,** *(3 dc, ch 1, 3 dc) in next st.* For **shell,** *(2 dc, ch 1, 2 dc) in next st.*

Rnd 2: Ch 3, (2 dc, ch 1, 3 dc) in same st, *skip next 2 sts, (shell, skip next 2 sts) 15 times, corner shell, skip next 2 sts, (shell in next st, skip next 2 sts) 17 times*, corner shell; repeat between **, join with sl st in top of ch-3.

Aran Popcorns

Size: 17" square.

Materials: Worsted-weight yarn — 8 oz. off-white; 15" square pillow form; 16" x 32" piece of matching fabric; sewing thread; sewing and tapestry needles; H crochet hook or size needed to obtain gauge.

Gauge: 11 sts = 4"; 1 sc row and 1 dc row = 1".

Skill Level: ☆☆ Average

PILLOW SIDE (make 2)

Row 1: Ch 42, sc in 2nd ch from hook, sc in each ch across, turn (41 sc). Front of row 1 is right side of work.

NOTES: For **cable,** *skip next 2 sts, tr in each of next 2 sts; working in back of sts just made, tr in last 2 skipped sts.*

Row 2: Ch 3, dc in each of next 3 sts, ch 1, skip next st, cable, ch 1, skip next st, dc in next 8 sts, pc, dc in next 8 sts, ch 1, skip next st, cable, ch 1, skip next st, dc in last 4 sts, turn (24 dc, 4 ch-1 sps, 2 cables, one pc).

Row 3: Ch 1, sc in each st and in each ch across, turn (45 sc).

Row 4: Ch 3, dc in each of next 3 sts, ch 1, skip next st, cable, ch 1, skip next st, dc in next 6 sts, pc, dc in each of next 3 sts, pc, dc in next 6 sts, ch 1, skip next st, cable, ch 1, skip next st, dc in last 4 sts, turn (23 dc, 4 ch-1 sps, 2 cables, 2 pc).

continued on page 35

Home Sweet Home

Designed by *Hazel Henry*

Sizes: When blocked, Chair Back Cover is 15" x 19" and Arm Covers are 6" x 12" each.

Materials For One Set: Size-20 crochet cotton — 1400 yds. ecru; tapestry needle; No. 10 steel crochet hook or size needed to obtain gauge.

Gauge: 14 dc = 1"; 6 dc rows = 1".

Skill Level: ☆☆☆ Advanced

SPECIAL NOTES: For **beginning increase block (beg inc block),** ch 5, dc in 4th ch from hook, dc in next ch, dc in first dc.

For **beginning 2-block inc (beg 2-block inc),** ch 8, dc in 4th ch from hook, dc in next 4 chs, dc in first dc.

For **mesh,** ch 2, skip next 2 chs or dc, dc in next dc.

For **beginning block (beg block),** ch 3, dc in each of next 2 dc or chs, dc in next dc.

For **block,** dc in each of next 2 chs or dc, dc in next ch or dc.

For **ending one-block increase (end one-block inc),** yo, insert hook in same st as last dc made, yo, draw lp through, yo, draw through one lp on hook, (yo, draw through 2 lps on hook) 2 times; *yo, insert hook in base of last st made (see illustration), yo, draw lp through , yo, draw through one lp on hook, (yo, draw through 2 lps on hook) 2 times; repeat from * one more time.

For **ending 2-block increase (end 2-block inc),** yo, insert hook in same st as last dc made, yo, draw lp through, yo, draw through one lp on hook, (yo, draw through 2 lps on hook) 2 times; *yo, insert hook in base of last st made (see illustration), yo, draw lp through , yo, draw through one lp on hook, (yo, draw through 2 lps on hook) 2 times; repeat from * 4 more times.

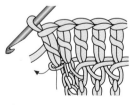

CHAIR BACK COVER

Row 1: For **first side,** ch 273, dc in 4th ch from hook, dc in each ch across, turn (271 dc).

Rows 2-69: Work according to Graph A on page 34, turn. At end of last row, fasten off.

Row 1: For **second side,** working in starting ch on opposite side of row 1, with right side facing you, join with sl st in first st, ch 3, dc in each of next 3 sts (first block made), complete row according to Graph B on page 34, turn.

Rows 2-9: Work according to graph, turn.

Row 10: For **first point,** work according to graph leaving remaining sts unworked, turn.

Rows 11-18: Work according to graph, turn. At end of last row, fasten off.

Row 10: For **2nd point,** skip next 5 dc on row 9, join with sl st in next dc, work according to graph leaving remaining sts unworked, turn.

Rows 11-13: Work according to graph, turn. At end of last row, fasten off.

Row 10: For **3rd point,** skip next 5 dc on row 9, join with sl st in next dc, work according to graph leaving remaining sts unworked, turn.

Rows 11-18: Repeat same rows of first point.

Row 10: For **4th point,** skip next 5 dc on row 9, join with sl st in next dc, work according to graph leaving remaining sts unworked, turn.

Rows 11-13: Work according to graph, turn. At end of last row, fasten off.

Row 10: For **5th point,** skip next 5 dc on row 9, join with sl st in next dc, work according to graph leaving remaining sts unworked, turn.

Rows 11-18: Work according to graph, turn. At end of last row, fasten off.

ARM COVER (make 2)

Row 1: Ch 12, dc in 4th ch from hook, dc in each ch across, turn (10 dc).

Rows 2-73: Work according to Graph C on page 35, turn. At end of last row, fasten off. ✂

graphs on pages 34 & 35

GRAPH A

GRAPH B

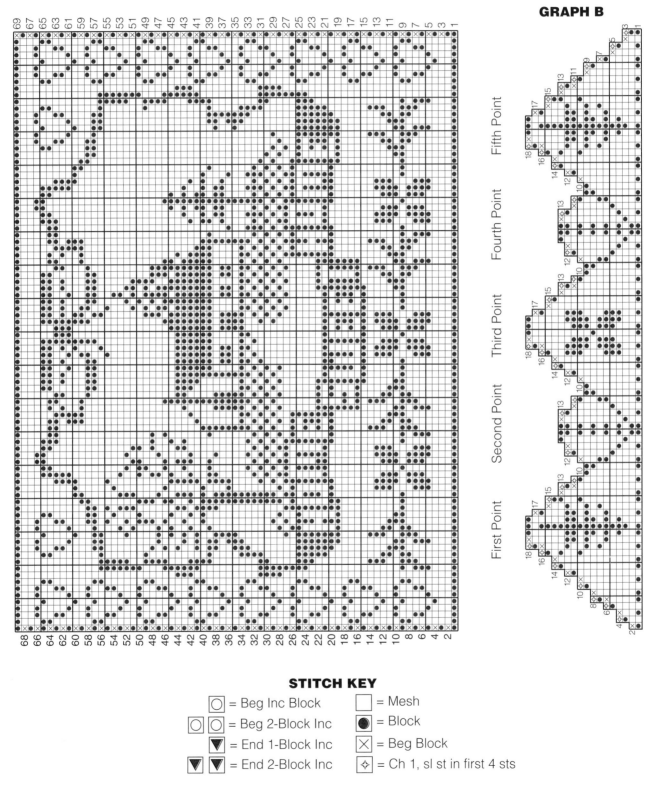

STITCH KEY

Ⓞ = Beg Inc Block   ☐ = Mesh

Ⓞ Ⓞ = Beg 2-Block Inc   ⬤ = Block

▼ = End 1-Block Inc   ☒ = Beg Block

▼ ▼ = End 2-Block Inc   ◈ = Ch 1, sl st in first 4 sts

GRAPH C

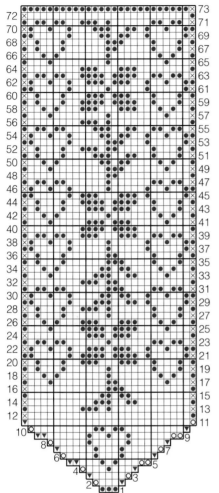

For **reverse popcorn stitch (rpc),** 4 dc in next st, drop lp from hook, insert hook from back to front in first st, draw dropped lp through.

Row 2: Ch 3, dc in each of next 3 sts, ch 1, skip next st, cable, ch 1, skip next st, dc in next 10 sts, rpc, dc in next 10 sts, ch 1, skip next st, cable, ch 1, skip next st, dc in last 4 sts, turn (28 dc, 4 ch-1 sps, 2 cables, one rpc).

Row 3: Ch 1, sc in each st and in each ch across, turn (41 sc).

Row 4: Ch 3, dc in each of next 3 sts, ch 1, skip next st, cable, ch 1, skip next st, dc in next 8 sts, rpc, dc in each of next 3 sts, rpc, dc in next 8 sts, ch 1, skip next st, cable, ch 1, skip next st, dc in last 4 sts, turn (27 dc, 4 ch-1 sps, 2 rpc, 2 cables).

Row 5: Repeat row 3.

Row 6: Ch 3, dc in each of next 3 sts, ch 1, skip next st, cable, ch 1, skip next st, dc in next 6 sts, rpc, dc in next 7 sts, rpc, dc in next 6 sts, ch 1, skip next st, cable, ch 1, skip next st, dc in last 4 sts, turn (27 dc, 4 ch-1 sps, 2 rpc, 2 cables).

Row 7: Repeat row 3.

Row 8: Ch 3, dc in each of next 3 sts, ch 1, skip next st, cable, ch 1, skip next st, dc in next 4 sts, rpc, (dc in next 5 sts, rpc) 2 times, dc in next 4 sts, ch 1, skip next st, cable, ch 1, skip next st, dc in last 4 sts, turn (26 dc, 4 ch-1 sps, 3 rpc, 2 cables).

Row 9: Repeat row 3.

Row 10: Repeat row 6.

Rows 11-13: Repeat rows 3 and 4 alternately, ending with row 3.

Row 14: Repeat row 8.

Row 15: Repeat row 3.

Row 16: Ch 3, dc in each of next 3 sts, ch 1, skip next st, cable, ch 1, skip next st, dc in each of next 2 sts, (rpc, dc in each of next 3 sts, rpc), dc in next 7 sts; repeat between ( ), dc in each of next 2 sts, ch 1, skip next st, cable, ch 1, skip next st, dc in last 4 sts, turn (25 dc, 4 ch-1 sps, 4 rpc, 2 cables).

Row 17: Repeat row 3.

Row 18: Repeat row 8.

Rows 19-29: Repeat rows 3-13.

Rows 30-31: Repeat rows 2 and 3. At end of last row, fasten off.

For **pillow form cover,** from fabric, cut 2 pieces each 16" square. Allowing ½" for seams, sew right sides

continued on page 36

together leaving one side open. Clip and trim edges, turn, stuff with pillow form. Sew opening closed.

Edging

Rnd 1: Holding Pillow sides wrong sides together with pillow form between; working through both thicknesses, in sts and in ends of rows, join with sc in first st, sc in same st, *sc in next 39 sts, 3 sc in next st, 2 sc in next dc row, (sc in next sc row, 2 sc in next dc row) 14 times*, 2 sc in next st; repeat between **, join with sl st in first sc (176 sc).

NOTE: For V-stitch (V-st), (sc, ch 4, sc) in next st.

Rnd 2: Ch 1, V-st in each of first 2 sts, *(skip next st, V-st in next st) 20 times, V-st in each of next 2 sts; repeat between ( ) 22 times*, V-st in each of next 2 sts; repeat between **, join, fasten off.

Orchid Shells

Size: 16" square.

Materials: Worsted-weight yarn — 8 oz. orchid; 14" square pillow form; 15" x 30" piece of matching fabric; sewing thread; sewing and tapestry needles; H crochet hook or size needed to obtain gauge.

Gauge: 7 sts = 2"; rows 1-6 = 3".

Skill Level: ☆☆ Average

PILLOW SIDE (make 2)

NOTE: For front cross stitch (fcr), skip next 3 chs or sts, dc in next ch or st, ch 3; working over dc just made, dc in 2nd skipped ch or st.

Row 1: Ch 53, dc in 5th ch from hook, skip next 2 chs, dc in next ch, (fcr, skip next ch, dc in next ch) across to last 3 chs, skip next 2 chs, (dc, ch 1, dc) in last ch, turn (26 dc, 7 ch-3 sps, 2 ch-1 sps).

Row 2: Ch 3, 3 dc in first ch sp, skip next dc, sc in next dc, (7 dc in next ch-3 sp, skip next dc, sc in next

dc) across to last ch sp, 3 dc in last ch sp, dc in top of ch-3, turn (57 dc, 8 sc).

Row 3: Ch 1, sc in each of first 2 sts, ch 1, skip next 2 sts, dc in next st, ch 1, skip next 2 sts, (sc in each of next 3 sts, ch 1, skip next 2 sts, dc in next st, ch 1, skip next 2 sts) across to last 2 sts, sc in each of last 2 sts, turn (25 sc, 8 dc, 16 ch-1 sps).

Row 4: Ch 3, fcr, skip next sc, dc in next st, (fcr, skip next sc, dc in next st) across, turn (25 dc, 8 ch-3 sps).

Row 5: Ch 1, sc in first st, (7 dc in next ch-3 sp, skip next st, sc in next st) across, turn (56 dc, 9 sc).

Row 6: Ch 4, (skip next 2 sts, sc in each of next 3 sts, ch 1, skip next 2 sts, dc in next st) across, turn (24 sc, 16 ch-1 sps, 9 dc).

Row 7: Ch 4, dc in same st, skip next sc, dc in next st, (fcr, skip next sc, dc in next st) 7 times, skip next sc, (dc, ch 1, dc) in 3rd ch of last ch-4, turn (26 dc, 7 ch-3 sps, 2 ch-1 sps).

Rows 8-27: Repeat rows 2-7 consecutively, ending with row 3. At end of last row, **do not** turn, fasten off.

Rnd 28: Working around outer edge, join with sc in first st, sc in same st, (sc in next 47 sts and chs, 2 sc in last st; working in ends of rows, evenly space 45 sc across), 2 sc in next st; repeat between ( ), join with sl st in first sc, fasten off (192).

For **pillow form cover**, from fabric, cut 2 pieces each 15" square. Allowing ½" for seams, sew right sides together leaving one side open. Clip and trim edges, turn, stuff with pillow form. Sew opening closed.

Edging

Rnd 1: Holding Pillow Sides wrong sides together with pillow form between; working through both thicknesses, join with sc in 2nd st on last rnd of Sides, sc in each st around with 3 sc in each corner st, join with sl st in first sc (200 sc).

Rnd 2: Ch 1, sc in first st, skip next st, 5 dc in next st, skip next st, (sc in next st, skip next st, 5 dc in next st, skip next st) around, join, fasten off. ✂

COLOR CHANGE GRAPH

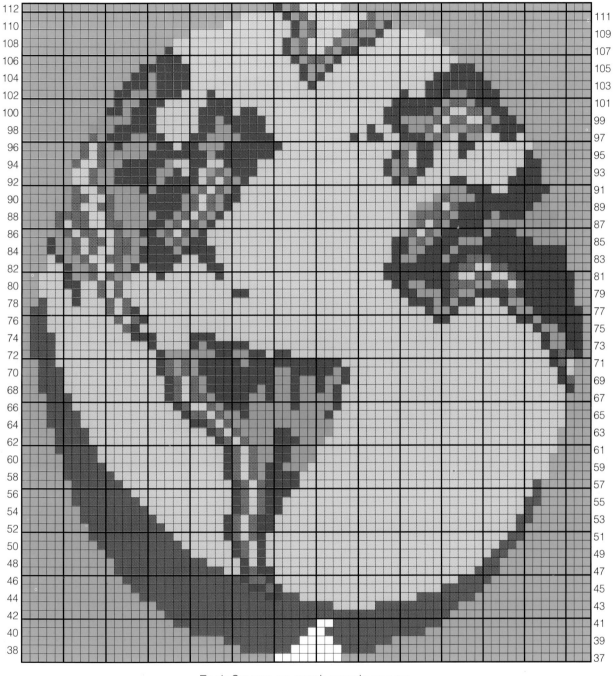

Each Square on graph equals one sc.

COLOR KEY

= Med. Blue   = Dk. Green

= White   = Med. Brown

= Dk. Blue   = Tan

= Lt. Blue   = Lt. Green

Tapestry Jewels

Designed by *Jennifer Christiansen McClain*

Size: 52" x 66".

Materials: Worsted-weight yarn — 28 oz. jeweltone variegated, 14 oz. blue and 13 oz. rose; H crochet hook or size needed to obtain gauge.

Gauge: 7 sts = 2"; rows 1 and 2 = 1½".

Skill Level: ☆☆ Average

FIRST PANEL

Row 1: With rose, ch 4, 3 dc in 4th ch from hook, turn (3 dc).

NOTE: Beginning ch-3 is not used or counted as a st.

Row 2: Ch 3, (yo, insert hook in next dc, yo, draw lp through, yo, draw through 2 lps on hook) 3 times, yo, draw through all 4 lps on hook, turn.

Row 3: Ch 4, 3 dc in 4th ch from hook, turn.

Rows 4-79: Repeat rows 2 and 3 alternately.

Row 80: Repeat row 2, ch 1, fasten off.

Rnd 81: Working in ends of rows with right side of row 80 facing you, join variegated with sc in first ch of ch-3 on row 80, sc in next ch, skip next ch, (hdc, dc) in next st, (3 tr, 3 dc, tr) in ch-1 of row 80, skip end of row 80, *sc in each of first 2 chs on ch-3 of next row, (hdc, dc) in next ch, tr in same ch as 3-dc group, skip next row*; repeat between ** across to last row, sc in each of first 2 chs of ch-3 on last row, (hdc, dc) in next ch, (3 tr, 3 dc, tr) in same ch as 3-dc group on row 1, skip opposite end of row 1; working in opposite ends of rows, repeat between ** across, join with sl st in first sc (412 sts).

Rnd 82: Ch 1, sc in first st, *2 sc in next st, (sc in next st, 2 sc in next st) 2 times, (2 sc in next st, sc in next st) 3 times*, sc in next 195 sts; repeat between **, sc in each st across, join, fasten off (424 sc).

NOTE: Beginning ch-2 or ch-3 is used and counted as first st.

Rnd 83: Join blue with sl st in first sc, ch 2, *(hdc in next st, 2 hdc in next st) 4 times, (2 hdc in next st, hdc in next st) 4 times*, hdc in next 195 sts; repeat between **, hdc in each st across, join with sl st in top of ch-2, fasten off (440 hdc).

NOTE: For shell, (sl st, ch 3, 2 dc) in next st.

Rnd 84: Join variegated with sl st in 13th st, ch 3, 2 dc in same st, *shell in next st, (skip next st, shell in next st) 3 times, (skip next 2 sts, shell in next st) 69 times*, (skip next st, shell in next st) 3 times; repeat between **, (skip next st, shell in next st) 2 times, skip last st, join with sl st in same st as first shell, fasten off (152 shells).

NEXT 11 PANELS

Rows/Rnds 1-83: Repeat same rows/rnds of First Panel.

NOTE: For joining shell, sl st in next st, ch 3, drop lp from hook; insert hook from front to back through top of ch-3 in corresponding shell on last Panel made, draw dropped lp through, 2 dc in same st as last sl st on this Panel.

Rnd 84: Join variegated with sl st in 13th st, ch 3, 2 dc in same st, shell in next st, (skip next st, shell in next st) 3 times, (skip next 2 sts, shell in next st) 69 times, (skip next st, shell in next st) 3 times, (shell in next st, skip next st) 3 times, work joining shell, (skip next 2 sts, work joining shell) 69 times, (skip next st, shell in next st) 2 times, skip last st, join with sl st in same st as first shell, fasten off (152 shells).

EDGING

Working around entire outer edge, join variegated with sl st in top of ch-3 on any shell on one long edge, ch 3, 2 dc in same st, [shell in top of ch-3 on each shell around to next joined shell, *skip next joined shell; working on next panel, shell in top of ch-3 on first unworked shell, shell in top of ch-3 on next 5 shells*; repeat between ** 10 more times]; repeat between [ ], shell in top of ch-3 on each shell around, join with sl st in same st as first shell, fasten off. ✂

Timeless Tablecloth

Designed by *Lucille LaFlamme*

Size: 54" after blocking.
Materials: Size-10 bedspread cotton — 2855 yds. white; tapestry needle; No. 8 steel crochet hook or size needed to obtain gauge.
Gauge: Rnd 1 = 1" across.
NOTE: Tablecloth may ruffle until blocked.
Skill Level: ☆☆☆☆ Challenging

TABLECLOTH

Rnd 1: Ch 10, sl st in first ch to form ring, ch 3, 23 dc in ring, join with sl st in top of ch-3 (24 dc).

Rnd 2: Ch 9, skip next dc, (tr in next dc, ch 5, skip next dc) around, join with sl st in 4th ch of ch-9 (12 ch sps).

Rnd 3: Sl st in first ch sp, ch 4, 6 tr in same sp, ch 1, (7 tr in next ch sp, ch 1) around, join with sl st in top of ch-4 (84 tr, 12 ch-1 sps).

Rnd 4: Ch 4, tr in next 6 tr, ch 3, (tr in next 7 tr, ch 3) around, join.

*NOTES: For **beginning small decrease (beg sm dec)**, ch 3, tr in next st.*

*For **small decrease (sm dec)**, tr next 2 sts tog.*

*For **beginning medium decrease (beg med dec)**, ch 3, *yo 2 times, insert hook in next st, yo, draw lp through, (yo, draw through 2 lps on hook) 2 times; repeat from * 3 more times, yo, draw through all 5 lps on hook, ch 1.*

*For **medium decrease (med dec)**, *yo 2 times, insert hook in next st, yo, draw lp through, (yo, draw through 2 lps on hook) 2 times; repeat from * 4 more times, yo, draw through all 6 lps on hook, ch 1.*

Rnd 5: Beg sm dec, tr in each of next 3 tr, sm dec, ch 3, tr in center ch of next ch sp, ch 3, *sm dec, tr in each of next 3 tr, sm dec, ch 3, tr in center ch of next ch sp, ch 3; repeat from * around, join with sl st in top of beg sm dec.

Rnd 6: Beg med dec, ch 5, tr in center ch of next ch sp, ch 3, tr in center ch of next ch sp, ch 5, *med dec, ch 5, tr in center ch of next ch sp, ch 3, tr in center ch of next ch sp, ch 5; repeat from * around, join with sl st in top of beg med dec (12 med dec).

Rnd 7: Ch 7, tr in center ch of next ch-5 sp, (ch 5, tr in center ch of next ch-5) 2 times, *ch 3, tr in top of next dec, ch 3, tr in center ch of next ch-5, (ch 5, tr in center ch of next ch-5) 2 times; repeat from * 10 more times; to **join,** ch 1, hdc in 4th ch of ch-7.

Rnds 8-9: Ch 9, tr in center ch of next ch sp, (ch 5, tr in center ch of next ch sp) around; to **join,** ch 2, dc in 4th ch of ch-9.

Rnd 10: Ch 4, 4 tr around joining dc, *ch 3, tr in center ch of next ch-5, ch 5, tr in center ch of next ch-5, ch 3*, [5 tr in center ch of next ch-5; repeat between **]; repeat between [ ] around, join (112 tr).

Rnd 11: Ch 4, tr in next tr, *2 tr in next tr, tr in each of next 2 tr, tr in each of next 3 chs, tr in next tr, tr in each of next 2 chs, 2 tr in next ch, tr in each of next 2 chs, tr in next tr, tr in each of next 3 chs*, [tr in each of next 2 tr; repeat between **]; repeat between [ ] around, join (320 tr).

*NOTES: For **beginning large decrease (beg lg dec)**, ch 3, *yo 2 times, insert hook in next st, yo, draw lp through, (yo, draw through 2 lps on hook) 2 times; repeat from * 4 more times, yo, draw through all 6 lps on hook, ch 1.*

*For **large decrease (lg dec)**, *yo 2 times, insert hook in next st, yo, draw lp through, (yo, draw through 2 lps on hook) 2 times; repeat from * 5 more times, yo, draw through all 7 lps on hook, ch 1.*

*For **beginning small cluster (beg sm cl)**, ch 3, *yo 2 times, insert hook in sp, yo, draw lp through, (yo, draw through 2 lps on hook) 2 times; repeat from * in same sp, yo, draw through all 3 lps on hook.*

*For **small cluster (sm cl)**, *yo 2 times, insert hook in sp, yo, draw lp through, (yo, draw through 2 lps on hook) 2 times; repeat from * 2 more times in same sp, yo, draw through all 4 lps on hook.*

Rnd 12: Beg lg dec, ch 7, skip next 3 tr, tr in next tr, ch 7, skip next 6 tr, tr in next tr, ch 7, skip next 3 tr, *lg dec, ch 7, skip next 3 tr, tr in next tr, ch 7, skip next 6 tr, tr in next tr, ch 7, skip next 3 tr; repeat from * around, join with sl st in top of beg lg dec (16 lg dec, 32 tr, 48 ch sps).

Rnd 13: (Beg sm cl, ch 3, sm cl) in top of beg lg dec, ch 5, skip next ch sp, 7 tr in center ch of next ch-7, ch 5, *(sm cl, ch 3, sm cl) in top of next dec, ch 5, skip next ch sp, 7 tr in center ch of next ch-7, ch 5; repeat from * around, join with sl st in top of beg sm cl (112 tr, 32 sm cls).

Rnd 14: Sl st in first ch-3 sp, (beg sm cl, ch 3, sm cl) in same sp, ch 5, 2 tr in next tr, tr in each of next 2 tr, 3 tr in next tr, tr in each of next 2 tr, 2 tr in next tr, ch 5, *(sm cl, ch 3, sm cl) in next ch-3 sp, ch 5, 2 tr in next tr, tr in each of next 2 tr, 3 tr in next tr, tr in each of next 2 tr, 2 tr in next tr, ch 5; repeat from * around, join as before (176 tr, 32 sm cls).

Rnd 15: Sl st in first ch-3 sp, (beg sm cl, ch 3, sm cl) in same sp, ch 5, tr in next tr, (ch 1, tr in next tr) 10 times, ch 5, *(sm cl, ch 3, sm cl) in next ch-3 sp, ch 5, tr in next tr, (ch 1, tr in next tr) 10 times, ch 5; repeat from * around, join.

Rnd 16: Sl st in first ch-3 sp, (beg sm cl, ch 3, sm cl) in same sp, ch 5, sm cl in next tr, (ch 3, skip next tr, sm cl in next tr) 5 times, ch 5, *(sm cl, ch 3, sm cl) in next ch-3 sp, ch 5, sm cl in next tr, (ch 3, skip next tr, sm cl in next tr) 5 times, ch 5; repeat from * around, join (128 sm cls).

Rnd 17: Sl st in first ch-3 sp, (beg sm cl, ch 3, sm cl) in same sp, ch 5, sc in top of next cl, (ch 6, sc in top of next cl) 5 times, ch 5, *(sm cl, ch 3, sm cl) in next ch-3 sp, ch 5, sc in top of next cl, (ch 6, sc in top of next cl) 5 times, ch 5; repeat from * around, join.

Rnd 18: Sl st in first ch-3 sp, (beg sm cl, ch 5, sm cl) in same sp, ch 7, skip next ch-5 sp, sc in next ch-6 sp, (ch 6, sc in next ch-6 sp) 4 times, ch 7, *(sm cl, ch 5, sm cl) in next ch-3 sp, ch 7, skip next ch-5 sp, sc in next ch-6 sp, (ch 6, sc in next ch-6 sp) 4 times, ch 7; repeat from * around, join.

continued on page 42

Rnd 19: Sl st in first ch-5 sp, (beg sm cl, ch 3, sm cl, ch 3, sm cl) in same sp, ch 7, skip next ch-7 sp, sc in next ch-6 lp, ch 6, sc in next ch-6 sp) 3 times, ch 7, *(sm cl, ch 3, sm cl, ch 3, sm cl) in next ch-5 sp, ch 7, skip next ch-7 sp, sc in next ch-6 lp, ch 6, sc in next ch-6 sp) 3 times, ch 7; repeat from * around, join (48 sm cls).

Rnd 20: Sl st in first ch-3 sp, (beg sm cl, ch 3, sm cl) in same sp, *ch 3, tr in top of next cl, ch 3, (sm cl, ch 3, sm cl) in next ch-3 sp, ch 7, skip next ch-7 sp, sc in next ch-6 sp, (ch 6, sc in next ch-6 sp) 2 times, ch 7*, [(sm cl, ch 3, sm cl) in next ch-3 sp; repeat between **]; repeat between [ ] around, join (64 sm cls).

Rnd 21: Sl st in first ch-3 sp, (beg sm cl, ch 3, sm cl) in same sp, *ch 5, (tr in center ch of next ch sp, ch 5) 2 times, (sm cl, ch 3, sm cl) in next ch-3 sp, ch 7, skip next ch-7 sp, sc in next ch-6 sp, ch 6, sc in next ch-6 sp, ch 7*, [(sm cl, ch 3, sm cl) in next ch-3 sp; repeat between **]; repeat between [ ] around, join.

Rnd 22: Sl st in first ch-3 sp, (beg sm cl, ch 3, sm cl) in same sp, *ch 5, (tr in center ch of next ch sp, ch 5) 3 times, (sm cl, ch 3, sm cl) in next ch-3 sp, ch 7, skip next ch-7 sp, (sc, ch 5, sc) in next ch-6 sp, ch 7*, [(sm cl, ch 3, sm cl) in next ch-3 sp; repeat between **]; repeat between [ ] around, join.

Rnd 23: Sl st in first ch-3 sp, (beg sm cl, ch 3, sm cl) in same sp, ch 5, (tr in center ch of next ch sp, ch 5) 4 times, (sm cl, ch 3, sm cl) in next ch-3 sp, *ch 3, skip next 2 ch-7 sps, (sm cl, ch 3, sm cl) in next ch 3 sp, ch 5, (tr in center ch of next ch sp, ch 5) 4 times, (sm cl, ch 3, sm cl) in next ch-3 sp; repeat from * 14 more times; to **join,** ch 1, dc in top of beg sm cl.

Rnd 24: (Beg sm cl, ch 3, sm cl) around joining dc just made, *ch 3, (tr in center ch of next ch sp, ch 5) 3 times, 7 tr in next ch sp, (ch 5, tr in center ch of next ch sp) 3 times, ch 3*, [(sm cl, ch 3, sm cl) in next ch sp; repeat between **]; repeat between [ ] around, join.

*NOTE: For **picot**, ch 6, sl st in **front lp** of last cl or sc made.*

Rnd 25: Sl st in first ch-3 sp, (beg sm cl, picot) in same sp, *ch 5, skip next ch-3 sp, tr in center ch of next ch sp, ch 5, tr in center ch of next ch sp, ch 7, skip next ch sp, 2 tr in each of next 3 tr, ch 2, skip next tr, 2 tr in each of next 3 tr, ch 7, skip next ch-3 sp, tr in center ch of next ch sp, ch 5, tr in center ch of next ch sp*, [ch 5, skip next ch-3 sp, (sm cl, picot) in next ch-3 sp; repeat between **]; repeat between [ ] around; to **join,** ch 2, dc in top of beg sm cl.

Rnd 26: Ch 9, *tr in center ch of next ch sp, (ch 5, tr in center ch of next ch sp) 2 times, ch 3, (tr in next 6 tr, ch 3) 2 times, tr in center ch of next ch sp, ch 5, tr in next ch of next ch sp*, [ch 5, tr in center ch of next ch sp, ch 5; repeat between **]; repeat between [ ] around; to **join,** ch 2, dc in 4th ch of ch-9.

Rnd 27: Ch 9, *(sm cl, picot) in center ch of next ch sp, ch 5, (tr in center ch of next ch sp, ch 5) 2 times, skip next ch-3 sp, (tr in next 6 tr, ch 5, skip next ch-3 sp) 2 times, tr in center ch of next ch sp*, [ch 5, tr in center ch of next ch sp, ch 5; repeat between **]; repeat between [ ] around, join as before.

Rnd 28: Ch 9, *tr in center ch of next ch sp, (ch 5, tr in center ch of next ch sp) 3 times, ch 3, tr in next 6 tr, ch 4, (sc, picot) in center ch of next ch sp, ch 4, tr in next 6 tr, ch 3, tr in center ch of next ch sp*, [ch 5, tr in center ch of next ch sp, ch 5; repeat between **]; repeat between [ ] around, join.

Rnd 29: Ch 9, *tr in center ch of next ch sp, ch 5, (sm cl, picot) in center ch of next ch sp, ch 5, (tr in center ch of next ch sp, ch 5) 2 times, skip next ch sp, tr in next 6 tr*, [ch 5, skip next ch sp, tr in center ch of next ch sp, ch 5; repeat between **]; repeat between [ ] around, join.

Rnd 30: Ch 9, *tr in center ch of next ch sp, (ch 5, tr in center ch of next ch sp) 4 times, ch 3, tr in next 6 tr, ch 5, sc in center ch of ch-11, ch 5, tr in next 6 tr, ch 3*, [tr in center ch of next ch sp, ch 5; repeat between **]; repeat between [ ] around, join with sl st in 4th ch of ch-9.

Rnd 31: Sl st in each of first 3 chs, ch 9, *tr in center ch of next ch sp, ch 5, (sm cl, picot) in center ch of next ch sp, ch 5, (tr in center ch of next ch sp, ch 5) 2 times, skip next ch sp, tr in next 6 tr, ch 5, (sm cl, picot) in next sc, ch 5, tr in next 6 tr, ch 5, skip next ch sp*, [tr in center ch of next ch sp, ch 5; repeat between **]; repeat between [ ] around, join as before.

Rnd 32: Sl st in first 3 chs, ch 9, *tr in center ch of next ch sp, ch 7, tr in center ch of next ch sp, (ch 5, tr in center ch of next ch sp) 2 times, ch 4, tr in next 6 tr, ch 4, sc in center ch of next ch sp, ch 7, sc in center ch of next ch sp, ch 4, tr in next 6 tr, ch 4, tr in center ch of next ch sp, ch 5*, [tr in center ch of next ch sp, ch 5; repeat between **]; repeat between [ ] around, join.

Rnd 33: Ch 4, *(tr in each of next 2 chs, 2 tr in next ch, tr in each of next 2 chs, tr in next tr), tr in each of next 3 chs, 2 tr in next ch, tr in each of next 3 chs, tr in next tr; repeat between ( ), ch 3, tr in center ch of next ch sp, ch 7, skip next ch sp, tr in next 6 tr, ch 5, sc in center ch of next ch-7 sp, ch 5, tr in next 6 tr, ch 7, skip next ch sp, tr in center ch of next ch sp, ch 3*, [tr in next tr; repeat between **]; repeat between [ ] around, join.

Rnd 34: Ch 4, *tr in next 5 tr, ch 7, skip next 4 tr, sc in next tr, ch 5, skip next 2 tr, sc in next tr, ch 7, skip next 4 tr, tr in next 6 tr, ch 5, skip next ch sp, tr in 3rd ch of ch-7, ch 5, tr in next 6 tr, ch 3, cl in next sc, ch 3, tr in next 6 tr, ch 5, tr in 5th ch of ch-7, ch 5, skip next ch-3 sp*, [tr in next tr; repeat between **]; repeat between [ ] around, join.

Rnd 35: Ch 4, *tr in next 5 tr, ch 6, 10 tr in next ch-5 sp, ch 6, tr in next 6 tr, ch 3, tr in center ch of next ch sp, ch 5, tr in center ch of next ch sp, ch 3, (tr in next 6 tr, ch 3) 2 times, tr in center ch of next ch sp, ch 5, tr in center ch of next ch sp, ch 3*, [tr in next tr; repeat between **]; repeat between [ ] around, join.

Rnd 36: Ch 4, *tr in next 5 tr, ch 5, sm cl in next tr, (ch 4, skip next 2 tr, sm cl in next tr) 3 times, ch 5, tr in next 6 tr, ch 5, skip next ch sp, tr in center ch of next ch sp, ch 7, skip next ch-3 sp, (tr next 3 sts tog) 2 times, ch 1, (tr next 3 sts tog) 2 times, ch 7, skip next ch-3 sp, tr in center ch of next ch sp, ch 5, skip next ch-3 sp*, [tr in next tr; repeat between **]; repeat between [ ] around, join.

*NOTES: For **double treble crochet (dtr**—see page 158), yo 3 times, insert hook in next st, yo, draw lp through, (yo, draw through 2 lps on hook) 4 times.*

*For **dtr next 5 sts tog**, *yo 3 times, insert hook in next st, yo, draw lp through (yo, draw through 2 lps on hook) 3 times; repeat from * 4 more times, yo, draw through all 6 lps on hook.*

Rnd 37: Ch 4, *tr in next 5 tr, ch 7, sc in next ch-4 sp, (ch 5, sc in next ch-4 sp) 2 times, ch 7, tr in next 6 tr, ch 3, tr in center ch of next ch sp, ch 5, tr in 3rd ch of ch-7, ch 5; working in sts and in ch-1 sp, dtr next 5 sts tog, ch 5, tr in 5th ch of ch-7, ch 5, tr in center ch of next ch sp, ch 3*, [tr in next tr; repeat between **]; repeat between [ ] around, join.

Rnd 38: Ch 4, *tr in next 5 tr, ch 5, sc in center ch of next ch sp, ch 5, sm cl in center ch of next ch sp, ch 7, sm cl in center ch of next ch sp, ch 5, sc in center ch of next ch sp, ch 5, tr in next 6 tr, ch 5, skip next ch-3 sp, tr in center ch of next ch sp, ch 7, skip next ch sp, (tr, ch 7, tr) in top of next dtr group, ch 7, skip next ch sp, tr in center ch of next ch sp, ch 5, skip next ch sp*, [tr in next tr; repeat between **]; repeat between [ ] around, join.

Rnd 39: Ch 4, *tr in next 5 tr, ch 7, (sc, ch 5, sc) in center ch of next ch-7, ch 7, tr in next 6 tr, ch 3, tr in center ch of next ch sp, ch 5, tr in 3rd ch of ch-7, ch 7, sc in center ch of next ch sp, ch 7, tr in 5th ch of next ch-7, ch

5, tr in center ch of next ch-5, ch 3*, [tr in next tr; repeat between **]; repeat between [ ] around, join.

Rnd 40: Ch 4, *tr in next 5 tr, ch 5, tr in next ch-5 sp, ch 5, tr in next 6 tr, ch 5, sm cl in next tr, ch 5, tr in next tr, ch 19, skip next 2 ch sps, tr in next tr, ch 5, sm cl in next tr, ch 5*, [tr in next tr; repeat between **]; repeat between [ ] around, join.

Rnd 41: Ch 4, *tr in next 5 tr, ch 5, sc in next tr, ch 5, tr in next 6 tr, ch 5, (sm cl, ch 3, sm cl) in next sm cl, ch 5, skip next tr, sc in first ch of next ch-19, (ch 5, skip next 2 chs, sc in next ch) 6 times, ch 5, (sm cl, ch 3, sm cl) in next sm cl, ch 5*, [tr in next tr; repeat between **]; repeat between [ ] around, join.

Rnd 42: Ch 4, *tr in next 5 tr, ch 3, tr in next 6 tr, ch 5, (sm cl in next cl, ch 5) 2 times, skip next ch-5 sp, (tr, ch 3, tr) in center ch of each of next 6 ch-5 sps, ch 5, (sm cl in next cl, ch 5) 2 times*, [tr in next tr; repeat between **]; repeat between [ ] around, join.

Rnd 43: Ch 4, *tr in next 11 tr, (ch 5, sm cl in next cl) 2 times, ch 3, (tr, ch 3, tr) in center ch of each of next 8 ch sps, ch 3, (sm cl in next cl, ch 5) 2 times*, [tr in next tr; repeat between **]; repeat between [ ] around, join.

Rnd 44: Ch 4, *tr in each of next 2 tr, skip next 6 tr, tr in each of next 3 tr, (ch 5, sm cl in next cl) 2 times, ch 7, (sc in next tr, 3 sc in next ch sp, sc in next tr) 8 times, ch 7, (sm cl in next cl, ch 5) 2 times*, [tr in next tr; repeat between **]; repeat between [ ] around, join.

*NOTES: For **beginning split decrease (beg split dec)**, ch 3, *yo 2 times, insert hook in next tr, yo, draw lp through, (yo, draw through 2 lps on hook) 2 times*, skip next 2 tr; repeat between ** 2 more times, yo, draw through all 4 lps on hook, ch 1.*

*For **split decrease (split dec)**, *yo 2 times, insert hook in next tr, yo, draw lp through, (yo, draw through 2 lps on hook) 2 times*; repeat between **, skip next 2 tr; repeat between ** 2 more times, yo, draw through all 5 lps on hook, ch 1.*

Rnd 45: Beg split dec, *ch 5, (sm cl in next cl, ch 7) 2 times, skip next 2 sc, sc in next sc, picot, (ch 6, skip next 4 sc, sc in next sc, picot) 7 times, (ch 7, sm cl in next cl) 2 times, ch 5*, [split dec; repeat between **]; repeat between [ ] around, join with sl st in top of beg split dec.

Rnd 46: Ch 1, sc in first st, *ch 6, sm cl in next cl, ch 7, sc in center ch of next ch sp, ch 7, sm cl in next cl, ch 8, sc in next ch-6 sp, picot, (ch 6, sc in next ch-6 sp, picot) 6 times, ch 8, sm cl in next cl, ch 7, sc in center ch of next ch sp, ch

continued on page 46

Mountain Laurel

Designed by *Lucille LaFlamme*

Size: 18" after blocking.

Materials: Size-20 bedspread cotton — 445 yds. ecru; tapestry needle; No. 12 steel crochet hook or size needed to obtain gauge.

Gauge: 3 tr rnds = 1" across.

NOTE: Doily may ruffle until blocked.

Skill Level: ☆☆☆ Advanced

DOILY

Rnd 1: Ch 9, sl st in first ch to form ring, ch 3, 4 dc in ring, ch 2, (5 dc, ch 2) 4 times in ring, join with sl st in top of ch-3 (25 dc, 5 ch-2 sps).

Rnd 2: Ch 4, tr in same st, 2 tr in each of next 4 dc, ch 3, (2 tr in each of next 5 dc, ch 3) around, join with sl st in top of ch-4 (50 tr, 5 ch-3 sps).

Rnds 3-4: Ch 5, tr in next tr, (ch 1, tr in next tr) 8 times, ch 3, *tr in next tr, (ch 1, tr in next tr) 9 times, ch 3; repeat from * around, join with sl st in 4th ch of ch-5.

*NOTES: For **beginning cluster (beg cl)**, ch 4, *yo 2 times, insert hook in sp, yo, draw lp through, (yo, draw through 2 lps on hook) 2 times; repeat from * in same sp, yo, draw through all 3 lps on hook.*

*For **cluster (cl)**, *yo 2 times, insert hook in sp, yo, draw lp through, (yo, draw through 2 lps on hook) 2 times; repeat from * 2 more times in same sp, yo, draw through all 4 lps on hook.*

Rnd 5: Sl st in first ch-1 sp, beg cl, (ch 2, cl in next ch-1 sp) 8 times, ch 5, *cl in next ch-1 sp, (ch 2, cl in next ch-1 sp) 8 times, ch 5; repeat from * around, join with sl st in top of beg cl (45 cls, 40 ch-2 sps).

Rnd 6: Sl st in first ch-2 sp, beg cl, (ch 2, cl in next ch-2 sp) 7 times, ch 9, *cl in next ch-2 sp, (ch 2, cl in next ch-2 sp) 7 times, ch 9; repeat from * around, join (40 cls).

*NOTE: For **small V-stitch (sm V-st)**, (tr, ch 5, tr) in ch.*

Rnd 7: Sl st in first ch-2 sp, beg cl, (ch 2, cl in next ch-2 sp) 6 times, ch 7, sm V-st in 5th ch of ch-9, ch 7, *cl in next ch-2 sp, (ch 2, cl in next ch-2 sp) 6 times, ch 7, sm V-st in 5th ch of ch-9, ch 7; repeat from * around, join (35 cls, 5 sm V-sts).

Rnd 8: Sl st in first ch-2 sp, beg cl, *[(ch 2, cl in next ch-2 sp) 5 times, ch 7, cl in next tr, ch 5, tr in 3rd ch of ch-5, ch 5, cl in next tr, ch 7], cl in next ch-2 sp; repeat from * 3 more times; repeat between [ ], join (40 cls, 5 tr).

Rnd 9: Sl st in first ch-2 sp, beg cl, *[(ch 2, cl in next ch-2 sp) 4 times, ch 7, (cl, ch 3, cl) in next cl, ch 5, (cl, ch 3, cl) in next tr, ch 5, (cl, ch 3, cl) in next cl, ch 7], cl in next ch-2 sp; repeat from * 3 more times; repeat between [ ], join (55 cls).

Rnd 10: Sl st in first ch-2 sp, beg cl, *[(ch 2, cl in next ch-2 sp) 3 times, ch 7, (cl in next cl, ch 3, cl in next ch-3 sp, ch 3, cl in next cl), 2 times, ch 7], cl in next ch-2 sp; repeat from * 3 more times; repeat between [ ], join (65 cls).

Rnd 11: Sl st in first ch-2 sp, beg cl, [◊(ch 2, cl in next ch-2 sp) 2 times, ch 7, *cl in next cl, (ch 3, cl in next cl) 2 times, ch 7; repeat from * 2 more times◊, cl in next ch-2 sp]; repeat between [ ] 3 more times; repeat between ◊◊, join (60 cls).

Rnd 12: Sl st in first ch-2 sp, beg cl, [◊ch 2, cl in next ch-2 sp, ch 9, *cl in next cl, (ch 1, cl in next cl) 2 times, ch 5, sm V-st in 4th ch of ch-7, ch 5; repeat from *, ch 5, cl in next cl, (ch 1, cl in next cl) 2 times, ch 9◊, cl in next ch-2 sp]; repeat between [ ] 3 more times; repeat between ◊◊, join (55 cls, 10 sm V-sts).

Rnd 13: Sl st in first ch-2 sp, beg cl, [◊ch 9, cl in next cl, ch 3, skip next cl, cl in next cl, *ch 7, tr in next tr, 11 tr in next ch-5 sp, tr in next tr, ch 7, cl in next cl, ch 3, skip next cl, cl in next cl; repeat from *, ch 9◊, cl in next ch-2 sp]; repeat between [ ] 3 more times; repeat between ◊◊, join (35 cls, 130 tr).

Rnd 14: Ch 15, [◊skip next cl, cl in next ch-3 sp, *ch 7, skip next cl, tr in next tr, (ch 1, tr in next tr) 12 times, ch 7, cl in next ch-3 sp; repeat from *, ch 11, skip next cl◊, tr in next cl, ch 11]; repeat between [ ] 3 more times; repeat between ◊◊, join with sl st in 4th ch of ch-15 (15 cls).

*NOTES: For **beginning large V-stitch (beg lg V-st)**, ch 11, tr in same st.*

*For **large V-stitch (lg V-st)**, (tr, ch 7, tr) in next st.*

Rnd 15: Beg lg V-st, [◊ch 5, lg V-st in next cl, ch 5, *sc in next ch-1 sp, (ch 3, sc in next ch-1 sp) 11 times, ch 5, lg V-st in next cl, ch 5; repeat from *◊, lg V-st in next tr]; repeat between [ ] 3 more times; repeat between ◊◊, join with sl st in 4th ch of ch-11 (20 lg V-sts).

Rnd 16: Beg cl, [◊ch 3, dc in 4th ch of ch-7, ch 3, cl

in next tr, *ch 5, dc in next tr, ch 3, sc in next ch-7 sp, ch 3, dc in next tr, ch 5, sc in next ch-3 sp, (ch 4, sc in next ch-3 sp) 10 times; repeat from *, ch 5, dc in next tr, ch 3, sc in next ch-7 sp, ch 3, dc in next tr, ch 5◊, cl in next tr]; repeat between [ ] 3 more times; repeat between ◊◊, join.

NOTE: *For shell, (2 tr, ch 3, 2 tr) in next st or ch sp.*
Rnd 17: (Beg cl, ch 3, cl) in beg cl, [◊ch 3, tr in next

dc, ch 3, (cl, ch 3, cl) in next cl, ch 5, shell in next sc, *ch 5, sc in next ch-4 sp, (ch 4, sc in next ch-4 sp) 9 times, ch 5*, shell in each of next 2 dc; repeat between **, shell in next sc, ch 5◊, (cl, ch 3, cl) in next cl]; repeat between [ ] 3 more times; repeat between ◊◊, join (20 cls, 20 shells).

Rnd 18: Beg cl in beg cl, [◊ch 3, cl in next cl, ch 3, tr

continued on page 46

Mountain Laurel

continued from page 45

in next tr, (ch 3, cl in next cl) 2 times, ch 5, shell in next shell, *ch 5, sc in next ch-4 sp, (ch 4, sc in next ch-4 sp) 8 times, ch 5*, shell in each of next 2 shells; repeat between**, shell in next shell, ch 5◊, cl in next cl]; repeat between [ ] 3 more times; repeat between ◊◊, join.

Rnd 19: Beg cl, [◊ch 3, cl in next ch-3 sp, ch 3, cl in next cl, ch 3, cl in next tr, ch 3, cl in next cl, ch 3, cl in next ch-3 sp, ch 3, cl in next cl, ch 5, *shell in next shell, ch 5, sc in next ch-4 sp, (ch 4, sc in next ch-4 sp) 7 times, ch 5, shell in next shell*, ch 3; repeat between **, ch 5◊, cl in next cl]; repeat between [ ] 3 more times; repeat between ◊◊, join (35 cls, 20 shells).

Rnd 20: Beg cl, [◊(ch 3, cl in next cl) 2 times, ch 5, (cl, ch 3, cl) in next cl, ch 5, cl in next cl, (ch 3, cl in next cl) 2 times, ch 5, shell in next shell, *ch 6, sc in next ch-4 sp, (ch 4, sc in next ch-4 sp) 6 times, ch 6, shell in next shell*, ch 3, 5 tr in 2nd ch of ch-3, ch 3, shell in next shell; repeat between **, ch 5◊, cl in next cl]; repeat between [ ] 3 more times; repeat between ◊◊ around, join.

Rnd 21: Beg cl, [◊(ch 3, cl in next cl) 2 times, ch 5, cl in next cl, ch 3, cl in next ch-3 sp, ch 3, cl in next cl, ch 5, cl in next cl, (ch 3, cl in next cl) 2 times, ch 6, *shell in next shell, ch 6, sc in next ch-4 sp, (ch 4, sc in next ch-4 sp) 5 times, ch 6, shell in next shell*, ch 5, tr in next tr, (ch 1, tr in next tr) 4 times, ch 5; repeat between **, ch 6◊, cl in next cl]; repeat between [ ] 3 more times; repeat between ◊◊, join.

Rnd 22: Beg cl, [◊ch 1, tr in next cl, ch 1, cl in next cl, ch 7, cl in next cl, (ch 3, cl in next cl) 2 times, ch 7, cl in next cl, ch 1, tr in next cl, ch 1, cl in next cl, ch 7, skip first 2 chs of ch-6, tr in each of next 2 chs, *ch 7, shell in next shell, ch 6, sc in next ch-4 sp, (ch 4, sc in next ch-4 sp) 4 times, ch 7, shell in next shell, ch 7*, tr in next tr, (ch 1, tr in next ch-1 sp, ch 1, tr in next tr) 4 times; repeat between **, skip next 2 chs of ch-6, tr in each of next 2 chs, ch 7◊, cl in next cl]; repeat between [ ] 3 more times; repeat between ◊◊, join.

Rnd 23: Beg cl, [◊ch 3, cl in next cl, ch 5, 3 tr in 4th ch of ch-7, ch 5, cl in next cl, ch 1, tr in next cl, ch 1, cl in next cl, ch 5, 3 tr in 4th ch of next ch-7, ch 5, cl in next cl, ch 3, cl in next cl, ch 7, 3 tr in each of next 2 tr, *ch 7, shell in next shell, ch 7, sc in next ch-4 sp, (ch 4, sc in next ch-4 sp) 3 times, ch 7, shell in next shell, ch 7*, tr in next tr, (ch 3, tr in next tr) 8 times; repeat between **, 3 tr in each of next 2 tr, ch 7◊, cl in next cl]; repeat between [ ] 3 more times; repeat between ◊◊ , join.

NOTE: *For **picot,** ch 5, sl st in **front lp** of last tr made.*

Rnd 24: Sl st in first ch-3 sp, beg cl in same sp, [◊ch 5, 3 tr in each of next 3 tr, ch 5, cl in next cl, ch 1, cl in next cl, ch 5, 3 tr in each of next 3 tr, ch 5, cl in next ch-3 sp, ch 5, 2 tr in each of next 6 tr, ch 7, *3 tr in next shell, ch 7, sc in next ch-4 sp, (ch 4, sc in next ch-4 sp) 2 times, ch 7, 3 tr in next shell*, ch 9, (2 tr, picot, 2 tr) in next ch-3 sp, (ch 3, 2 tr, picot, 2 tr) in each of next 7 ch-3 sps, ch 9; repeat between **, ch 7, 2 tr in each of next 6 tr, ch 5◊, cl in next ch-3 sp]; repeat between [ ] 3 more times; repeat between ◊◊, join.

Rnd 25: Ch 1, sc in same st, *◊ch 5, (tr, picot) in next tr, tr in next tr, ch 5, skip next 2 tr, sc in next tr, ch 5, skip next 2 tr, (tr, picot) in next tr, tr in next tr, ch 5◊, sc in next ch-1 sp; repeat between ◊◊, sc in next cl, ch 5, **(tr, picot) in next tr, tr in next tr, ch 5, skip next tr, sc in next tr, ch 5, skip next tr; repeat from **, (tr, picot) in next tr, tr in next tr, ch 7, sc in 2nd tr of next 3-tr group, ch 2, (tr, picot) in next ch-4 sp, tr in next ch-4 sp, ch 2, sc in 2nd tr of next 3-tr group, ch 13, •(tr, picot, tr) in next ch-3 sp, ch 7, sc in next ch-3 sp, ch 7; repeat from • 2 more times, (tr, picot, tr) in next ch-3 sp, ch 13, sc in 2nd tr of next 3-tr group, ch 2, (tr, picot) in next ch-4 sp, tr in next ch-4 sp, ch 2, sc in 2nd tr of next 3-tr group, ch 7, (tr, picot) in next tr, ♦tr in next tr, ch 5, skip next tr, sc in next tr, ch 5, skip next tr, (tr, picot) in next tr; repeat from ♦, tr in next tr, ch 5*, [sc in next cl; repeat between **]; repeat between [ ] around, join. ✄

Timeless Tablecloth

continued from page 43

7, sm cl in next cl*, [ch 6, sc in next dec; repeat between **]; repeat between [ ] around, to **join,** dtr in first sc.

Rnd 47: Beg sm cl in first st, *sm cl in next cl, ch 7,

(sc in next ch sp, ch 7) 2 times, sm cl in next cl, ch 8, sc in next ch-6 sp, picot, (ch 6, sc in next ch-6 sp, picot) 5 times, ch 8, sm cl in next cl, (ch 7, sc in next ch sp) 2 times, ch 7*, [sm cl in next cl; repeat between **]; repeat between [ ] around; to **join,** ch 3, skip beg sm cl, tr in top of next sm cl.

Rnd 48: Ch 1, sc around joining tr just made, *ch 9, (sc in next ch sp, ch 9) 3 times, sm cl in next cl, ch 9, sc in next ch-6 sp, picot, (ch 8, sc in next ch-6 sp, picot) 4 times, ch 9, sm cl in next cl, ch 9, (sc in next ch sp, ch 9) 2 times*, [sc in next ch sp; repeat between **]; repeat between [ ] around, join.

Rnd 49: Sl st in first 4 chs, ch 1, sc in same ch sp, *ch 9, (sc in next ch sp, ch 9) 3 times, sm cl in next cl, ch 9, sc in next ch-8 sp, picot, (ch 8, sc in next ch-8 sp, picot) 3 times, ch 9, sm cl in next cl, ch 9, (sc in next ch sp, ch 9) 3 times*, [sc in next ch sp; repeat between **]; repeat between [ ] around, join.

Rnd 50: Sl st in first 4 chs, ch 1, sc in same ch sp, *ch 9, (sc in next ch sp, ch 9) 3 times, sm cl in next cl, ch 9, sc in next ch-8 sp, picot, (ch 8, sc in next ch-8 sp, picot) 2 times, ch 9, sm cl in next cl, ch 9, (sc in next ch sp, ch 9) 4 times *, [sc in next ch sp; repeat between **]; repeat between [ ] around, join.

Rnd 51: Sl st in first 4 chs, ch 1, sc in same ch sp, *ch 10, (sc in next ch sp, ch 10) 3 times, sm cl in next cl, ch 9, sc in next ch-8 sp, picot, ch 8, sc in next ch-8 sp, picot, ch 9, sm cl in next cl, ch 10, (sc in next ch sp, ch 10) 5 times*, [sc in next ch sp; repeat between **]; repeat between [ ] around, join.

Rnd 52: Sl st in first 5 chs, ch 1, sc in same ch sp, *ch 10, (sc in next ch sp, ch 10) 3 times, sm cl in next cl, ch 9, sc in next ch-8 sp, ch 9, sm cl in next cl, ch 10, (sc in next ch sp, ch 10) 6 times*, [sc in next ch sp; repeat between **]; repeat between [ ] around, join.

Rnd 53: Sl st in first 5 chs, ch 1, sc in same ch sp, *ch 10, (sc in next ch sp, ch 10) 3 times, sm cl in next cl, ch 9, sc in next sc, ch 9, sm cl in next cl, ch 10, (sc in next ch sp, ch 10) 7 times*, [sc in next ch sp; repeat between **]; repeat between [ ] around, join.

Rnd 54: Sl st in first 5 chs, ch 1, sc in same ch sp, *ch 10, (sc in next ch sp, ch 10) 3 times, sm cl in each of next 2 cls, (ch 10, sc in next ch sp) 8 times*, [ch 10, sc in next ch sp; repeat between **]; repeat between [ ] around; to **join,** ch 5, dtr in first sc.

Rnd 55: Ch 1, sc around joining dtr just made, ch 3, sm cl in same sc as joining of last rnd, *ch 3, (sm cl, ch 3) 4 times in each of next 2 ch sps, sm cl in next sc, ch 3, sc in next ch sp, ch 7, sc in next ch sp, ch 3, (3 tr in next cl, ch 3) 2 times, sc in next ch sp, ch 7, sc in next ch sp, ch 3, sm cl in next sc, ch 3, (sm cl, ch 3) 4 times in each of next 2 ch sps, sm cl in next sc, ch 3, sc in next ch sp, ch 7, sc in next ch sp, ch 3, skip first 4 chs of next ch-10, 3 tr in next ch, ch 3, 3 tr in next ch, ch 3, sc in next ch sp*, [ch 7, sc in next ch sp, ch 3, sm cl in next sc; repeat

between **]; repeat between [ ] around, to **join,** ch 3, tr in first sc (320 cls).

NOTES: *For **beginning V-stitch (beg V-st),** ch 7, tr in same st.*

*For **V-stitch (V-st),** (tr, ch 3, tr) in next st.*

Rnd 56: Beg V-st in top of joining tr just made, *ch 3, (sm cl in next cl, ch 3) 10 times, V-st in 4th ch of next ch-7, ch 3, shell in next shell, ch 3*, [V-st in 4th ch of next ch-7; repeat between **]; repeat between [ ] around, join with sl st in 4th ch of ch-7.

Rnd 57: Sl st in each of first 2 chs, ch 4, 2 tr in same ch, *ch 4, sc in top of next cl, (ch 5, sc in top of next cl) 9 times, ch 4, 3 tr in 2nd ch of next V-st, ch 3, shell in next shell, ch 3, skip next ch-3 sp*, [3 tr in 2nd ch of next V-st; repeat between **]; repeat between [ ] around, join.

Rnd 58: Sl st in next tr, ch 4, 2 tr in same st, *ch 5, sc in next ch-5 sp, (ch 6, sc in next ch-5 sp) 8 times, ch 5, skip next tr, 3 tr in next tr, ch 3, shell in next shell, ch 3*, [skip next tr, 3 tr in next tr; repeat between **]; repeat between [ ] around, join.

Rnd 59: Sl st in next tr, ch 4, 2 tr in same st, *ch 5, sc in next ch-6 sp, (ch 6, sc in next ch-6 sp) 7 times, ch 5, skip next tr, 3 tr in next tr, ch 3, (3 tr, ch 3, 3 tr, ch 3, 3 tr) in next shell, ch 3*, [skip next tr, 3 tr in next tr; repeat between **]; repeat between [ ] around, join.

Rnd 60: Sl st in next tr, ch 4, 2 tr in same st, *ch 5, sc in next ch-6 sp, (ch 6, sc in next ch-6 sp) 6 times, ch 5, skip next tr, 3 tr in next tr, ch 3, skip next ch-3 sp, 3 tr in next ch-3 sp, ch 3, skip next tr, 3 tr in next tr, ch 3, 3 tr in next ch-3 sp, ch 3*, [skip next tr, 3 tr in next tr; repeat between **]; repeat between [ ] around, join.

Rnd 61: Sl st in next tr, ch 4, 2 tr in same st, *ch 5, sc in next ch-6 sp, ch 6, sc in next ch-6 sp) 5 times, ch 5, skip next tr, 3 tr in next tr, ch 3, skip next ch-3 sp, shell in each of next 2 ch-3 sps, ch 3*, [skip next tr, 3 tr in next tr; repeat between **]; repeat between [ ] around, join.

Rnd 62: Sl st in next tr, ch 4, 2 tr in same st, *ch 5, sc in next ch-6 sp, (ch 6, sc in next ch-6 sp) 4 times, ch 5, skip next tr, 3 tr in next tr, ch 3, skip next ch-3 sp, shell in next shell, ch 5, shell in next shell, ch 3*, [skip next tr, 3 tr in next tr; repeat between **]; repeat between [ ] around, join.

Rnd 63: Sl st in next tr, ch 4, 2 tr in same st, *ch 5, sc in next ch-6 sp, (ch 6, sc in next ch-6 sp) 3 times, ch 5, skip next tr, 3 tr in next tr, ch 3, skip next ch-3 sp, shell in next shell, ch 5, 3 tr in 3rd ch of ch-5, ch 5, shell in next shell, ch 3*, [skip next tr, 3 tr in next tr; repeat between **]; repeat between [ ] around, join.

Rnd 64: Sl st in next tr, ch 4, 2 tr in same st, *ch 5, sc in next ch-6 sp, (ch 6, sc in next ch-6 sp) 2 times, ch 5, skip next tr, 3 tr in next tr, ch 3, skip next ch-3 sp, shell

continued on page 49

Ruffled Bath Set

Designed by _Kathy Wigington_

Sizes: Basket is 4" tall without Handle. Soap Dispenser Cover fits 7½" tall liquid soap dispenser. Toilet Tissue Cover fits standard toilet tissue roll.

Materials For One Set: Worsted-weight yarn — 9 oz. green; 4 yds. burgundy ⅜" satin ribbon; 6 burgundy 2½" silk roses; 2 pieces of 18" 16-gauge wire; 3-lb. plastic margarine container; 7½" tall liquid soap dispenser; craft glue or hot glue gun; tapestry needle; G crochet hook or size needed to obtain gauge.

Gauge: Rnds 1-2 of Basket = 2½" across.

Skill Level: ☆☆ Average

BASKET

Rnd 1: Starting at **bottom,** ch 4, 11 dc in 4th ch from hook, join with sl st in top of ch-3 (12 dc).

Rnd 2: Ch 3, dc in same st, 2 dc in each st around, join (24).

Rnd 3: Ch 3, 2 dc in next st, (dc in next st, 2 dc in next st) around, join (36).

Rnd 4: Ch 3, dc in next st, 2 dc in next st, (dc in each of next 2 sts, 2 dc in next st) around, join (48).

Rnd 5: Ch 3, dc in each of next 2 sts, 2 dc in next st, (dc in each of next 3 sts, 2 dc in next st) around, join (60).

Rnd 6: Working this rnd in **back lps** only, ch 3, 2 dc in same st, 3 dc in each st around, join (180).

Rnds 7-10: Ch 3, dc in each st around, join.

Rnd 11: Ch 2, dc next 2 sts tog, (dc next 3 sts tog) around, join with sl st in top of first dc (60).

Rnd 12: Ch 1, sc in first st, skip next st, (sc in next st, skip next st) around, join with sl st in first sc, fasten off.

Cut margarine container to measure 3¾" tall. Place inside Basket. Weave 48" piece ribbon through sts of rnd 11, pull to fit around container, tie ends into a bow on one side. Glue top of Basket to container.

Handle

Row 1: Join with sc around first wire (see illustration), work 78 more sc over wire, turn (79 sc).

Row 2: Ch 4, skip next st, dc in next st, (ch 1, skip next st, dc in next st) across, turn (40 dc, 39 ch sps).

Row 3: Working over second wire, sc in each st and in each ch sp across, fasten off.

Weave 24" piece ribbon through sts of row 2; glue ends to secure. Glue ends of Handle inside margarine container. Glue one rose to Handle just above Basket on each side.

SOAP DISPENSER COVER

Rnd 1: Ch 10, 4 hdc in 3rd ch from hook, dc in next ch, tr in next 4 chs, dc in next ch, 5 hdc in end ch; working on opposite side of ch, dc in next ch, tr in next 4 chs, dc in next ch, join with sl st in top of ch-2 (22 sts).

Rnd 2: Working this rnd in **back lps** only, ch 3, 2 dc in same st, 3 dc in each st around, join with sl st in top of ch-3 (66).

Rnds-3-9: Ch 3, dc in each st around, join.

Rnd 10: Repeat rnd 11 of Basket (22).

Rnd 11: Ch 4, skip next st, (dc in next st, ch 1, skip next st) around, join with sl st in 3rd ch of ch-4, fasten off.

Place dispenser inside Cover. Weave 30" piece ribbon through sts of rnd 11, pull to fit around top of dispenser; tie ends into a bow. Glue one rose over center of bow.

TOILET TISSUE COVER

Rnd 1: Starting at **top**, ch 4, 11 dc in 4th ch from hook, join with sl st in top of ch-3 (12 dc).

Rnd 2: Ch 3, dc in same st, 2 dc in each st around, join (36).

Rnd 3: Ch 3, 2 dc in next st, (dc in next st, 2 dc in next st) around, join (36).

Rnd 4: Ch 3, dc in next st, 2 dc in next st, (dc in each of next 2 sts, 2 dc in next st) around, join (48).

Rnd 5: Repeat rnd 6 of Basket (144).

Rnds 6-11: Ch 3, dc in each st around, join.

Rnd 12: Repeat rnd 11 of Basket (48).

Rnd 13: Ch 4, skip next st, (dc in next st, ch 1, skip next st) around, join with sl st in 3rd ch of ch-4, fasten off.

For **drawstring**, ch 90, fasten off. Weave through sts of rnd 13. Place toilet tissue inside cover, pull drawstring to fit, tie ends into a bow. Weave 36" piece ribbon through sts of rnd 5, tie ends into a bow. Glue 3 roses over center of rnd 1. ✄

Timeless Tablecloth

continued from page 47

in next shell, ch 5, 3 tr in 3rd ch of ch-5, ch 1, skip next tr, 3 tr in next tr, ch 1, 3 tr in 3rd ch of ch-5, ch 5, shell in next shell, ch 3*; [skip next tr, 3 tr in next tr; repeat between **]; repeat between [ ] around, join.

Rnd 65: Sl st in next tr, ch 4, 2 tr in same st, *ch 5, sc in next ch-6 sp, ch 6, sc in next ch-6 sp, ch 5, skip next tr, 3 tr in next tr, ch 3, skip next ch-3 sp, shell in next shell, ch 5, 3 tr in 3rd ch of ch-5, ch 1, skip next tr, 3 tr in next tr, (ch 1, skip next 2 tr, 3 tr in next tr) 2 times, ch 1, 3 tr in 3rd ch of ch-5, ch 5, shell in next shell, ch 3*, [skip next tr, 3 tr in next tr; repeat between **]; repeat between [ ] around, join.

Rnd 66: Sl st in next tr, ch 4, 2 tr in same st, *ch 5, sc in next ch-6 sp, ch 5, skip next tr, 3 tr in next tr, ch 3, shell in next shell, ch 5, 3 tr in 3rd ch of ch-5, ch 1, skip next tr, 3 tr in next tr, (ch 1, skip next 2 tr, 3 tr in next tr) 4 times, ch 1, 3 tr in 3rd ch of ch-5, ch 5, shell in next shell,

ch 3*; [skip next tr, 3 tr in next tr; repeat between **]; repeat between [ ] around, join.

Rnd 67: Sl st in next tr, ch 4, 2 tr in same st, tr in next sc, skip next tr, 3 tr in next tr, ch 3, shell in next shell, ch 5, 3 tr in 3rd ch of ch-5, ch 1, skip next tr, 3 tr in next tr, (ch 1, skip next 2 tr, 3 tr in next tr) 6 times, ch 1, 3 tr in 3rd ch of ch-5, ch 5, shell in next shell*, [ch 3, skip next tr, 3 tr in next tr; repeat between **]; repeat between [ ] around, to **join,** dc in top of ch-4, **turn.**

Rnd 68: Sl st in each of next 3 tr, sl st in each of next 3 chs, **turn,** (ch 4, 2 tr, ch 3, 3 tr) in same sp, *shell in next shell, ch 7, skip next tr, (sc, picot) in next tr, ch 5, skip next 2 tr, (tr, picot) in next tr, ◊ch 5, skip next 2 tr, sc in next tr, ch 5, skip next 2 tr, (tr, picot) in next tr; repeat from ◊ 2 more times, ch 5, skip next 2 tr, (sc, picot) in next tr, ch 7*, [shell in next shell; repeat between **]; repeat between [ ] around, join, fasten off. ✄

Berry Ripples

Designed by *Diane Simpson*

Size: 49" x 66½" not including Tassels.

Materials: Worsted-weight yarn — 40 oz. pale rose, 5 oz. each burgundy, plum and steel blue; tapestry needle; I crochet hook or size needed to obtain gauge.

Gauge: 3 dc = 1"; 3 dc rows = 2".

NOTE: Ch-3 at beginning of each row counts as first st.

Skill Level: ☆☆ Average

AFGHAN

Row 1: With pale rose, ch 221, dc in 7th ch from hook, dc in next 11 chs, (2 dc, ch 1, 2 dc) in next ch, dc in next 12 chs, *skip next 6 chs, dc in next 12 chs, (2 dc, ch 1, 2 dc) in next ch, dc in next 12 chs; repeat from * across to last 4 chs, skip next 3 chs, dc in last ch, turn (198 dc, 7 ch-1 sps).

Rows 2-5: Ch 3, skip next 2 sts, *dc in next 12 sts, (2 dc, ch 1, 2 dc) in next ch-1 sp, dc in next 12 sts*, [skip next 4 sts; repeat between **]; repeat between [ ] across to last 3 sts, skip next 2 sts, dc in last st, turn. At end of last row, fasten off.

*NOTE: For **berry stitch (berry st),** insert hook in next st, yo, draw lp through, (yo, draw through first lp on hook) 3 times, yo, draw through both lps on hook.*

Row 6: Join plum with sc in first st, ch 1, skip next 2 sts, *(sc in next st, berry st) 6 times, (sc, ch 3, sc) in next ch-1 sp, (berry st, sc in next st) 6 times*, [ch 2, skip next 4 sts; repeat between **]; repeat between [ ] across to last 3 sts, ch 1, skip next 2 sts, sc in last st, turn, fasten off.

Row 7: Join steel blue with sc in first st, ch 1, skip next ch-1 sp, skip next st, *(sc in next st, berry st) 6 times, (sc, ch 3, sc) in next ch-3 sp, (berry st, sc in next st) 6 times*, [ch 2, skip next st, skip next ch-2 sp, skip next st; repeat between **]; repeat between [ ] across to last 2 sts, ch 1, skip next st, skip next ch-1 sp, sc in last st, turn, fasten off.

Row 8: With burgundy, repeat row 7.

Row 9: Join pale rose with sl st in first st, ch 3, skip next ch-1 sp, skip next st, *dc in next 12 sts, (2 dc, ch 1, 2 dc) in next ch-3 sp, dc in next 12 sts*, [skip next st, skip next ch-2 sp, skip next st; repeat between **]; repeat between [ ] across to last 2 sts, skip next st, skip next ch-1 sp, dc in last st, turn.

Rows 10-93: Repeat rows 2-9 consecutively, ending with row 5.

TASSEL

For **each Tassel,** cut 17 strands pale rose each 14" long. Tie separate strand tightly around middle of all strands. Wrap 30" strand ¾" from top of Tassel, secure. Trim ends. Tie one Tassel to each point on short ends of Afghan. ✂

Beautiful Baby

Welcome each blessed new creation with a special creation of your own to start their journey through life wrapped in love. Snuggly comfort and peaceful dreams await your most precious possession when you fashion charming projects to fill their world with softness and beauty. Stitch cozy afghans and handy helpers that soothe the everyday tears or heirloom outfits for special occasions that will be cherished for generations to come.

continued from page 55

Holding wrong sides of last rows together, sew sts of each front to matching sts of back for shoulder seams.

Sleeve (make 2)

Rnd 1: With white, ch 34 [36, 38], sl st in first ch to form ring, ch 2, hdc in each ch around, join with sl st in top of ch-2, **turn** (34) [36, 38].

Rnd 2: Ch 3, working over ch-3, dc back into last st of last rnd, cross st around, join with sl st in top of ch-3, **turn,** fasten off.

Rnd 3: Join lt. green with sc in first st, hdc in same st, skip next st, *(sc, hdc) in next st, skip next st; repeat from * around, join with sl st in first sc, **turn,** fasten off.

Rnd 4: Skip first 2 sts, join white with sl st in next st, ch 3, working over ch-3, dc back into 2nd skipped st, cross st around, join, **turn,** fasten off.

Rnd 5: With pink, repeat rnd 3.

Rnd 6: Repeat rnd 4.

Rnd 7: With yellow, repeat rnd 3.

Rnd 8: Repeat rnd 4.

Rnd 9: With lt. blue, repeat rnd 3.

Rnd 10: Repeat rnd 4, **do not** fasten off.

Row 11: For **0-3 mos. only,** sl st in next st, ch 2, hdc next 2 sts tog, hdc in next 27 sts, hdc next 2 sts tog leaving last and first st unworked, turn (30).

Row [11]: For **3-6 mos. only,** sl st in next st, ch 2, hdc next 2 sts tog, hdc in next 31 sts leaving last and first st unworked, turn [33].

Row [11]: For **6-9 mos. only,** sl st in next st, ch 2, hdc in next 35 sts leaving last and first st unworked, turn [36].

Rows 12-19 [12-20, 12-21]: For **all sizes,** ch 2, hdc next 2 sts tog, hdc in each st across to last 3 sts, hdc next 2 sts tog leaving last st unworked, turn, ending with (6) [6, 6] sts in last row. For **0-3 mos. only,** fasten off.

[Row 21, 22]: Ch 1, sc in first st, hdc in each st across to last st, sc in last st, turn. For **3-6 mos. only,** fasten off.

[Row 23]: Ch 1, sc in each of first 2 sts, hdc in each st across to last 2 sts, sc in each of last 2 sts, fasten off.

For **trim,** working in starting ch on opposite side of row 1, join white with sl st in first ch; working from left to right, **reverse sc** (see page 159) in each ch around, join with sl st in first sc, fasten off.

With skipped sts of row 11 matching center sts of skipped sts on row 14 [16, 18] of Sweater and 6 sts of last row on Sleeve matching 3 rows on each side of shoulder seam, sew Sleeves to armholes.

Finishing

1: For **Sweater trim,** join white with sl st in last ch at bottom left edge of Sweater, reverse sc in each ch, in each st and in end of each sc row around with 2 reverse sc in end of each hdc row, join with sl st in first sc, fasten off.

2: For **waist tie,** with lt. green, ch 100 [110, 120], fasten off. Weave through sts of row 12 [14, 16].

3: For **2nd tie** (make 2), with pink, ch 50 [55, 60], fasten off. Sew one end of each tie to last st (next to Sleeve) of row 14 [16, 18].

4: For **3rd tie** (make 2), with yellow, ch 45 [50, 55], fasten off. Sew one end of each tie to last st of row 16 [18, 20].

5: For **4th tie** (make 2), with lt. blue, ch 40 [45, 50], fasten off. Sew one end of each tie to last st of row 18 [20, 22].

Weave all ties through sts to center front.

BONNET

Row 1: With white, ch 55 [59, 63], hdc in 3rd ch from hook, hdc in each ch across, turn (54 hdc) [58 hdc, 62 hdc].

Rows 2-10: Repeat rows 2-10 of Sweater.

Row 11 [11-12, 11-13]: Ch 2, hdc in each st across, turn.

Row 12 [13, 14]: Ch 2, hdc in next st, (hdc next 2 sts tog, hdc in each of next 2 sts) across, turn (41) [44, 47].

Row 13 [14, 15]: Ch 2, hdc in next 6 [9, 13] sts, (hdc next 2 sts tog, hdc in next st) 9 [8, 7] times, hdc in last 7 [10, 12] sts, turn (32) [36, 40].

Row 14 [15, 16]: Ch 2, hdc in next 7 [9, 11] sts, (hdc next 2 sts tog, hdc in each of next 2 sts) 4 times, hdc in last 8 [10, 12] sts, turn (28) [32, 36].

Row 15 [16, 17]: Ch 2, hdc in next 7 [9, 11] sts, (hdc next 2 sts tog) 6 times, hdc in last 8 [10, 12] sts, turn (22) [26, 30].

Row 16 [17, 18]: Ch 2, hdc in next 7 [9, 11] sts, (hdc next 2 sts tog) 3 times, hdc in last 8 [10, 12] sts, join with sl st in top of ch-2, fasten off (19) [23, 27].

Finishing

1: For **trim,** with right side of row 1 facing you, join white with sl st in last ch at left corner, ch 1, reverse sc in each ch and 2 reverse sc in end of each row around leaving remaining sts of last row unworked for back opening, join with sl st in first sc, fasten off.

2: For **tie,** with lt. green, ch 100 [110, 120], fasten off. Weave through ends of rows.

BOOTIE (make 2)

Rnd 1: With white, ch 9 [11, 13], 3 sc in 2nd ch from hook, sc in each of next 3 [4, 5] chs, hdc in each of next 3 [4, 5] chs, 8 hdc in last ch; working on opposite side of ch, hdc in each of next 3 [4, 5] chs, sc in each of next 3 [4, 5] chs, 3 sc in same ch as first 3 sc, join with sl st in first sc, **turn** (26) [30, 34].

Rnd 2: Ch 1, sc in each of first 2 sts, 2 sc in next st, sc in next 4 [5, 6] sts, hdc in next 4 [5, 6] sts, 2 hdc in next st, hdc in next st, 2 hdc in each of next 2 sts, hdc in next st, 2 hdc in next st, hdc in next 4 [5, 6] sts, sc in next 4 [5, 6] sts, 2 sc in last st, join, **turn** (32) [36, 40].

Rnd 3: Ch 1, 2 sc in first st, sc in next 9 [11, 13] sts, 2 sc in next st, sc in each of next 2 sts, 2 sc in next st, sc in next st, 2 sc in each of next 2 sts, sc in next st, 2 sc in next st, sc in each of next 2 sts, 2 sc in next st, sc in next 9 [11, 13] sts, 2 sc in last st, join, **turn** (40) [44, 48].

Rnd 4 [4-5, 4-6]: Ch 2, hdc in each st around, join with sl st in top of ch-2, **turn.**

Rnd 5 [6, 7]: Ch 2, hdc in next 11 [13, 15] sts, (hdc next 2 sts tog, hdc in each of next 2 sts) 2 times, (hdc in each of next 2 sts, hdc next 2 sts tog) 2 times, hdc in last 12 [14, 16] sts, join, **turn** (36) [40, 44].

Rnd 6 [7, 8]: Ch 2, hdc in next 13 [15, 17] sts, (hdc next 2 sts tog, hdc in next st, hdc next 2 sts tog) 2 times, hdc in last 12 [14, 16] sts, join, **turn** (32) [36, 40].

Rnd 7 [8, 9]: Ch 2, hdc in next 11 [13, 15] sts, (yo, insert hook in next st, yo, draw through st) 8 times, yo, draw through all lps on hook, hdc in last 12 [14, 16] sts, join, **turn** (25) [29, 33].

Rnd 8 [9, 10]: Ch 2, hdc in next 9 [11, 13] sts, hdc first and last of next 5 sts tog, hdc in last 10 [12, 14] sts, join, **turn** (21) [25, 29].

Rnd 9 [10, 11]: Ch 2, hdc next 2 sts tog, hdc in each st around, join, **turn** (20) [24, 28].

Rnds 10-17 [11-18, 12-19]: Repeat rnds 2-9 of Sleeve.

Rnd 18 [19, 20]: Join white with sc in first st, sc in each st around, join, fasten off. Turn right side out.

For **tie,** with lt. green, ch 70 [75, 80], fasten off. Weave through sts of rnd 8 [9, 10].

Afghan

Size: 32" x 33".

Materials: Pompadour baby yarn — 8 oz. white, 3 oz. each lt. green, lt. blue, pink and yellow; tapestry needle; F crochet hook or size needed to obtain gauge.

Gauge: 7 (sc, hdc) = 3"; 7 cross sts = 3"; 2 (sc, hdc) rows and 1 cross st row = 1".

Skill Level: ☆☆ Average

Row 1: With white, ch 161, hdc in 3rd ch from hook, hdc in each ch across, turn (160 hdc).

*NOTE: For **cross st,** skip next st, dc in next st, working over last dc made, dc in skipped st.*

Row 2: Ch 2, cross st across to last st, hdc in last st, turn, fasten off (79 cross sts).

Row 3: Join lt. green with sc in first st, hdc in same st, *skip next st, (sc, hdc) in next st; repeat from * across to last st, sc in last st, turn, fasten off.

Row 4: Join white with sl st in first st, ch 2, skip next st, cross st across to last st, hdc in last st, turn, fasten off.

Row 5: With pink, repeat row 3.

Row 6: Repeat row 4.

Row 7: With yellow, repeat row 3.

Row 8: Repeat row 4.

Row 9: With lt. blue, repeat row 3.

Row 10: Repeat row 4.

Rows 11-98: Repeat rows 3-10 consecutively. At end of last row, **do not** fasten off.

Row 99: Ch 2, hdc in each st across, **do not** turn or fasten off.

Rnd 100: Working around outer edge, ch 1; working from left to right, **reverse sc** (see page 159) in each st and in end of each row around, join with sl st in first sc, fasten off. ✄

Heirloom Baby Dress

Designed by *Erma Fielder*

Sizes: Instructions given fit up to 18" chest. Changes for chests up to 19" and 20" are in [ ].

Materials: Size-20 crochet cotton — 1450 yds. white; pink and green embroidery floss; 2 yds. pink ¼" satin picot ribbon; three ⅜" buttons; white sewing thread; sewing and tapestry needles; No. 10 steel crochet hook or size needed to obtain gauge.

Gauge: 9 dc = 1"; 4 dc rows = 1".

Skill Level: ☆☆ Average

DRESS

*NOTE: For **shell**, (2 dc, ch 2, 2 dc) in next ch or ch sp.*

Row 1: Starting at **neck**, ch 146, dc in 4th ch from hook, dc in next 19 chs, *shell in next ch, dc in next 31 chs, shell in next ch*, dc in next 36 chs; repeat between **, dc in last 21 chs, turn (140 dc, 4 shells).

Rows 2-11 [2-12, 2-13]: Ch 3, dc in each dc across with shell in ch sp of each shell, turn, ending with 300 [316, 332] dc and 4 shells in last row.

Rnd 12 [13, 14]: Working in rnds, ch 3, dc in next 42 [44, 46] dc, *2 dc in next ch sp; for **armhole**, skip next 75 [79, 83] sts; 2 dc in next ch sp*, dc in next 80 [84, 88] dc; repeat between **, dc in last 41 [43, 45] sts, join with sl st in top of ch-3, **turn** (174) [182, 190].

Rnd 13 [14, 15]: Ch 3, dc in next st, (ch 1, skip next st, dc in next st) across, join, **turn** (88 dc, 86 ch sps) [92 dc, 90 ch sps; 96 dc, 94 ch sps].

Rnd 14 [15, 16]: Ch 3, dc in each dc and in each ch sp around, join, **turn** (174 dc) [182 dc, 190 dc].

Rnd [16, 17-18]: For **19" and 20" chest only**, ch 3, dc in each st around, join, **turn.**

Rnd 15 [17, 19]: For **all sizes**, for **skirt**, ch 3, dc in same st, 2 dc in each st around, join, **turn** (348) [364, 380].

Rnds 16-47 [18-51, 20-55]: Ch 3, dc in each st around, join, **turn.** At end of last rnd, **do not** turn.

Rnd 48 [52, 56]: Ch 1, sc in each st around, join with sl st in first sc.

*NOTES: For **beginning V-stitch (beg V-st)**, ch 4, dc in same st.*

*For **V-stitch (V-st)**, (dc, ch 1, dc) in next st.*

*For **picot**, ch 3, sl st in 3rd ch from hook.*

Rnd 49 [53, 57]: Beg V-st, V-st in each st around, join with sl st in 3rd ch of beg V-st.

Rnd 50 [54, 58]: Sl st in first ch sp, ch 4, (tr, ch 2, 2 tr) in same sp, tr in next sp between V-sts, *(2 tr, ch 2, 2 tr) in ch sp of next V-st, tr in next sp between V-sts; repeat from * around, join with sl st in top of ch-4.

Rnd 51 [55, 59]: Ch 1, sc in each tr around with (sc, picot, sc) in each ch sp, join with sl st in first sc, fasten off.

Neck Trim

Row 1: Working in starting ch on opposite side of row 1, join white with sc in first ch, sc in each ch across, turn.

Row 2: Working this row in **front lps** only, ch 3, dc in next st, (ch 1, skip next st, dc in next st) across, turn (73 dc, 71 ch sps).

Row 3: Ch 1, sc in each of first 2 dc, picot, (sc in each of next 2 dc, picot) across to last dc, sc in last dc, fasten off.

Neck Ruffle

Row 1: Working in **back lps** of row 1 on Neck Trim, with right side of work facing you, join with sl st in first st, beg V-st, V-st in each st across, turn.

Row 2: Sl st in first ch sp, ch 4, (tr, ch 2, 2 tr) in same sp, *tr in next sp between V-sts, (2 tr, ch 2, 2 tr) in ch sp of next V-st; repeat from * across, turn.

Row 3: Ch 1, sc in each tr across with (sc, picot, sc) in each ch sp, fasten off.

Sleeve Ruffles

Rnd 1: Working around one armhole, join with sc in any underarm st, sc in each st around, join with sl st in first sc (75) [79, 83].

Rnds 2-4: Repeat rnds 49-51 [53-55, 57-59] of Dress. Repeat on other armhole.

Finishing

1: With pink, using French Knot (see page 159), embroider rosebuds according to Embroidery Diagram on page 59. With green, using Lazy Daisy Stitch (see page 159), embroider leaves according to diagram. Embroider 5 sets of rosebuds and leaves 1" apart across front of bodice as shown in photo.

2: Starting at center back, weave 14" piece ribbon through dc of row 2 on Neck Trim to center front. Repeat on opposite side. Turn ribbon ends under at center back and tack in place; tie opposite ends into a bow at center front.

3: Starting at center front, weave 30" piece ribbon through dc of rnd 13 [14, 15] on Dress; tie ends into a bow at center front.

4: Sew buttons evenly spaced down left back using corresponding sps between sts on right back as button holes. ✀

EMBROIDERY DIAGRAM

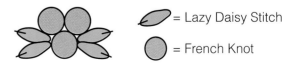

⬯ = Lazy Daisy Stitch

⬤ = French Knot

Pastel Nursery Set

Designed by *Rosemarie Walter*

Diaper Stacker

Size: 18" x 26" when hanging.

Materials: Worsted-weight yarn — 20 oz. white, 4 oz. green and 1 oz. yellow; 3 yds. yellow ⅜" satin ribbon; 9½ yds. yellow ⅛" satin ribbon; plastic clothes hanger; 9" x 13½" piece plastic canvas; 4 stitch markers; tapestry needle; I crochet hook or size needed to obtain gauge.

Gauge: 8 sc = 3"; 8 sc rows = 3".

Skill Level: ☆☆ Average

BASE

Row 1: With 2 strands white held together, ch 36, sc in 2nd ch from hook, sc in each ch across, turn (35 sc).

Rows 2-23: Ch 1, sc in each st across, turn.

Rnd 24: Working around outer edge, ch 1, sc in each st and in end of each row around with 3 sc in each corner, join with sl st in first sc, fasten off (120).

SIDES

Row 1: With 2 strands white held together, working in **back lps** only, skip first 20 sts of one long edge on Base, join with sc in next st, sc in each st around Base leaving last 5 sts unworked, turn (115 sc).

Rows 2-4: Ch 1, sc in each st across, turn. At end of last row, fasten off.

*NOTE: For **tr front post** (**tr fp**—see page 159), yo 2 times, insert hook from front to back around post of next st on designated row, yo, draw lp through, (yo, draw through 2 lps on hook) 3 times. Skip next st on last row.*

Row 5: With 2 strands green held together, join with sc in first st, sc in each of next 2 sts, (tr fp around next st on row 1, sc in each of next 3 sts on last row) across, turn (87 sc, 28 tr fp).

Row 6: Ch 1, sc in each st across, turn, fasten off (115).

Row 7: With 2 strands yellow held together, join with sc in first st, tr fp around next st on row 3, (sc in each of next 3 sts, tr fp around next st on row 3) across to last st, sc in last st, turn.

Row 8: Repeat row 6.

Row 9: With 2 strands green held together, join with sc in first st, sc in same st, sc in each of next 2 sts, tr fp around next fp on row 5, (sc in each of next 3 sts, tr fp around next fp on row 5) across to last 3 sts, sc in each of next 2 sts, 2 sc in last st, turn (89 sc, 28 tr fp).

Row 10: Working this row in **back lps** only, (ch 1, sl st in next st) across, turn, fasten off.

NOTES: Work remainder of pattern with one strand yarn.

*For **shell**, 7 dc in next st.*

Row 11: Working in **front lps** of row 9, join white with sl st in first st, ch 3, 4 dc in same st, skip next st, sc in next st, skip next st, (shell in next st, skip next st, sc in next st, skip next st) across to last st, 5 dc in last st, turn (29 sc, 28 shells, 10 dc).

*NOTES: For **dc back post (dc bp)**, yo, insert hook from back to front around post of next st, yo, draw lp through, complete as dc.*

*For **dc front post (dc fp)**, yo, insert hook from front to back around post of next st, yo, draw lp through, complete as dc.*

Row 12: Ch 3, 4 dc in same st, dc bp around next sc or fp, (shell in 4th st of next shell, dc bp around next sc or fp) across to last 5-dc group, 5 dc in last st of same group, turn.

Row 13: Ch 3, 4 dc in same st, dc fp around next bp, (shell in 4th st of next shell, dc fp around next bp) across to last 5-dc group, 5 dc in last st of same group, turn.

Rows 14-28: Repeat rows 12 and 13 alternately, ending with row 12.

Row 29: Ch 1, sc in same st, ch 2, dc fp around next bp, ch 2, (sc in 4th st of next shell, ch 2, dc fp around next bp, ch 2) across to last 5-dc group, sc in last st of same group, **do not** turn, fasten off (58 ch sps).

NOTE: Hold shells of row 29 wrong sides together with stitch markers.

For **first pleat**, fold 3rd and 14th ch sps together. For **2nd pleat**, fold 15th and 26th ch sps together. For **3rd pleat**, fold 44th and 55th ch sps together. For **4th pleat**, fold 45th and 56th ch sps together.

To **join**, with front opening facing you, working through all 4 thicknesses of pleats, join with sc in ends of 3rd and 4th pleats according to Pleat Diagram on page 61, 2 sc in each ch sp and sc in each dc across

PLEAT DIAGRAM

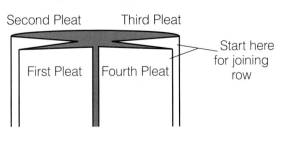

Second Pleat

Third Pleat

First Pleat

Fourth Pleat

Start here for joining row

working through only 2 thicknesses of back and front opening.

Cut 10 pieces ⅛" ribbon each 23" long. Leaving pleats and back unworked, wrap each piece around post sts on front of Bag with 5 on each side of opening as shown in photo. With ends on inside, tie in knot around one st to secure, trim.

continued on page 62

Pastel Nursery Set

continued from page 61

TOP

Row 1: For **front,** with opening of Bag facing you, join green with sl st in upper right corner of flattened joining rnd, ch 3, dc in next 53 sts and chs across to opposite corner leaving remaining sts unworked, turn (54 dc).

Row 2: Ch 1, (sc first 2 sts tog) 2 times, sc in each st across to last 4 sts, (sc next 2 sts tog) 2 times, turn (50).

Row 3: Ch 1, sc in each st across, turn.

Rows 4-11: Repeat row 2, ending with 18 sts in last row.

Rows 12-15: Ch 1, sc first 2 sts tog, sc in each st across to last 2 sts, sc last 2 sts tog, turn, ending with 10 sts in last row.

Row 16: Repeat row 3.

Row 17: Ch 3, dc in each st across, turn, fasten off.

Row 18: With right side of row 1 facing you, working in ends of rows, join green with sc in first row, sc in same row, sc in each sc row, 2 sc in each dc row and sc in each st of row 17 across to opposite end of row 1, fasten off.

For **back,** with back of Bag facing you, repeat Top. With tapestry needle and green, sew front and back of Top together with clothes hanger in between leaving 9 sts on front and back unsewn.

For **trim,** working around hanger opening above row 17, join with sl st in any st, ch 3, (sl st in next st, ch 3) around, join with sl st in first sl st, fasten off. Cut one yd. ⅜" ribbon. Weave through dc sts of row 1 on Top around front and back, secure ends. Weave 18" piece ⅛" ribbon through row 17 around front and back of Top, tie in front leaving ends long. Fold remaining ⅜" ribbon into bow measuring 4" across. Cut four pieces ⅛" ribbon each 18" long, place on back of bow. Wrap separate 18" piece ⅛" ribbon around center of bow and ends. Tie into a bow to Top near hanger. Place plastic canvas inside Base.

Dressing Tray

Size: 6" x 10".

Materials: Worsted-weight yarn — 2½ oz. green, 1 oz. white and small amount yellow; 1½ yds. yellow ⅜" satin ribbon; yellow sewing thread; one sheet plastic canvas; sewing and tapestry needles; G crochet hook or size needed to obtain gauge.

Gauge: 4 sc = 1"; 4 sc rows = 1".

Skill Level: ☆☆ Average

BASE

With one strand green, work same as Diaper Stacker Base on page 63. Using crocheted piece as pattern, cut one piece from plastic canvas.

SIDES

Rnd 1: Working this rnd in **back lps** only, join white with sc in first st, sc in each st around, join with sl st in first sc, **turn** (120 sc).

Rnds 2-4: Ch 1, sc in each st around, join, **turn.** At end of last rnd, fasten off.

*NOTE: For **treble front post (tr fp**— see page 159), yo 2 times, insert hook from front to back around post of next st on designated rnd, yo, draw lp through, (yo, draw through 2 lps on hook) 3 times. Skip next st on last rnd.*

Rnd 5: Join green with sc in first st, sc in each of next 2 sts, tr fp around next st on rnd 1, (sc in each of next 3 sts, tr fp around next st on rnd 1) around, join, **turn.**

Rnd 6: Repeat rnd 2, fasten off.

Rnd 7: Join yellow with sc in first sc, tr fp around next st on rnd 3, (sc in each of next 3 sts, tr fp around next st on rnd 3) around to last 2 sts, sc in each of last 2 sts, join, **turn.**

Rnd 8: Repeat rnd 2, fasten off.

Rnd 9: Join green with sc in first st, sc in each of next 2 sts, tr fp around next fp on rnd 5, (sc in each of next 3 sts, tr fp around next fp on rnd 5) around, join, **turn.**

Rnd 10: (Ch 1, sl st in next st) around, join with sl st in first ch-1, fasten off.

For **long sides,** cut 2 pieces from plastic canvas each 2" x 10".

For **short sides,** cut 2 pieces from plastic canvas each 2" x 6".

FINISHING

1: Whipstitch (see illustration) plastic canvas sides and base together to form box.

WHIPSTITCH

2: For **long dividers (A),** cut 2 pieces from plastic canvas each 2" x 5". For **short dividers (B),** cut 2 pieces from plastic canvas each 2" x 3". Whipstitch together according to Dividers Diagram.

DIVIDERS DIAGRAM

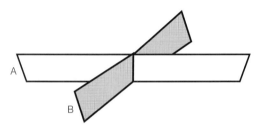

3: Place plastic canvas box inside crocheted piece, place divider inside box. With tapestry needle and green, sew upper edges of box to rnd 9, working through top corners of dividers to secure.

4: Cut 1 yd. piece from ribbon, tie into a 4" wide bow leaving ends long. Wrap remaining ribbon around center of all lps, tie to secure. With sewing needle and thread, sew bow centered over one long side.

Wipes Cozy

Size: Holds up to 3" x 6" round wipes container.

Materials: Worsted-weight yarn — 2 oz. white, 1 oz. green and small amount yellow; 3 yds. ⅛" yellow satin ribbon; tapestry needle; F and G crochet hooks or sizes needed to obtain gauges.

Gauges: With **F hook,** 9 sc = 2"; 9 sc rows = 2". With **G hook,** 4 sc = 1"; 4 sc rows = 1".

Skill Level: ☆☆ Average

BASE

NOTE: Do not join rnds unless otherwise stated. Mark first st of each rnd.

Rnd 1: With G hook and green, ch 2, 6 sc in 2nd ch from hook (6 sc).

Rnd 2: 2 sc in each st around (12).

Rnd 3: (Sc in next st, 2 sc in next st) around (18).

Rnd 4: (Sc in each of next 2 sts, 2 sc in next st) around (24).

Rnd 5: (Sc in each of next 3 sts, 2 sc in next st) around (30).

Rnd 6: (Sc in next 4 sts, 2 sc in next st) around, join with sl st in first sc, fasten off (36).

SIDES

Rnd 1: Working this rnd in **back lps** only, with G hook, join white with sc in any st, sc in each st around, join, **turn.**

Rnds 2-9: Repeat same rnds of Dressing Tray Sides. At end of last rnd, **do not** turn.

Rnd 10: Working this rnd in **front lps** only; for **trim,** repeat same rnd of Dressing Tray Sides.

*NOTES: For **double crochet front post (dc fp**—see page 159), yo, insert hook from front to back around post of next st , yo, draw lp through, complete as dc.*

*For **shell,** 7 dc in next st.*

Ch-3 at beginning of each rnd does not count as first st.

Use F hook for remainder of pattern.

Rnd 11: Working in **back lps** of rnd 9, join white with sl st in any tr fp, ch 3, dc in same st, skip next st, shell in next st, skip next st, (dc in next st, skip next st, shell in next st, skip next st) around, join with sl st in top of ch-3, **do not** turn.

Rnds 12-14: Ch 3, dc fp around first dc or dc fp, shell in 4th st of next shell, (dc fp around next dc or dc fp, shell in 4th st of next shell) around, join.

Rnd 15: Ch 3, dc fp around first dc fp, ch 2, sc in center st of next shell, ch 2, (dc fp around next dc fp, ch 2, sc in center st of next shell, ch 2) around, join.

Rnd 16: Ch 1, sc in top of first dc fp, 2 sc in each ch-2 sp, in each sc and in each dc fp around, join with sl st in first sc, fasten off (54 sc).

Rnd 17: Join green with sl st in first st, ch 3, dc in each st around, join with sl st in top of ch-3.

Rnd 18: Ch 1, sc in each st around, join with sl st in first sc.

Rnd 19: (Ch 1, sl st in next st) around, join with sl st in first ch-1, fasten off.

Cut 9 pieces ribbon each 8" long. Wrap around dc fp same as Diaper Stacker on page 60. Weave remaining 1 yd. ribbon through dc on rnd 17, tie into a bow leaving ends long.✄

Antique Bib & Booties

Designed by *Pearl Gaither*

Sizes: Bib fits up to 18" chest. Changes for chest up to 20" are in [ ]. Bootie fits up to 3" sole. Changes given fit up to 4" are in [ ].

Materials For Both: Size-20 crochet cotton — 250 [300] yds. white; 2¼ yds. satin ¼" ribbon; 1¼ yds. ruffled ¾" lace ribbon; sewing thread; sewing and tapestry needles; No. 9 steel crochet hook or size needed to obtain gauge.

Gauge: 11 sc = 1"; 12 sc rows = 1".

NOTE: To **achieve a decorative antique look,** follow Tea Dyeing Crochet below.

Skill Level: ☆☆ Average

BIB
Front

Row 1: Ch 8 [10], sc in 2nd ch from hook, sc in each of next 2 [3] chs, 3 sc in next ch, sc in each of last 3 [4] chs, turn (9 sc) [11 sc].

Row 2: Ch 1, sc in first 4 [5] sts, 3 sc in next st, sc in last 4 [5] sts, turn (11) [13].

Row 3: Ch 1, sc in first 5 [6] sts, 3 sc in next st, sc in last 5 [6] sts, turn (15) [17].

Row 4: Ch 1, sc in first 6 [7] sts, 3 sc in next st, sc in last 6 [7] sts, turn (15) [17].

Rows 5-62 [5-79]: Working in established pattern, ch 1, sc in each st across with 3 sc in middle st, turn, ending with (131) [167] sts in last row.

Row 63 [80]: For **first shoulder,** ch 1, sc in first 10 sts leaving remaining sts unworked, turn (10).

Rows 64-121 [81-153]: Ch 1, sc in each st across, turn. At end of last row, leaving long end for sewing, fasten off.

For **first armhole,** skip next 20 [35] sts on row 62 [79], sew last row made to next 10 sts on same row.

Row 63 [80]: For **first shoulder,** skip next 81 [102] sts, join with sc in next st, sc in last 9 sts, turn (10).

Rows 64-121 [81-153]: Repeat same rows of first shoulder.

For **2nd armhole,** skip next 20 [35] unworked sts on row 62 [79], sew last row made to next 10 sts on same row.

Sleeve Edgings

Rnd 1: Working around one armhole, in sts and in ends of rows, join with sc in first unworked sc on row 62 [79], ch 2, skip next 2 sc, (sc in next sc, ch 2, skip next 2 sc) around, join with sl st in first sc.

Rnd 2: Sl st in first ch-2 sp, ch 1, 2 sc in same sp, 2 sc in each ch-2 sp around, join, fasten off.

Repeat on other armhole.

Finishing

Cut 2 pieces ribbon each 18" long. Weave one ribbon through rnd 1 of each Sleeve Edging. Tie into a bow at top of shoulder.

Fold back remaining unworked sts on row 62 [79] between Sleeves, tack in place. Tie 9" of ribbon into a bow; sew to fold. Easing to fit, sew lace around outer edge of Bib.

BOOTIE (make 2)

Row 1: Ch 46 [56], sc in 2nd ch from hook, sc in each ch across, turn (45 sc) [55 sc].

Rows 2-29 [2-41]: Working these rows in **back lps** only, ch 1, sc in each st across, turn.

Rnd 30 [42]: Working in rnds, ch 3, dc in each st around, join with sl st in top of ch-3 (45) [55].

Rnds 31-35 [43-47]: Ch 3, dc in each st around, join.

Rnd 36 [48]: Draw up long lp in each st around; to **close,** yo, draw through all 45 [55] lps, fasten off. Sew back seam.

Edging

Working around one ankle opening, join with sc in end of any row, ch 5, work 12 [14] (sc, ch 5) evenly spaced around opening, join with sl st in first sc, fasten off.

Easing to fit, sew lace around ankle opening. Weave one 18" piece ribbon through ch-5 sps on Edging, tie ends into a bow. ✂

TEA DYEING CROCHET

If you're making the *"Antique Bib & Booties"* for decorative purposes, tea dyeing will make them look as though they came from your great-grandmother's trunk! Tea dyeing will also give a uniform cream color to real antique crochet pieces.

First, hand wash the crochet with mild soap powder or hand wash product in warm water. Then, prepare your tea solution. Stronger tea gives a darker color which may be necessary to cover stains on older pieces. For new pieces, warm, half-strength tea will work nicely. Place the clean and wet crochet into a bowl, cover items completely with tea solution and allow to soak about one hour. Rinse in cold water, shape on blocking board or thick toweling and allow to dry.

Baby Bubbles

Designed by *Sandra Miller Maxfield*

Sizes: Instructions given are for 0-3 mos. Changes for 3-6 mos., 6-9 mos., 9-12 mos are in [ ].

Materials For Set: 100% cotton sport-weight yarn — 5 [7, 9, 11] oz. Main Color (MC) and 1¾ oz. white; 6 small appliqués; elastic thread; three ⅜" buttons; 2¼" strip ¾" Velcro™ fastener; sewing thread; sewing and tapestry needles; F crochet hook or size needed to obtain gauge.

Gauge: 9 hdc = 2"; 3 hdc rows = 1".

Skill Level: ☆☆ Average

BUBBLE SUIT

Front Bodice

Row 1: With white, ch 31, [33, 35, 37], hdc in 3rd ch from hook, hdc in each ch across, turn (30 hdc) [32 hdc, 34 hdc, 36 hdc].

Rows 2-5: Ch 2, hdc in each st across, turn. At end of last row, fasten off.

Row 6: With right side of yoke facing you, working in starting ch on opposite side of row 1, join MC with sc in first ch, sc in each ch across, turn.

Row 7: For **first shoulder,** ch 2, hdc in next 8 sts leaving remaining sts unworked, turn (9).

Rows 8-11: Ch 2, hdc in each st across, turn. At end of last row, **do not** turn, fasten off.

Row 7: For **2nd shoulder,** skip next 12 [14, 16, 18] sts on row 6, join MC with sl st in next st, ch 2, hdc in each st across, turn (9).

Rows 8-11: Ch 2, hdc in each st across, turn. At end of last row, fasten off.

Back Bodice

Row 1: For **first side,** with MC, ch 16 [17, 18, 19], hdc in 3rd ch from hook, hdc in each ch across, turn (15) [16, 17, 18].

Rows 2-6: Ch 2, hdc in each st across, turn.

Row 7: For **first shoulder,** ch 2, hdc in next 8 sts leaving remaining sts unworked, turn (9).

Rows 8-11: Repeat row 2. At end of last row, fasten off.

Rows 1-6: For **second side,** repeat same rows of first side (15) [16, 17, 18].

Row 7: Sl st in first 7 [8, 9, 10] sts; for **2nd shoulder,** ch 2, hdc in each st across, turn (9).

Rows 8-11: Repeat same rows of first shoulder. Sew shoulder seams.

Body

Row 1: To **assemble,** with right side facing you, starting at **center back,** working in starting ch on opposite side of row 1 of Back Bodice on first side, join MC with sc in first ch, sc in next 13 [14, 15, 16] chs, 2 sc in next ch; for **first armhole,** ch 6 [7, 8, 9], 2 sc in first st on row 5 of Front Bodice, sc in next 28 [30, 32, 34] sts, 2 sc in next st; for **2nd armhole,** ch 6 [7, 8, 9]; working in starting ch on opposite side of row 1 of Back Bodice on second side, 2 sc in next ch, sc in each ch across, turn (64 sts and 2 ch sps) [68, 72, 76 sts and 2 ch sps].

Row 2: Ch 2, hdc in each st and in each ch across, turn (76) [82, 88, 94].

Row 3: Ch 2, hdc in next 4 [7, 4, 7] sts, 2 hdc in next st, *hdc in next 5 [5, 6, 6] sts, 2 hdc in next st; repeat from * 10 more times, hdc in last 4 [7, 5, 8] sts, turn (88) [94, 100, 106].

Row 4: Ch 2, hdc in each st across, turn.

Row 5: Ch 2, hdc in next 4 [7, 3, 6] sts, 2 hdc in next st, *hdc in next 5 [5, 6, 6] sts, 2 hdc in next st; repeat from * 12 more times, hdc in last 4 [7, 4, 7] sts, turn (102) [108, 114, 120].

Rnds 6-22 [6-24, 6-26, 6-28] or to desired length: Working in rnds, ch 2, hdc in each st around, join with sl st in top of ch-2. At end of last rnd, fasten off.

Row 23 [25, 27, 29]: For **front crotch,** skip first 46 [49, 52, 55] sts, join MC with sl st in next st, ch 2, hdc in next 9 sts leaving remaining sts unworked, turn (10)

Row 24 [26, 28, 30]: Ch 2, hdc next 2 sts tog, hdc in each st across to last 2 sts, hdc last 2 sts tog, turn, fasten off (8).

Row 23 [25, 27, 29]: Skip next 41 [44, 47, 50] sts on row 22 [24, 26, 28]; for **back crotch,** join MC with sl st in next st, ch 2, hdc in next 9 sts leaving remaining sts unworked, turn (10).

Row 24 [26, 28, 30]: Ch 2, hdc next 2 sts tog, hdc in each st across to last 2 sts, hdc last 2 sts tog, turn (8).

Row 25 [27, 29, 31]: Ch 2, hdc in each st across, **do not** turn.

Rnd 26 [28, 30, 32]: Working around opening, sc in end of next 3 rows, (sc next 2 sts tog) 20 [21, 23, 24]

continued on page 71

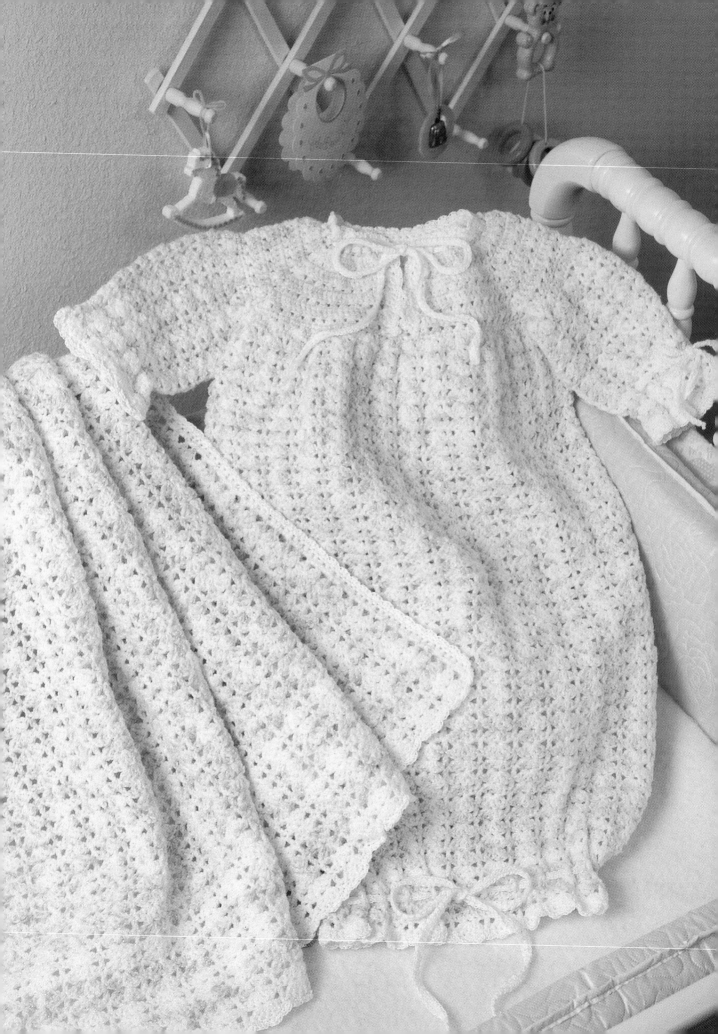

Afghan & Bunting

Designed by *Donna Piglowski*

Afghan

Sizes: 35" x 37½".

Materials: Pompadour baby yarn — 12 oz. candy print and 2½ oz. white; 225 yds. white bedspread cotton; tapestry needles; No. 0 steel and F crochet hooks or size needed to obtain gauge.

Gauge: With **F hook and baby yarn,** 1 dc and 1 shell = 1"; 2 dc rows = 1".

Skill Level: ☆☆ Average

NOTES: Use F hook and baby yarn unless otherwise stated.

*For **shell,** 5 dc in next st or ch.*

Row 1: With white, ch 177, 5 dc in 6th ch from hook, skip next 2 chs, dc in next ch, (skip next 2 chs, shell in next st, skip next 2 chs, dc in next ch) across, turn, fasten off. (29 shells, 30 dc)

Row 2: Join print with sl st in first st, ch 3, (skip next 2 sts, shell in next st, skip next 2 sts, dc in next st) across, turn.

Row 3: Ch 3, (skip next 2 sts, shell in next st, skip next 2 sts, dc in next st) across, turn, fasten off.

Rows 4-5: With white, repeat rows 2 and 3.

Rows 6-7: Repeat rows 2 and 3.

Rows 8-9: With white, repeat rows 2 and 3.

Row 10: Repeat row 2

Rows 11-61: Ch 3, (skip next 2 sts, shell in next st, skip next 2 sts, dc in next st) across, turn. At end of last row, fasten off.

Rows 62-71: Repeat rows 4-7 consecutively, ending with row 5.

Row 72: Working in starting ch on opposite side of row 1, join white with sl st in 3rd ch of ch-5, ch 3, (skip next 2 chs, shell in next ch, skip next 2 chs, dc in next ch) across, fasten off.

Border

Working in ends of rows on one short end, join white with sc in first row, 2 hdc in same row, 2 hdc in each row across with (2 hdc, sc) in last row, fasten off.

Repeat on other short end.

Edging

Rnd 1: Working around outer edge, with No. 0 steel hook and bedspread cotton, join with sc in any corner st, ch 1, (sc in next st, ch 1) around, join with sl st in first sc.

Rnd 2: Ch 2, 2 hdc in first sc, sl st in next sc, (3 hdc in next sc, sl st in next sc) around, join with sl st in top of ch-2, fasten off.

Bunting

Sizes: Instructions are given fit 0-3 mos. Change for 6-9 mos. are in [ ].

Materials: Pompadour baby yarn — 9 oz. candy print and 1 oz. white; 420 yds. white bedspread cotton; tapestry needle; No. 0 steel and F crochet hooks or size needed to obtain gauge.

Gauge: With **F hook and baby yarn,** 1 dc and 1 shell = 1"; 2 dc rows = 1".

Skill Level: ☆☆ Average

Yoke

NOTES: Use F hook and baby yarn unless otherwise stated.

*For **cross st (cr st),** skip next st, dc in next st; working behind last dc made, dc in skipped st.*

*For **V-st,** (dc, ch 1, dc) in next ch sp.*

Row 1: Starting at **neckline,** with print, ch 53 [57] loosely, dc in 4th ch from hook, dc in each ch across, turn (51 dc) [55 dc].

Row 2: Ch 3, 2 dc in each st across to last 2 sts, skip next st, dc in last st, turn (98) [106].

Row 3: Ch 3, cr st across to last st, dc in last st, turn (48 cr sts, 2 dc) [52 sc sts, 2 dc].

Row 4: Ch 3, (dc in next 14 [16] sts, 2 dc in next st, ch 1, 2 dc in next st) 2 times, dc in next 32 sts, (2 dc in next st, ch 1, 2 dc in next st, dc in next 14 [16] sts) 2 times, dc in last st, turn (106) [114].

Row 5: For **right front,** ch 3, cr st 8 [9] times, V-st in next ch sp; for **sleeve,** cr st 9 [10] times, V-st; for **back,** cr st 18 times, V-st; for **sleeve,** cr st 9 [10] times, V-st; for **left front,** cr st 8 [9] times; dc

continued on page 70

in last st, turn (52 cr sts, 10 dc) [56 cr sts, 10 dc].

Row 6: Ch 3, dc in next 17 [19] sts, V-st, dc in next 20 [22] sts, V-st, dc in next 38 sts, V-st, dc in next 20 [22] sts, V-st, dc in next 17 [19] sts, dc in last st, turn (122 [130]).

Row 7: Ch 3, cr st 9 [10] times, V-st, cr st 11 [12] times, V-st, cr st 20 times, V-st, cr st 11 [12] times, V-st, cr st 9 [10] times, dc in last st, turn (60 cr sts, 10 dc) [64 cr sts, 10 dc].

Row 8: Ch 3, dc in next 19 [21] sts, V-st, dc in next 24 [26] sts, V-st, dc in next 42 sts, V-st, dc in next 24 [26] sts, V-st, dc in next 19 [21] sts, dc in last st, turn (138) [146].

Row 9: Ch 3, cr st 10 [11] times, V-st, cr st 13 [14] times, V-st, cr st 22 times, V-st, cr st 13 [14 times], V-st, cr st 10 [11] times, dc in last st, turn (68 cr sts, 10 dc) [72 cr sts, 10 dc], fasten off.

Edging

Row 1: With No. 0 hook and white baby yarn, working in ends of rows, with right side of last row facing you, join with sl st in row 9, ch 3, dc in same row, (sc in next row, 3 dc in next row) 4 times; working in starting ch on opposite side of row 1, sc in each ch across neck, (3 dc in next row, sc in next row) 4 times, 2 dc in last row, turn, fasten off (87) [91].

Row 2: Join white bedspread cotton with sc in first st, (ch 1, sc) in each st across, turn.

Row 3: Ch 2, hdc in same sc, sl st in next sc, (3 hdc in next sc, sl st in next sc) across to last st, 2 hdc in last st, fasten off.

Body

Rnd 1: Starting at **right front,** join print with sc in end of row 1 on Edging, 2 sc in same row, sc in next 22 [24] sts on row 9, sc in next ch sp; *for **armhole,** ch 4 [6], skip next 28 [30] sts; sc in next ch sp*, sc in next 46 sts, sc in next ch sp; repeat between **, sc in next 22 [24] sts, 3 sc in opposite end of row 1 on Edging, join with sl st in first sc, **do not** turn (100) [104].

Rnd 2: Ch 3, (skip next st, shell in next st, skip next st, dc in next st) around skipping last st, join with sl st in top of ch-3, **turn** (27 shells, 27 dc) [29 shells, 29 dc].

Rnds 3-39 [3-43]: Ch 3, shell in center st of next shell, (dc in next dc, shell in center st of next shell) around, join, **turn.** At end of last rnd, fasten off.

Rnd 40 [44]: Join white with sl st in first st, repeat rnd 3, fasten off.

Rnds 41-43 [45-47]: Join print with sl st in first st, repeat rnd 3. At end of last rnd, fasten off.

Rnd 44 [48]: Repeat rnd 40 [44].

Rnd 45 [49]: With No. 0 hook and white bedspread cotton, join with sc in first st, ch 1, (sc, ch 1) in each st around, join, **turn** (162) [174].

Rnd 46 [50]: Ch 2, hdc in same sc, sl st in next sc, (3 hdc in next sc, sl st in next sc) around, join with sl st in top of ch-2, fasten off.

Sleeve

Rnd 1: Working around one armhole, join print with sc in first ch, sc in each ch and in each st around, join with sl st in first sc, **do not** turn (32) [36].

Rnd 2: Repeat rnd 2 of Body (8 shells, 8 dc) [9 shells, 9 dc].

Rnds 3-10 [3-12]: Repeat rnd 3 of Body. At end of last rnd, fasten off.

Rnd 11 [13]: Join white with sl st in first st, repeat rnd 3 of Body, fasten off.

Rnd 12 [14]: Join print with sl st in first st, repeat rnd 3 of Body, fasten off.

Rnds 13-15 [15-17]: Repeat rnds 9 and 10 [13 and 14] alternately, ending with row 9 [13].

Rnds 16-17 [18-19]: Repeat rnds 45 and 46 [49 and 50] of Body.

Repeat on other armhole.

Ties

Row 1: For **neck,** with F hook and white baby yarn, ch 175 loosely, fasten off.

Row 2: Working in back bar of ch (see illustration), with No. 0 hook and white bedspread cotton, join with sc in first ch, (ch 1, sc) in each ch across, fasten off. Weave through sts of row 1 on Yoke.

For **wrist** (make 2), ch 82, repeat rows 1 and 2 of neck. Weave through sts of rnd 11 [15] on Sleeve.

For **bottom,** ch 200, repeat rows 1 and 2 of neck. Weave through sts of rnd 38 [42] on Body. ✂

BACK BAR OF CHAIN

times, sc in next 1 [2, 1, 2] st, sc in end of next 2 rows, 3 sc in next st, sc in next 6 sts, 3 sc in next st, sc in end of next 2 rows, sc in next 1 [2, 1, 2] st, (sc next 2 sts tog) 20 [21, 23, 24] times, sc in end of next 3 rows, 3 sc in next st, sc in next 6 sts, 3 sc in next st, join with sl st in first sc, **do not** turn.

Rnd 27 [29, 31, 33]: Ch 1, sc in each st around, join fasten off.

Trim

For **neck and back opening Trim,** working in sts and in ends of rows, join MC with sc in end of last row on back, evenly space 92 more sc around to opposite end of last row, fasten off.

For **armhole Trim,** join MC with sc in center ch at underarm on one armhole, working in sts and in ends of rows, evenly space 40 more sc around, join with sl st in first sc. Repeat on other armhole.

Finishing

1: Sew one side of Velcro™ to inside of front crotch and other side of Velcro™ to outside of back crotch.

2: Sew buttons evenly spaced down back opening using space between sts for buttonholes.

3 : Sew 3 appliqués across yoke on Front Bodice.

BONNET

Row 1: With MC, ch 15 [17, 19, 21] hdc in 3rd ch from hook, hdc in each ch across, turn (14 hdc) [16 hdc, 18 hdc, 20 hdc]

Rows 2-4: Ch 2, hdc in same st, hdc in each st across to last st, 2 hdc in last st, ending with 20 [22, 24, 26] sts in last row, turn.

Rows 5-8 [5-10, 5-11, 5-12]: Ch 2, hdc in each st across, turn.

Rows 9-11 [11-13, 12-14, 13-15]: Ch 2, hdc next 2 sts tog, hdc in each st across to last 2 sts, hdc last 2 sts tog, ending with 14 [16, 18, 20] sts in last row, turn.

Rnd 12 [14, 15, 16]: Working in rnds, ch 1, sc in first 14 [16, 18, 20] sts; (working in ends of rows, evenly sp 16 [18, 20, 22] sc across next 12 [14, 15, 16] rows); working in starting ch on opposite side of row 1, sc in next 14 [16, 18, 20] chs; repeat between ( ), join with sl st in first sc, **turn** (60) [68, 76, 84].

Row 13 [15, 16, 17]: Working in rows, ch 2, hdc in same st, hdc in next 44 [50, 56, 62] sts, 2 hdc in next st leaving remaining sts unworked, turn (48) [54, 60, 66].

Row 14 [16, 17, 18]: Ch 2, hdc in next 9 sts, 2 hdc in next st, (hdc in next 8 [10, 12, 14] sts, 2 hdc in next st) 3 times, hdc in last 10 sts, turn (52) [58, 64, 70].

Row 15 [17-18, 18-20, 19-22]: Ch 2, hdc in each st across, turn. At end of last row, fasten off.

Row 16 [19, 21, 23]: Join white with sl st in first st, ch 2, hdc in each st across, turn.

Rows 17-19 [20-22, 22-24, 24-26]: Ch 2, hdc in each st across, turn. At end of last row, fasten off.

Row 20 [23, 25, 27]: Join MC with sl st in first st, ch 2, hdc in each st across, turn.

Row 21 [24, 26, 28]: For **boy's only,** ch 2, hdc in each st across, fasten off.

Row 22 [25, 27, 29]: For **boy's only,** ch 1, sc in each of first 2 sts, hdc in each of next 2 sts, 2 dc in each st across to last 4 sts, hdc in each of next 2 sts, sc in each of last 2 sts, fasten off.

Row 21 [24, 26, 28]: For **girl's only,** ch 1, sc in each st across.

Row 22 [25, 27, 29]: For **girl's only,** ch 1, sc in each of first 2 sts, hdc in each of next 2 sts, 2 dc in each st across to last 4 sts, hdc in each of next 2 sts, sc in each of last 2 sts, fasten off.

Trim

For **first tie,** with MC, ch 35, join with sc in end of last hdc row on Hat, sc in each row and in each st across to opposite end of last hdc row; for **2nd tie,** ch 35, fasten off. Sew 3 appliqués evenly spaced across white band. ✄

Baby Blocks

Designed by *Aline Suplinskas*

Size: 29½" x 36½".

Materials: Pompadour 3-ply sport yarn — 10½ oz. variegated, 6½ oz. pink and 2 oz. orchid; tapestry needle; F crochet hook or size needed to obtain gauge.

Gauge: Each Motif = 3½" square.

Skill Level: ☆☆ Average

Motif (make 80)

Rnd 1: With orchid, ch 4, sl st in first ch to form ring, ch 4, (dc, ch 1) 11 times in ring, join with sl st in 3rd ch of ch-4, fasten off (12 dc, 12 ch-1 sps).

*NOTES: For **beginning cluster (beg cl)**, ch 3, (yo, insert hook in same sp, yo, draw lp through, yo, draw through 2 lps on hook) 2 times, yo, draw through all 3 lps on hook.*

*For **cluster (cl)**, *yo, insert hook in next ch sp, yo, draw lp through, yo, draw through 2 lps on hook; repeat from * 2 more times in same sp, yo, draw through all 4 lps on hook.*

Rnd 2: Join variegated with sl st in any ch sp, beg cl, ch 2, (cl in next ch sp, ch 2) around, join with sl st in top of ch-3 (12 cls, 12 ch-2 sps).

*NOTES: For **beginning shell (beg shell)**, ch 3, (2 dc, ch 3, 3 dc) in same sp.*

*For **shell**, (3 dc, ch 3, 3 dc) in next ch sp.*

Rnd 3: Sl st in next ch sp, beg shell, 3 dc in each of next 2 ch sps, (shell in next ch sp, 3 dc in each of next 2 ch sps) around, join, fasten off (24 dc, 4 shells).

Rnd 4: Join pink with sl st in any corner ch sp, beg shell, ch 1, (2 dc between next two 3-dc groups, ch 1) 3 times, *shell in next corner ch sp, ch 1, (2 dc between next two 3-dc groups, ch 1) 3 times; repeat from * around, join, fasten off.

ASSEMBLY

Strip

To **join first two Motifs,** holding right sides together, working through both thicknesses, join pink with sc in any corner ch sp, *ch 3, sc in next ch sp, (ch 2, sc in next ch sp) 3 times, ch 3, sc in next corner ch sp*, [ch 3; to **join next two Motifs,** holding right sides together, working through both thicknesses, sc in first corner ch sp; repeat between **]; repeat between [ ] 8 more times for a total of 2 Strips of 10 Motifs each, fasten off.

To **join next Motif to first Motif on last Strip made,** holding right sides together, working through both thicknesses, join pink with sc in first corner ch sp, *ch 3, sc in next ch sp, (ch 2, sc in next ch sp) 3 times, ch 3, sc in next corner ch sp*, [ch 3; to **join next Motif on to same Strip,** holding right sides together, working through both thicknesses, sc in first corner ch sp; repeat between **]; repeat between [ ] 8 more times, fasten off. Repeat for a total of 8 Strips.

Joining Strips

To **join first two Strips,** holding right sides together, working through both thicknesses, join pink with sc in first corner ch sp, *ch 3, sc in next ch sp, (ch 2, sc in next ch sp) 3 times, ch 3, sc in next corner ch sp*, [ch 2, sc in next corner ch sp; repeat between **]; repeat between [ ] across, fasten off.

To **join next Strip,** holding right sides of last joined Strip and next Strip together, work same as before.

Repeat for a total of 8 joined Strips.

EDGING

Rnd 1: Working around entire outer edge, join pink with sc in any corner ch sp, (ch 3, sc, ch 3) in same sp, (sc, ch 3) in each ch sp around with (sc, ch 3, sc, ch 3) in each corner ch sp, join with sl st in first sc, fasten off.

Rnd 2: Join variegated with sc in first corner ch sp, (ch 3, sc, ch 3) in same sp, (sc, ch 3) in each ch sp around with (sc, ch 3, sc, ch 3) in each corner ch sp, join.

Rnd 3: Sl st in next ch sp, ch 1, (sc, ch 3, sc, ch 3) in same sp, (sc, ch 3) in each ch sp around with (sc, ch 3, sc, ch 3) in each corner ch sp, join, fasten off. ✀

Sun-Kissed Gardens

Brighten your heart as well as your home with ever-blooming designs that capture the essence of spring throughout the year. Dainty butterflies and colorful blooms lend an enchanting beauty to any room, surrounding everyone with nature's peaceful calm. Cultivate your own relaxing retreat with bountiful crochet creations that will blossom before your eyes.

Rose Cafe Curtain

Designed by *Lucille LaFlamme*

Size: 21" x 38" not including hanging loops.

Materials: Size-20 crochet cotton — 1940 yds. white; tapestry needle; No. 12 steel crochet hook or size needed to obtain gauge.

Gauge: 14 dc = 1"; 5 dc rows = 1".

NOTES: For **mesh**, ch 2, skip next 2 chs or dc, dc in next ch or dc.

For **block**, 2 dc in next ch sp, dc in next st, **or,** dc in each of next 3 sts, **or,** dc in each of next 3 chs.

For **beginning block (beg block),** ch 3, dc in each of next 2 chs or dc, dc in next dc. Use beg block as first block on each row.

Work each row on graph from right to left, then return to right on same row.

Work center mesh indicated by gray area of each row only once, **do not** repeat.

Curtain may ruffle until blocked.

For those who chain tightly, a larger hook may be needed to crochet the starting chain.

Skill Level: ☆☆☆ Advanced

CURTAIN

Row 1: Ch 539, dc in 4th ch from hook, dc in each of next 2 chs (first block made), complete row according to Filet Graph on page 81, turn.

Rows 2-105: Work according to graph turning as stated in Notes.

Row 106: Ch 1, sc in first dc, ch 33, sc in each of next 3 dc, (2 sc in next ch sp, sc in next dc) 9 times, ch 33, *(2 sc in next ch sp, sc in next dc or sc in each dc of block) 10 times, ch 33; repeat from * across to last 8 mesh, (2 sc in next ch sp, sc in next dc) 8 times, sc in each of next 3 dc, ch 33, sc in last dc, fasten off.

For **edging,** working in starting ch on opposite side of row 1, with wrong side facing you, join with sc in first dc, sc in each of next 3 dc, 2 sc in next ch sp, ch 4; working a sc in each dc and 2 sc in each ch sp, (work 6 sc, ch 4) across to last ch sp, sc in next dc, 2 sc in next ch sp, sc in last 4 dc, fasten off. ✂

Butterflies in Flight

Designed by *Frances Hughes*

Size: 45½" x 55".

Materials: Worsted-weight yarn — 25 oz. pink and 13 oz. off-white; tapestry needle; H crochet and H-20" flexible afghan crochet hooks or sizes needed to obtain gauges.

Gauges: With **afghan hook,** 5 afghan sts = 1"; 4 afghan st rows = 1". With **crochet hook,** 5 sc = 1".

Skill Level: ☆☆ Average

AFGHAN

Row 1: With afghan hook and pink, ch 187, leaving all lps on hook, insert hook in 2nd ch from hook, yo, draw lp through, (insert hook in next ch, yo, draw lp through) across, **do not** turn; to **work lps off hook,** yo, draw through one lp on hook (see illustration a), (yo, draw through 2 lps on hook) across leaving one lp on hook at end of row (see illustration b), **do not** turn (187 vertical bars).

Rows 2-187: For **afghan st,** skip first vertical bar, insert hook under next vertical bar (see illustration c), yo, draw lp through, afghan st in each vertical bar across to last bar; for **last st,** insert hook under last bar and st directly behind it (see illustration d), yo, draw lp through; work sts off hook.

Row 188: Skip first vertical bar, (insert hook under next vertical bar, yo, draw lp through bar and one lp on hook) across, **do not** fasten off.

BORDER

Rnd 1: With H crochet hook, working around outer edge, ch 1, 3 sc in same sp, sc in end of each row and in each st around with 3 sc in each corner, join with sl st in first sc, **turn,** fasten off.

Rnd 2: With wrong side of rnd 1 facing you, join off-white with sl st in any center corner st, ch 4, (dc, ch 1, dc, ch 1, dc) in same st, [skip next st, *(dc, ch 1, dc) in next st, skip next 2 sts; repeat from * across to next center corner st], ◊(dc, ch 1, dc, ch 1, dc, ch 1, dc) in next st; repeat between [ ]; repeat from ◊ around, join with sl st in 3rd ch of ch-4, **do not** turn (256 ch sps).

*NOTES: For **beginning shell (beg shell),** ch 4, (tr, ch 1, 2 tr) in same sp.*

*For **V-stitch (V-st),** (tr, ch 1, tr) in next sp.*

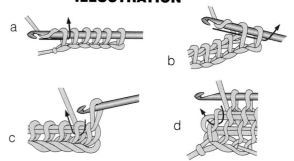

*For **shell,** (2 tr, ch 1, 2 tr) in next sp.*

Rnd 3: Sl st in first ch sp, beg shell, *V-st in next ch sp, shell in next ch sp, sc in next ch sp, ch 3, sc in next ch sp, (shell in next ch sp, sc in next ch sp, ch 3, sc in next ch sp) 20 times*, [shell in next ch sp; repeat between **]; repeat between [ ] around, join with sl st in top of ch-4 (88 shells, 88 sc, 84 ch-3 sps, 4 V-sts).

Rnd 4: Sl st in next st, sl st in next ch sp, beg shell, shell in next V-st, shell in next shell, *ch 3, sc in next ch-3 sp, ch 3, (shell in next shell, ch 3, sc in next ch-3 sp, ch 3) 20 times*, [shell in each of next 2 shells and one V-st; repeat between **]; repeat between [ ] around, join (168 ch-3 sps, 92 shells).

Rnd 5: Ch 4, tr in same st, 2 tr in next st, *2 tr in next ch-1 sp, 2 tr in each of next 2 sts, ch 3, sc in next shell, ch 3, (2 tr in each of next 2 sts, 2 tr in next ch-1 sp, 2 tr in each of next 2 sts, skip next 2 ch-3 sps) 21 times*, [2 tr in each of next 2 sts; repeat between **]; repeat between [ ] around, join (880 tr, 8 ch-3 sps).

Rnd 6: Sl st in next st, ch 1, sc in same st, (ch 3, skip next st, sc in next st) 4 times, (ch 3, sc in next ch-3 sp) 2 times, *(ch 3, skip next st, sc in next st) around to next ch-3 sp, (ch 3, sc in next ch-3 sp) 2 times; repeat from * 2 more times, (ch 3, skip next st, sc in next st) around; to **join,** ch 1, hdc in first sc (448 ch sps).

Rnds 7-8: Ch 1, sc around joining hdc, (ch 3, sc in next ch sp) around, join as before. At end of last rnd, **turn,** fasten off.

*NOTE: For **picot,** ch 3, sl st in 3rd ch from hook.*

Rnd 9: With wrong side of rnd 8 facing you, join pink with sc in any ch sp, (picot, sc) in same sp, (sc, picot, sc) in each ch sp around, join, fasten off.

continued on page 80

EMBROIDERY

With off-white, using Cross Stitch (see illustration), embroider butterfly design as follows:

For **rows 1-94,** work each row on Embroidery Diagram from right to left, then return to right on same row. Work center indicated by arrow of each row only once, **do not** repeat. For **rows 95-187,** turn graph upside down; work each row from left to right, then return to left on same row. ✄

CROSS STITCH OVER AFGHAN STITCH ILLUSTRATION

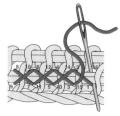

EMBROIDERY DIAGRAM

Center row of Afghan   (one quarter of design)

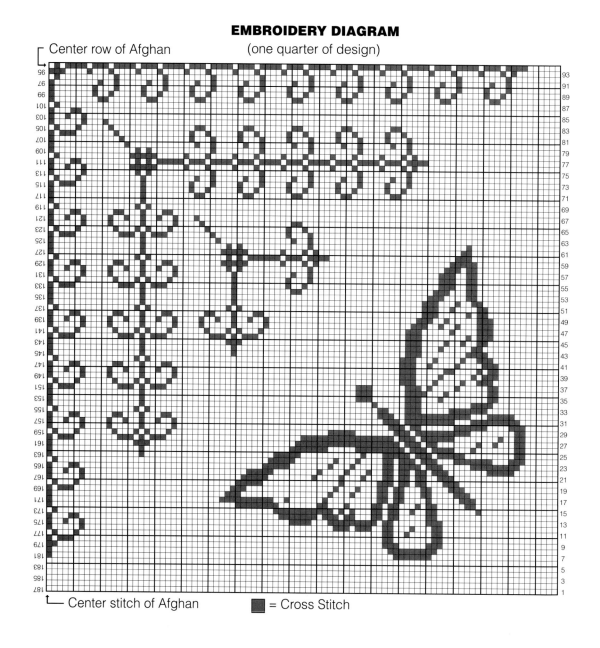

⌐ Center stitch of Afghan   ■ = Cross Stitch

Rose Cafe Curtain

instructions on page 77

□ = Mesh
● = Block
X = Beg block or last block made

FILET GRAPH

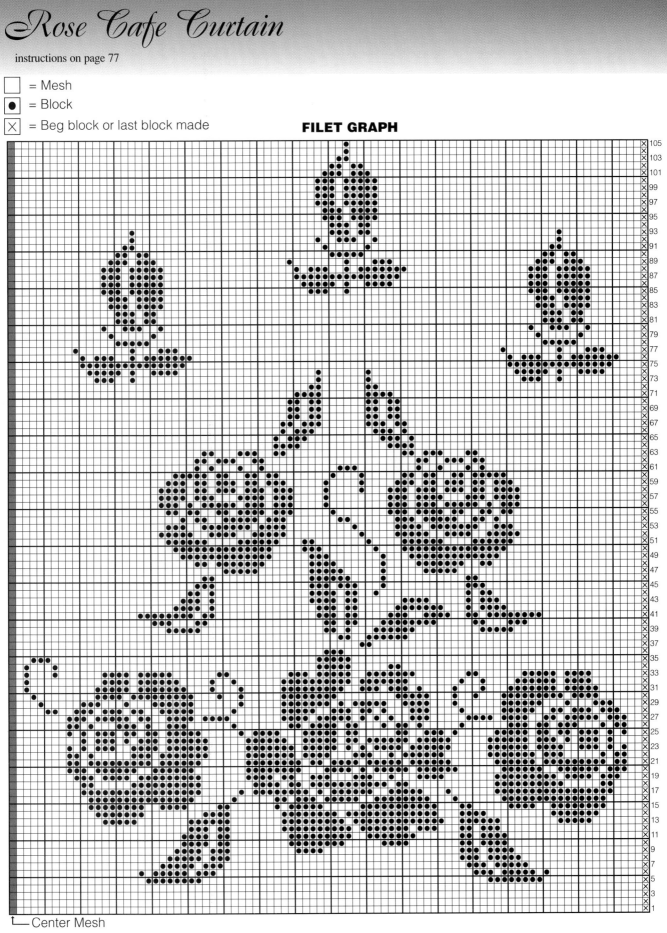

└─ Center Mesh

Floral Jewels

Designed by *Sandra Smith*

Size: Flower is 4½" across. Afghan is 44" x 66".

Materials: Worsted-weight yarn — 21 oz. black, 5 oz. each lt. and dk. shades of purple, rose, blue, green, gold and rust; tapestry needle; G crochet hook or size needed to obtain gauge.

Gauge: 4 sc = 1".

Notes: Make Large Flower No. 1 first, then make one Small Flower, joining to Large Flower just made. Alternate joining Large and Small Flowers.

For **Large Flower,** make 8 each color according to instructions and make 8 each color reversing shades. For example, you will have 8 with dk. blue centers and 8 with lt. blue centers. Repeat with each color, ending with a total of 96 Large Flowers.

Skill Level: ☆☆ Average

LARGE FLOWER NO. 1

Rnd 1: With dk. shade, ch 4, sl st in first ch to form ring, (ch 8, sl st) 8 times in ring, join with sl st in first ch of first ch-8 (8 ch sps).

Rnd 2: Sl st in first ch sp, ch 1, (4 sc, hdc, 5 dc, hdc, 4 sc) in same sp, sl st in next sl st, *(4 sc, hdc, 5 dc, hdc, 4 sc) in next ch sp, sl st in next sl st; repeat from * around, join with sl st in first sc, fasten off (8 petals).

Rnd 3: Working this rnd in **back lps** only, join lt. shade with sl st in first hdc of any petal, sc in next dc, hdc in next dc, 3 dc in next dc, hdc in next dc, sc in next dc, sl st in next hdc, *sl st in first hdc of next petal, sc in next dc, hdc in next dc, 3 dc in next dc, hdc in next dc, sc in next dc, sl st in next hdc; repeat from * around, join with sl st in first sl st, fasten off (72 sts).

Rnd 4: Working this rnd in **back lps** only, join black with sl st in 2nd dc of any 3-dc group, ch 5, *sl st in 2nd dc of next 3-dc group, ch 5; repeat from * around, join.

*NOTE: For **picot,** ch 2, sl st in 2nd ch from hook.*

Rnd 5: Sl st in first ch sp, ch 1, (5 sc, picot, 5 sc) in same sp, sl st in next sl st, *(5 sc, picot, 5 sc) in next ch sp, sl st in next sl st; repeat from * around, join, fasten off.

LARGE FLOWER NOS. 2-96

*NOTES: For joining **picot,** ch 1, sl st in picot of next flower, ch 1, sl st in first ch-1.*

Join Large Flowers in 8 rows of 12 Flowers each according to Assembly Diagram.

Rnds 1-4: Repeat same rnds of Large Flower No. 1.

Rnd 5: Repeat same rnd of Large Flower No. 1 using joining picot when joining Flowers.

SMALL FLOWER (*make 77*)

Rnd 1: With black, ch 5, sl st in first ch to form ring, ch 1, 16 sc in ring, join with sl st in first sc (16 sc).

Rnd 2: Ch 6, skip next 3 sts, * sl st in **back lp** of next st, ch 6, skip next 3 sts; repeat from * around, join with sl st in first ch of first ch-6 (4 ch sps).

NOTE: Join Small Flowers to Large Flowers according to diagram.

Rnd 3: Sl st in first ch sp, ch 1, (5 sc, joining picot in space between next 2 Large Flowers, 5 sc) in same sp, sl st in next sl st, *(5 sc, joining picot, 5 sc) in next ch sp, sl st in next sl st; repeat from * around, join with sl st in first sc, fasten off. ✂

ASSEMBLY DIAGRAM

⬤ = Lt. Shades

⬤ = Dk. Shades

▲ = Small Flower Joining Picot

| = Large Flower Joining

Irish Mint Doily

Designed by *Carol Smith*

Size: 12½" across.

Materials: Size-10 bedspread cotton — 150 yds. mint and 50 yds. white; tapestry needle; No. 9 steel crochet hook or size needed to obtain gauge.

Gauge: 9 dc = 1"; 4 dc rows = 1".

Skill Level: ☆☆ Average

DOILY

Rnd 1: With white, for **flower,** ch 4, sl st in first ch to form ring, ch 6, (dc in ring, ch 3) 4 times, join with sl st in 3rd ch of ch-6 (5 dc, 5 ch-3 sps).

Rnd 2: Ch 1; for **petal,** (sc, hdc, 2 dc, 3 tr, 2 dc, hdc, sc) in each ch-3 sp around, join with sl st in first sc (5 petals).

Rnd 3: Ch 1, sc in same st, ch 4, skip next 10 sts, (sc in next st, ch 4, skip next 10 sts) around, join (5 sc, 5 ch-4 sps).

Rnd 4: Ch 1, (sc, 2 hdc, 3 dc, 3 tr, 3 dc, 2 hdc, sc) in each ch-4 sp around, join.

Rnd 5: Ch 1, sc in same st, ch 6, skip next 14 sts, (sc in next st, ch 6, skip next 14 sts) around, join (5 sc, 5 ch-6 sps).

Rnd 6: Ch 1, (sc, 2 hdc, 3 dc, 5 tr, 3 dc, 2 hdc, sc) in each ch-6 sp around, join, fasten off.

Rnd 7: Join mint with sc in center tr of any petal, ch 7, skip next 8 sts, dc in next st, (ch 7, skip next 7 sts, sc in next st, ch 7, skip next 8 sts, dc in next st) across to last 7 sts; to **join,** ch 4, skip last 7 sts, dc in first sc (5 sc, 5 dc, 10 ch sps).

Rnd 8: Ch 3, dc around joining dc just made, ch 7, (2 dc in next ch-7 sp, ch 7) around, join with sl st in top of ch-3 (20 dc, 10 ch-7 sps).

Rnd 9: (Sl st, ch 3, dc, ch 5, 2 dc, ch 5) in first ch-7 sp, (2 dc, ch 5, 2 dc, ch 5) in each ch-7 sp around, join (40 dc, 20 ch-5 sps).

Rnd 10: (Sl st, ch 3, dc, ch 5, 2 dc, ch 3) in first ch-5 sp, dc in next ch-5 sp, ch 3, *(2 dc, ch 5, 2 dc, ch 3) in next ch-5 sp, dc in next ch-5 sp, ch 3; repeat from * around, join (50 dc, 20 ch-3 sps, 10 ch-5 sps).

Rnd 11: (Sl st, ch 3, dc, ch 5, 2 dc) in first ch-5 sp, ch 3, skip next ch-3 sp, (dc, ch 2, dc) in next dc, ch 3, skip next ch-3 sp, *(2 dc, ch 5, 2 dc,) in next ch-5 sp, ch 3, skip next ch-3 sp, (dc, ch 2, dc) in next dc, ch 3, skip next ch-3 sp; repeat from * around, join (60 dc, 20 ch-3 sps, 10 ch-5 sps, 10 ch-2 sps).

Rnd 12: (Sl st, ch 3, dc, ch 4, 2 dc) in first ch-5 sp, ch 3, skip next ch-3 sp, 3 dc in next dc, ch 3, dc in next ch-2 sp, ch 3, 3 dc in next dc, ch 3, skip next ch-3 sp, *(2 dc, ch 4, 2 dc) in next ch-5 sp, ch 3, skip next ch-3 sp, 3 dc in next dc, ch 3, dc in next ch-2 sp, ch 3, 3 dc in next dc, ch 3, skip next ch-3 sp; repeat from * around, join (110 dc, 40 ch-3 sps, 10 ch-4 sps).

Rnd 13: Sl st in next dc, (sl st, ch 3, dc) in first ch-4 sp, *ch 3, skip next ch-3 sp, dc in next dc, 3 dc in next dc, dc in next dc, ch 3, skip next ch-3 sp, (dc, ch 2, dc) in next dc, ch 3, skip next ch-3 sp, dc in next dc, 3 dc in next dc, dc in next dc, ch 3, skip next ch-3 sp*, [2 dc in next ch-4 sp; repeat between **]; repeat between [ ] around, join (140 dc, 40 ch-3 sps, 10 ch-2 sps).

Rnd 14: Ch 3, dc in next dc, *ch 3, skip next ch-3 sp, skip next dc, dc in each of next 3 dc, ch 3, skip next dc, skip next ch-3 sp, 3 dc in next dc, ch 3, dc in next ch-2 sp, ch 3, 3 dc in next dc, ch 3, skip next ch-3 sp, skip next dc, dc in each of next 3 dc, ch 3, skip next dc, skip next ch-3 sp*, [dc in each of next 2 dc; repeat between **]; repeat between [ ] around, join (150 dc, 60 ch-3 sps).

Rnd 15: Ch 3, dc in next dc, *ch 5, skip next ch-3 sp and next dc, dc in next dc, ch 3, skip next dc and next ch-3 sp, dc in next dc, 3 dc in next dc, (dc in next dc, ch 3)

2 times, dc in next dc, 3 dc in next dc, dc in next dc, ch 3, skip next ch-3 sp and next dc, dc in next dc, ch 5, skip next dc and next ch-3 sp*, [dc in each of next 2 dc; repeat between **]; repeat between [ ] around, join (150 dc, 54 ch-3 sps, 20 ch-5 sps).

Rnd 16: Ch 3, dc in next dc, *2 dc in next ch-5 sp, ch 3, skip next dc, skip next ch-3 sp, skip next dc, dc in each of next 3 dc, ch 3, skip next dc, 3 dc in next dc, ch 3, skip next dc, dc in each of next 3 dc, ch 3, skip next dc, skip next ch-3 sp, skip next dc, 2 dc in next ch-5 sp*, [dc in each of next 2 dc; repeat between **]; repeat between [ ] around, join (150 dc, 40 ch-3 sps).

Rnd 17: Ch 3, dc in each of next 3 dc, *2 dc in next ch-3 sp, ch 3, skip next dc, dc in next dc, ch 3, skip next dc, skip next ch-3 sp, dc in next dc, 3 dc in next dc, dc in next dc, ch 3, skip next ch-3 sp, skip next dc, dc in next dc, ch 3, skip next dc, 2 dc in next ch-3 sp, dc in each next 2 dc*, [dc in next 4 dc; repeat between **]; repeat between [ ] around, join (170 dc, 40 ch-3 sps).

Rnd 18: Ch 3, dc in next 5 dc, *2 dc in next ch-3 sp, ch 5, skip next dc, skip next ch-3 sp, skip next dc, dc in each of next 3 dc, ch 5, skip next dc, skip next ch-3 sp, skip next dc, 2 dc in next ch-3 sp, dc in next 4 dc*, [dc in next 6 dc; repeat between **]; repeat between [ ] around, join (170 dc, 20 ch-5 sps).

Rnd 19: Ch 3, dc in next 7 dc, 2 dc in next ch-5 sp, ch 4, skip next dc, dc in next dc, ch 4, skip next dc, 2 dc in next ch-5 sp, dc in next 6 dc, [dc in next 8 dc, 2 dc in next ch-5 sp, ch 4, skip next dc, dc in next dc, ch 4, skip next dc, 2 dc in next ch-5 sp, dc in next 6 dc]; repeat between [ ] around, join (190 dc, 20 ch-4 sps).

Rnd 20: Ch 3, dc in next 9 dc, *2 dc in next ch-4 sp, ch 5, skip next dc, 2 dc in next ch-4 sp, dc in next 8 dc*, [dc in next 10 dc; repeat between **]; repeat between [ ] around, join (220 dc, 10 ch-5 sps).

Rnd 21: Ch 3, dc in next 11 dc, 6 dc in next ch-5 sp, dc in next 10 dc, (dc in next 12 dc, 6 dc in next ch-5 sp, dc in next 10 dc) around, join (280 dc).

Rnd 22: Ch 3, dc in next 13 dc, 2 dc in each of next 2 dc, dc in next 12 dc, (dc in next 14 dc, 2 dc in each of next 2 dc, dc in next 12 dc) around, join, fasten off (300 dc).

Rnd 23: Join white with sl st in first dc, ch 8, skip next 2 dc, (dc in each of next 2 dc, ch 5, skip next 2 dc) around to last st, dc in last st, join with sl st in 3rd ch of ch-8 (150 dc, 75 ch-5 sps).

Rnd 24: (Sl st, ch 3, dc) in first ch-5 sp, ch 5, (2 dc in next ch-5 sp, ch 5) around, join with sl st in top of ch-3, fasten off.

Rnd 25: Join mint with sc in first ch-5 sp, (2 sc, ch 3, 3 sc) in same sp, (3 sc, ch 3, 3 sc) in each ch-5 sp around, join with sl st in first sc, fasten off. ✂

Petite Petals Runner

Designed by *Lucille LaFlamme*

Size: 18" x 35".

Materials: Size-10 bedspread cotton — 1000 yds. ecru; tapestry needle; No. 9 steel crochet hook or size needed to obtain gauge.

Gauge: Motif is 4¼" across.

Skill Level: ☆☆☆ Advanced

FIRST ROW

First Motif

Rnd 1: Ch 8, sl st in first ch to form ring, ch 4, 7 tr in ring, ch 20, sl st in 15th ch from hook, ch 5, (8 tr in ring, ch 20, sl st in 15th ch from hook, ch 5) 3 times, join with sl st in top of ch-4 (32 tr, 8 ch-5 sps, 4 ch-15 lps).

*NOTES: For **beginning double treble cluster (beg dtr cl)**, ch 5, *yo 3 times, insert hook in next st, yo, draw lp through, (yo, draw through 2 lps on hook) 3 times; repeat from * 6 more times, yo, draw through all 8 lps on hook.*

*For **double treble cluster (dtr cl)**, *yo 3 times, insert hook in next st, yo, draw lp through, (yo, draw through 2 lps on hook) 3 times; repeat from * 7 more times, yo, draw through all 9 lps on hook.*

*For **treble cluster (tr cl)**, *yo 2 times, insert hook in next st or ch lp, yo, draw lp through, (yo, draw through 2 lps on hook) 2 times; repeat from * 2 more times in same st or lp, yo, draw through all 4 lps on hook.*

Rnd 2: Beg dtr cl, ch 7, skip first 5 chs of ch-20 lp, (tr cl, ch 7) 5 times in next ch-15 lp, skip next ch-5, [dtr cl, ch 7, skip first 5 chs of ch-20 lp, (tr cl, ch 7) 5 times in next ch-15 lp, skip next ch-5]; repeat between [ ] around, join with sl st in top of beg dtr cl (24 ch-7 sps, 20 tr cls, 4 dtr cls).

Rnd 3: Sl st in first 4 chs, ch 1, sc in same ch, *ch 5, (sc, ch 4, sc) in 4th ch of next ch-7, ch 5, (sc, ch 7, sc) in 4th ch of next ch-7, ch 5, (sc, ch 7, sc) in 4th ch of next ch-7, ch 5, (sc, ch 4, sc) in 4th ch of next ch-7, ch 5, sc in 4th ch of next ch-7, ch 15*, [sc in 4th ch of next ch-7; repeat between **]; repeat between [ ] around, join with sl st in first sc, fasten off (20 ch-5 sps, 8 ch-7 sps, 8 ch-4 sps, 4 ch-15 lps).

Second Motif

Rnds 1-2: Repeat same rnds of First Motif.

*NOTES: To **join Motif in ch-7 sp**, sc in 4th ch of next ch-7, ch 3, sl st in corresponding ch-7 sp on other Motif according to Assembly Diagram, ch 3, sc in same ch on this Motif.*

*To **join Motif in ch-15 lps**, sc in 4th ch of next ch-7, ch 7, sl st in corresponding ch-15 lp on other Motif according to diagram, ch 7, sc in 4th ch of next ch-7 on this Motif.*

Rnd 3: Repeat rnd 3 of First Motif join in ch-7 sps and ch-15 lps according to diagram.

Repeat First Row Second Motif for a total of 8 Motifs.

SECOND ROW

Repeat First Row Second Motif for a total of 8 Motifs.

Repeat Second Row 2 more times for a total of 4 rows.

EDGING

Rnd 1: Join with sc in 7th ch of ch-15 to right of corner on First Row (see diagram), *ch 9, skip next ch-5 sp, sc in next ch-4 sp, ch 7, skip next ch-5 sp, sc in next ch-7 sp, ch 5, tr cl in 3rd ch of next ch-5, ch 5, sc in next ch-7 sp, ch 7, sc in next ch-4 sp, ch 9, (sc in next ch-15 lp, ch 9, sc in next ch-4 sp, ch 7, sc in next ch-7 sp, ch 9, skip next 2 ch-5 sps and joining, sc in next ch-7 sp, ch 7, sc in next ch-4 sp, ch 9) across to ch-15 lp before next corner*, [sc in next ch-15 lp; repeat between **]; repeat between [ ] around, join with sl st in first sc (124 ch sps, 120 sc, 4 tr cls).

*NOTES: For **beginning treble cluster (beg tr cl)**, ch*

MOTIF ASSEMBLY DIAGRAM

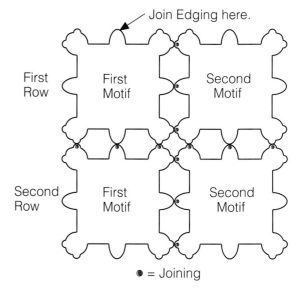

● = Joining

3, *yo 2 times, insert hook in same st, yo, draw lp through, (yo, draw through 2 lps on hook) 2 times; repeat from *, yo, draw through all 3 lps on hook.

For **picot,** ch 5, sl st in top of last st made.

Rnd 2: Beg tr cl, *picot, ch 11, sc in next sc, ch 9, tr cl in next sc, picot, ch 5, tr cl in 4th ch of next ch-5, picot, ch 5, tr cl in next cl, picot, ch 5, tr cl in 2nd ch of next ch-5, picot, ch 5, tr cl in next sc, picot, ch 9, sc in next sc, ch 11, (tr cl in next sc, picot, ch 11, sc in next sc, ch 9, tr cl in next sc, picot, ch 7, sc in 5th ch of next ch-9, ch 7, tr cl in next sc, picot, ch 9, sc in next sc, ch 11) across to 3 sc before next corner cl*, [tr cl in next sc; repeat between **]; repeat between [ ] around, join with sl st in top of beg cl, fasten off. ✂

Enchanted Garden Quilt

Designed by *Jennifer Christiansen McClain*

Size: 50¾" x 70¼".

Materials: Worsted-weight yarn — 29 oz. each off-white and lt. purple, 21½ oz. lt. rose, 12 oz. lt. blue, 6 oz. dk. green and 3½ oz. lt. green; I crochet hook or size needed to obtain gauge.

Gauge: 3 sts = 1"; rnds 1-6 = 3¾". Each Block is 9¾" square.

Skill Level: ☆☆☆ Advanced

AFGHAN
Block (make 35)

Rnd 1: With lt. green, ch 4, sl st in first ch to form ring, ch 1, 8 sc in ring, join with sl st in first sc, fasten off (8 sc).

Rnd 2: Join lt. rose with sl st in any st, (ch 2, 2 dc, ch 2, sl st) in same st, (sl st, ch 2, 2 dc, ch 2, sl st) in each st around, join with sl st in first sl st, fasten off (8 petals).

Rnd 3: Join dk. green with sl st in **back lp** of first sl st on any petal; working behind petals, ch 3, sl st in **back lp** of first sl st on next petal, ch 1, (sl st in **back lp** of first sl st on next petal, ch 3, sl st in **back lp** of first sl st on next petal, ch 1) around, join (4 ch-3 sps, 4 ch-1 sps).

*NOTE: For picot, ch 2, sl st in **front lp and left bar** of last st made.*

Rnd 4: Sl st in first ch sp, *[(ch 2, dc, tr, picot, dc, ch 2, sl st) in same sp, (sl st, ch 1, hdc, dc, picot, hdc, ch 1, sl st) in next ch-1 sp], sl st in next ch-3 sp; repeat from * 2 more times; repeat between [ ], join, fasten off (4 small leaves, 4 large leaves).

Rnd 5: Working behind leaves, join off-white with sl st in **back lp** of first sl st on any large leaf, (*ch 3, sl st in **back lp** of first sl st on next small leaf, ch 2*, sl st in **back lp** of first sl st on next large leaf) 3 times; repeat between **, join (4 ch-3 sps, 4 ch-s sps).

Rnd 6: Sl st in first ch sp, ch 3, (2 dc, ch 2, 3 dc) in same sp, 3 dc in next ch sp, *(3 dc, ch 2, 3 dc) in next ch sp, 3 dc in next ch sp; repeat from * around, join with sl st in top of ch-3, fasten off (36 dc, 4 ch sps).

Rnd 7: Join lt. blue with sc in any corner ch sp, (*sc in picot on corresponding leaf and in same sp on this rnd at same time, sc in same sp on this rnd, sc in next 4 sts, sc in picot on corresponding leaf and in next st on this rnd at same time, sc in next 4 sts*, sc in next cor-

ner ch sp) 3 times; repeat between **, join with sl st in first sc (48 sc).

Rnd 8: (Sl st in next st, ch 6, skip next st) around, join with sl st in first sl st, fasten off (24 ch sps).

Rnd 9: Working in skipped sts on rnd 7 and behind ch lps on rnd 8, join lt. purple with sl st in any corner st, ch 3, (dc, ch 2, 2 dc) in same st, 2 dc in each of next 5 skipped sts, *(2 dc, ch 2, 2 dc) in next skipped corner st, 2 dc in each of next 5 skipped sts; repeat from * around, join with sl st in top of ch-3 (56 dc, 4 ch sps).

Rnd 10: Sl st in next st, sl st in next ch sp, ch 1, (sc, ch 3, sc) in same sp, *[ch 3, skip next 2 sts, (sc in next st, ch 3, skip next 2 sts) 4 times], (sc, ch 3, sc) in next ch sp; repeat from * 2 more times; repeat between [ ], join with sl st in first sc (24 sc, 24 ch sps).

Rnd 11: Join lt. rose with sc in first st; *[working behind next ch sp, (dc, ch 3, dc) in next ch lp on rnd 8, (sc in next sc on last rnd; working behind next ch sp, 2 dc in next ch sp on rnd 8) 5 times], sc in next sc on last rnd; repeat from * 2 more times; repeat between [ ], join with sl st in first sc.

Rnd 12: Ch 1, sc in each st around with (2 hdc, ch 2, 2 hdc) in each corner ch sp, join with sl st in first sc, fasten off (88 sts, 4 ch sps).

Rnd 13: Join off-white with sc in any corner ch sp, (sc, ch 2, 2 sc) in same sp, *[skip next 2 sts, hdc in next st, dc in next 18 sts, hdc in next st], (2 sc, ch 2, 2 sc) in next ch sp; repeat from * 2 more times; repeat between [ ], join (96 sts, 4 ch sps).

Rnd 14: Ch 1, sc in first st, ch 2, skip next st, *[(sc, ch 2, sc) in next ch sp, ch 2, skip next 2 sts, (sc in next st, ch 2, skip next st) across] to next ch sp; repeat from * 2 more times; repeat between [ ], join, fasten off (52 sc, 52 ch sps).

Rnd 15: Join lt. purple with sc in first sc on any corner; *[working behind ch sp on last rnd, (dc, ch 2, dc) in next ch sp on rnd before last between sc, sc in next sc on last rnd, skip next skipped st on rnd before last]; (working behind last rnd, dc in next skipped st on rnd before last, sc in next sc on last rnd) across to next corner ch sp; repeat from * 2 more times; repeat between [ ]; working behind last rnd, dc in next skipped st on rnd before last, (sc in next sc on last rnd; working behind last rnd, dc in next skipped st on rnd before last) across, join, fasten off (27 sts on each edge between corner ch sps).

continued on page 91

Flower Coasters

Designed by *Judy Teague Treece*

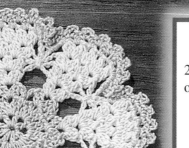

Size: 4¾" across.

Materials For One: Size-10 bedspread cotton —
20 yds. each color A and B; No. 6 steel crochet hook
or size needed to obtain gauge.

Gauge: Rnds 1-3 = 1¾" across.

NOTE: Coaster may ruffle until blocked.

Skill Level: ☆☆ Average

COASTER

Rnd 1: With A, ch 5, sl st in first ch to form ring, ch 4, (dc in ring, ch 1) 7 times, join with sl st in 3rd ch of ch-4 (8 dc, 8 ch sps).

*NOTES: For **beginning shell (beg shell)**, ch 3, (dc, ch 2, 2 dc) in same sp.*

*For **shell**, (2 dc, ch 2, 2 dc) in next ch sp.*

Rnd 2: Sl st in next ch sp, beg shell, ch 1, (shell in next ch sp, ch 1) around, join with sl st in top of ch-3 (8 shells, 8 ch-1 sps).

Rnd 3: Sl st in next st, sl st in next ch sp, beg shell, ch 2, sc in next ch-1 sp, ch 2, (shell in ch sp of next shell, ch 2, sc in next ch-1 sp, ch 2) around, join, fasten off (16 ch-2 sps, 8 shells).

*NOTES: For **beginning cluster (beg cl)**, ch 3, (yo, insert hook in same ch sp, yo, draw lp through, yo, draw through 2 lps on hook) 2 times, yo, draw through all 3 lps on hook.*

*For **cluster (cl)**, yo, insert hook in next ch sp, yo, draw lp through, yo, draw through 2 lps on hook, (yo, insert hook in same ch sp, yo, draw lp through, yo, draw through 2 lps on hook) 2 times, yo, draw through all 4 lps on hook.*

Rnd 4: Join B with sl st in first shell, (beg cl, ch 2, cl) in same shell, ch 6, skip next 2 ch-2 sps, *(cl, ch 2, cl) in next shell, ch 6, skip next 2 ch-2 sps; repeat from *

around, join with sl st in top of beg cl (16 cls, 8 ch-6 sps, 8 ch-2 sps).

Rnd 5: Sl st in first ch sp, (beg cl, ch 2, cl, ch 2, cl) in same sp, ch 6, skip next ch-6 sp, *(cl, ch 2, cl, ch 2, cl) in next ch-2 sp, ch 6, skip next ch-6 sp; repeat from * around, join (24 cls).

Rnd 6: Sl st in next ch-2 sp, beg cl, *[ch 2, cl in same sp, ch 2, (cl, ch 2, cl) in next ch-2 sp, ch 6, skip next ch-6 sp], cl in next ch-2 sp; repeat from * 6 more times; repeat between [ ], join (32 cls).

Rnd 7: Sl st in next ch sp, beg cl, *[ch 2, cl in same sp, ch 2, cl in next ch-2 sp, ch 2, (cl, ch 2, cl) in next ch-2 sp, ch 5, sc around all 3 ch-6 lps of last 3 rnds at same time, ch 5], cl in next ch-2 sp; repeat from * 6 more times; repeat between [ ], join, fasten off (40 cls).

Rnd 8: Join A with sc in first ch-2 sp, *[ch 2, (sc in next ch-2 sp, ch 2) 3 times, 5 sc in each of next 2 ch-5 sps, ch 2], sc in next ch-2 sp; repeat from * 6 more times; repeat between [ ], join with sl st in first sc.

Rnd 9: Sl st in next ch-2 sp, ch 1, (sc, ch 3, sc) in same sp, (sc, ch 3, sc) in each of next 3 ch-2 sps, *[skip next st, sc in next st, ch 3, sc in next st, sl st in each of next 2 sts, sc in next st, (ch 3, skip next st, sc in next st) 2 times], (sc, ch 3, sc) in each of next 5 ch-2 sps; repeat from * 6 more times; repeat between [ ], (sc, ch 3, sc) in last ch-2 sp, join, fasten off. ✄

Enchanted Garden Quilt

continued from page 89

ASSEMBLY

Holding 2 Blocks right sides together, matching sts, working through both thicknesses, join lt. purple with sc in corner ch sp, sc in each st across to next corner ch sp, sc in next corner ch sp, ch 1; holding two more Blocks right sides together, sc in first corner ch sp, sc in each st across to next corner ch sp, sc in next corner ch sp, ch 1. Continue joining Blocks in same manner until 14 Blocks are joined in 2 strips of 7 Blocks each, fasten off. Repeat with remaining Blocks, making a total of 5 joined strips of 7 Blocks each. Working across strips, join remaining edges in same manner.

BORDER

Rnd 1: Working around outer edge, join lt. purple with sl st in any corner ch sp, ch 4, hdc in same sp, *[sc in next 27 sts, (2 hdc in each of next 2 ch sps, sc in next

27 sts) across] to next corner ch sp, (hdc, ch 2, hdc) in next ch sp; repeat from * 2 more times; repeat between [ ], join with sl st in 2nd ch of ch-4, fasten off (153 sts on each short end between corner ch sps, 215 sts on each long edge between corner ch sps).

Rnd 2: Join off-white with sc in any corner ch sp, ch 2, sc in same sp, *[ch 2, skip next st, (sc in next st, ch 2, skip next st) across] to next corner ch sp; repeat from * 2 more times; repeat between [ ], join with sl st in first sc, fasten off.

Rnd 3: Join lt. purple with sc in first sc after any corner ch sp; *[working behind next ch sp, (dc in next skipped st on rnd before last, picot, sc in next sc on last rnd) across to next corner ch sp; working behind next ch sp, (dc, picot, dc) in next ch sp on rnd before last between sc], sc in next sc on last rnd; repeat from * 2 more times; repeat between [ ], join, fasten off. ✄

Coleus

Designed by *Barbara Anderson*

Size: Basket is 7" long.

Materials: Worsted-weight yarn — 2 oz. gray, ½ oz. each pink, white, brown, lt. and dk. green; 2-ply baby yarn — ½ oz. white; 1¾ yds. pink ¼" satin ribbon; pink sewing thread; 12" chenille stem — 8 pink and 1 gray; polyester fiberfill (optional; small bag of popcorn or pebbles); pliers; sewing and tapestry needles; No. 4 steel, E and G crochet hooks or sizes needed to obtain gauges.

Gauges: With **G hook and worsted-weight,** 4 sc = 1"; 4 sc rows = 1". With **No. 4 hook and baby yarn,** two (dc, ch 2, dc) sts = 1"; 4 dc rows = 3½".

Skill Level: ☆☆ Average

BASKET

Bottom

Row 1: With G hook and gray, ch 26, sc in 2nd ch from hook, sc in each ch across, turn (25 sc).

Rows 2-16: Ch 1, sc in each st across, turn.

Row 17: Working around outer edge, ch 1, 2 sc in first st, sc in each st and in end of each row around with 2 sc in each corner st, join with sl st in first sc (84).

Rnd 18: Working this rnd in **back lps** only, ch 2, hdc in each st around, join with sl st in top of ch-2.

NOTES: For front post (fp—see page 159), yo, insert hook from front to back around post of next st, yo, draw lp through, complete as dc.

For back post (bp—see page 159), yo, insert hook from back to front around post of next st, yo, draw lp through, complete as dc.

Rnd 19: Ch 2, fp around each of next 2 sts, *bp around next st, fp around each of next 2 sts; repeat from * around, join (27 bp, 56 fp).

Rnd 20: Ch 2, bp around each of next 2 fp, (fp around next bp, bp around each of next 2 fp) around, join.

Rnds 21-24: Repeat rnds 19 and 20 alternately.

Rnd 25: Ch 1, sc in each st around, join.

Rnd 26: Working this rnd in **back lps** only, ch 1, sc in each st around, join.

Rnd 27: Working this rnd in **back lps** only, ch 3, dc in each st around, join with sl st in top of ch-3, leaving long end for sewing, fasten off.

For **rim,** fold rnd 27 to inside, working in **back lps,** sew to secure.

Rnd 28: With bottom of Basket facing you, working in **front lps** of rnd 17, join gray with sl st in any st, sl st in each st around, join with sl st in first sl st, fasten off.

Bottom Lace

Rnd 1: Working in **front lps** of rnd 25, with inside of Basket Bottom facing you, with No. 4 hook and white baby yarn, join with sc in any st, sc in same st, 2 sc in each st around, join with sl st in first sc (168 sc).

Rnd 2: Working this rnd in **back lps** only, ch 4, skip next st, (dc in next st, ch 1, skip next st) around, join with sl st in 3rd ch of ch-4 (84 dc).

Rnd 3: Sl st in next ch sp, ch 5, dc in same sp, skip next ch sp, *(dc, ch 2, dc) in next ch sp, skip next ch sp; repeat from * around, join with sl st in 3rd ch of ch-5 (84 dc).

Rnd 4: Sl st in first ch sp, ch 3, (dc, ch 2, 2 dc) in same sp, (2 dc, ch 2, 2 dc) in each ch sp around, join with sl st in top of ch-3 (168).

Rnd 5: Sl st in next st, sl st in next ch sp, ch 2, (hdc, ch 3, 2 hdc) in same sp, ch 1, (2 hdc, ch 3, 2 hdc, ch 1) in each ch sp around, join with sl st in top of ch-2, fasten off.

Rnd 6: Working in **front lps** of rnd 1 on Bottom Lace, with Bottom of Basket facing you, join white with sc in any st, (sc, ch 4, 2 sc) in same st, skip next 3 sts, *(2 sc, ch 4, 2 sc) in next st, skip next 3 sts; repeat from * around, join, fasten off.

Handle

Row 1: With G hook and gray, ch 43, holding gray chenille stem over ch, starting ¼" from end of stem and working over stem (see illustration), sc in 2nd ch from hook, sc in each ch across, **do not** turn (42 sc).

To **secure,** with pliers, fold ¼" stem back over sts at each end.

SC OVER STEM

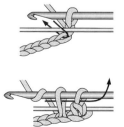

continued on page 94

FLOWERS OF FRIENDS   Brownlow

McDANIEL
Garden of Hope
CARPENTER   BOUQUET OF MEMORIES FOR MOTHER   C. R. GIBSON   MARK

Rnd 2: Working in starting ch on opposite side of row 1, ch 2, sl st in first ch, ch 1, sc in same ch, sc in each ch across, ch 2, sl st in first sc on row 1, ch 1, sc in same st, sc in last 13 sts, join with sl st in first ch of ch-2, fasten off.

Handle Lace

Row 1: With No. 4 hook and white baby yarn, ch 70, dc in 4th ch from hook, (ch 1, skip next ch, dc in next ch) across, **do not** turn (35 dc).

Rnd 2: Working around outer edge, in starting ch on opposite side of row 1, ch 3, sl st in first ch, sl st in sp of unworked ch, ch 2, (hdc, ch 4, 2 hdc) in same sp, ch 2, skip sp of next unworked ch, *(2 hdc, ch 4, 2 hdc) in sp of next unworked ch, ch 2, skip sp of next unworked ch*; repeat between ** across, 3 hdc over end ch-3 sp, ch 2, skip next ch sp; repeat between ** 16 times, (2 hdc, ch 4, 2 hdc) in last ch sp, ch 2, 3 hdc over end ch-3 sp, ch 2, join with sl st in top of first ch-2, fasten off.

Cut 13" from ribbon, weave through sts of row 1; fold back ¼" of ribbon on each end, with sewing thread and needle, sew to Lace. With white worsted-weight and tapestry needle, sew Lace to Handle. With gray, sew Handle ends to rnd 27 on inside of Basket in center of long sides.

Weave remaining ribbon through sts of rnd 1 on Basket Lace, tie ends into a bow at Handle.

SOIL

Rows 1-8: With G hook and brown, repeat same rows of Basket Bottom (25 sc).

Row 9: Ch 1, sc in first 6 sts, (ch 3, skip next 3 sts, sc in each of next 2 sts) 2 times, ch 3, skip next 3 sts, sc in last 6 sts, turn.

Row 10: Ch 1, sc in each st and in each ch across, turn.

Rows 11-17: Ch 1, sc in each st across, turn. At end of last row, fasten off.

Stuff Basket up to rim with fiberfill or bag of popcorn or pebbles. Easing to fit, sew to **front lps** in rnd 27 of inside Bottom.

DARK COLEUS (make 2)
Small Leaf

NOTE: For **small Leaf stem,** cut one 12" pink chenille stem in half.

Row 1: For **first Leaf,** with E hook and dk. green, ch 5, holding 6" stem over ch, starting ¼" from end of stem and working over stem, sc in 2nd ch from hook, hdc in next ch, dc in next ch, sc in last ch, **do not** turn, fasten off (4 sc).

To **secure,** with pliers, fold ¼" stem back over sts.

Rnd 2: Join lt. green with sl st in first st, ch 2, sl st in same st, (ch 2, sl st in next st) 3 times, (sc, ch 2, sl st in 2nd ch from hook, sc) in end of row 1; working in starting ch on opposite side of row 1, ch 2, sl st in first ch, (ch 2, sl st in next ch) 3 times, ch 2, sl st in same ch as last sl st, fasten off.

For **second Leaf,** repeat on opposite end of same stem.

Medium Leaf

Row 1: For **first Leaf,** with E hook and pink, ch 9, holding 12" stem over ch, starting ¼" from end of stem and working over stem, sc in 2nd ch from hook, sc in next ch, hdc in next ch, dc in next ch, tr in each of next 2 chs, dc in each of last 2 chs, turn (8 sc).

Secure same as Small Leaf.

Row 2: Ch 1, sc in first 8 sts, (sc, ch 2, sc) in end of row 1; working in starting ch on opposite side of row 1, sc in last 8 chs, turn, fasten off (18).

*NOTES: For **long double crochet (ldc),** yo, insert hook in next st on row before last, yo, draw through st drawing up long lp, (yo, draw through 2 lps on hook) 2 times.*

*For **long treble crochet (ltr),** yo 2 times, insert hook in next st on row before last, yo, draw through st drawing up long lp, (yo, draw through 2 lps on hook) 3 times.*

*For **long half double crochet (lhdc),** yo, insert hook in next st on row before last, yo, draw through st drawing up long lp, yo, draw through all 3 lps on hook.*

Row 3: Join dk. green with sc in first st, sc in same st, hdc in next st, ldc in next st, tr in next st, ltr in next st, tr in next st, ldc in next st, hdc in next st, sc in next st, (sc, ch 2, sc) in next ch-2 sp, sc in next st, lhdc in next st, ldc in next st, tr in next st, ltr in next st, tr in next st, dc in next st, lhdc in next st, 2 sc in last st, **do not** turn, fasten off (22).

Row 4: Join lt. green with sl st in end of row 1, ch 2, sl st in same row, sl st in first st of row 3, (ch 2, sl st in next st) 10 times, (sc, ch 2, sl st in 2nd ch from hook, sc) in next ch-2 sp, sl st in next st, (ch 2, sl st in next st) 10 times, (sl st, ch 2, sl st) in end of row 3, fasten off.

For **second Leaf,** repeat on opposite end of same stem.

Large Leaf

Rows 1-2: For **first Leaf,** repeat same rows of Medium Leaf, **do not** fasten off.

Row 3: Ch 1, sc in first 9 sts, (sc, ch 2, sc) in next ch sp, sc in last 9 sts, **do not** turn, fasten off (20).

*NOTE: For **long single crochet (lsc),** insert hook in next st on row before last, yo, draw through st drawing up long lp, yo, draw through **both lps** on hook.*

Row 4: Join dk. green with sc in first st, sc in same st, lhdc in next st, dc in next st, tr in next st, ltr in each of next 2 sts, dc in next st, lhdc in next st, lsc in next st, sc in next st, (sc, ch 2, sc) in next ch sp, lsc in next st, sc in next st, lhdc in next st, dc in next st, tr in next st, ltr in next st, tr in next st, ldc in next st, hdc in next st, 2 sc in last st, **do not** turn, fasten off (24).

Row 5: Join lt. green with sl st in end of row 2, ch 2, sl st in end of same row, (sl st, ch 2) in first st of row 4, (ch 2, sl st in next st) 11 times, (sc, ch 2, sl st in 2nd ch from hook, sc) in next ch sp, sl st in next st, (ch 2, sl st in next st) 11 times, (sl st, ch 2) in end of next row, (sl st, ch 2, sl st) in end of row 1, fasten off.

For **second Leaf,** repeat on opposite end of same stem.

Holding 1 stem of each Leaf together, fold all stems in half. Starting with Small Leaves on top, twist folded ends together forming stem and leaving ½" next to Leaves; twist Medium Leaves around stem, leaving 1" next to Leaves; twist Large Leaves around stem, leaving 1" next to Leaves.

LIGHT COLEUS
Small Leaf

With pink and lt. green, work same as Small Leaf of Dark Coleus.

Medium Leaf

Row 1: For **first Leaf,** with E hook and pink, ch 10, holding 12" stem over ch, starting ¼" from end of stem and working over stem, sc in 2nd ch from hook, sc in each ch across, **do not** turn, fasten off (9 sc).

Secure same as Small Leaf of Dark Coleus.

Row 2: Join white worsted-weight with sc in first st, *hdc in next st, dc in next st, tr in each of next 3 sts, dc in next st, hdc in next st, sc in next st*, (sc, ch 2, sc) in end of row 1; repeat between **, **do not** turn, fasten off (11 sts).

Row 3: Join lt. green with sl st in end of row 1, ch 2, sl st in same st, sl st in first st of row 2, (ch 2, sl st in next st) 9 times, (sc, ch 2, sl st in 2nd ch from Hook, sc) in ch sp, sl st in next st, (ch 2, sl st in next st) 9 times, (sl st, ch 2, sl st) in end of row 1, fasten off.

For **second Leaf,** repeat on opposite end of same stem.

With pink, using Straight Stitch (see page 159), embroider veins on Leaves as desired.

Large Leaf

Rows 1-2: For **first Leaf,** repeat same rows of Medium Leaf, turn, **do not** fasten off.

Row 3: Ch 1, sc in first 10 sts, (sc, ch 2, sc) in next ch sp, sc in last 10 sts, turn, fasten off.

Row 4: Join lt. green with sl st in end of row 1, ch 2, sl st in same row, (sl st, ch 2, sl st) in end of row 2, sl st in first st of row 3, (ch 2, sl st in next st) 9 times, (sc, ch 2, sl st in 2nd ch from hook, sc) in next ch sp, sl st in next st, (ch 2, sl st in next st) 10 times, (sl st, ch 2, sl st) in end of last 2 rows, fasten off.

For **second Leaf,** repeat on opposite end of same stem.

With pink, using Straight Stitch, embroider veins on Leaves as desired.

Arrange leaves same as Dark Coleus.

With Light Coleus in center, fit plants in soil through ch-3 sps; with brown, tack stems to soil.✄

Playful Pets

Fuzzy, friendly, cuddly and cute, animals enrich our lives in wonderous ways, even if they're only made of yarn. Treat a little one to a soft, fuzzy friend to calm their fears in the night or gift an apartment dweller to a companionable menagerie that's quiet and clean. Stitch your own version of Nature's perscription for perpetual smiles when you craft any or all of these simply sensational critters.

Claudia Cottontail

Designed by *Carolyn Christmas*

Size: 14" sitting.

Materials: Fuzzy worsted-weight yarn — 9 oz. brown; fuzzy sport-weight yarn — 6 oz. each pink and white; pink 15-mm animal nose with washer; two 18-mm animal eyes with washers; 1 yd. pink 1" satin ribbon; 3" square piece of cardboard; soft-sculpture needle; polyester fiberfill; G crochet hook or size needed to obtain gauge.

Gauge: 4 sc = 1"; 4 sc rows = 1".

Note: **Do not** join rnds unless otherwise stated. Mark first st of each rnd.

Skill Level: ☆☆ Average

BUNNY

Head & Body

Rnd 1: With brown, ch 2, 6 sc in 2nd ch from hook (6 sc).

Rnd 2: 2 sc in each st around (12).

Rnd 3: (2 sc in next st, sc in next st) around (18).

Rnd 4: Sc in first st, 2 sc in next st, (sc in each of next 2 sts, 2 sc in next st) 5 times, sc in last st (24).

Rnd 5: (2 sc in next st, sc in each of next 3 sts) around (30).

Rnd 6: Sc in each of first 2 sts, 2 sc in next st, (sc in next 4 sts, 2 sc in next st) 5 times, sc in each of last 2 sts (36).

Rnd 7: (2 sc in next st, sc in next 5 sts) around (42).

Rnd 8: Sc in each of first 3 sts, 2 sc in next st, (sc in next 6 sts, 2 sc in next st) 5 times, sc in each of last 3 sts (48).

Rnd 9: (2 sc in next st, sc in next 7 sts) around (54).

Rnd 10: Sc in first 4 sts, 2 sc in next st, (sc in next 8 sts, 2 sc in next st) 5 times, sc in last 4 sts (60).

Rnds 11-20: Sc in each st around.

Attach eyes with washers 2" apart over rnds 11 and 12.

Attach nose with washers between eyes over bottom of rnd 14. Stuff.

Rnd 21: Sc in first 4 sts, sc next 2 sts tog, (sc in next 8 sts, sc next 2 sts tog) 5 times, sc in last 4 sts (54).

Rnd 22: (Sc next 2 sts tog, sc in next 7 sts) around (48).

Rnd 23: Sc in each of first 3 sts, sc next 2 sts tog, (sc in next 6 sts, sc next 2 sts tog) 5 times, sc in each of last 3 sts (42).

Rnd 24: (Sc next 2 sts tog, sc in next 5 sts) around (36).

Rnd 25: Sc in each of first 2 sts, sc next 2 sts tog, (sc in next 4 sts, sc next 2 sts tog) 5 times, sc in each of last 2 sts (30).

Rnd 26: (Sc next 2 sts tog, sc in each of next 3 sts) around (24).

With soft-sculpture needle, make small indent ½" from outer edge of each eye.

With pink, using Straight Stitch (see page 158), embroider mouth lines as shown in photo.

Rnd 27: (2 sc in next st, sc in each of next 3 sts) around (30).

Rnd 28: (Sc in each of next 2 sts, 2 sc in next st) around (40).

Rnd 29: (Sc in next 9 sts, 2 sc in next st) around (44).

Rnds 30-42: Sc in each st around. Stuff.

Rnd 43: Sc first 2 sts tog, (sc in next 4 sts, sc next 2 sts tog) around (36).

Rnds 44-45: Repeat rnds 25 and 26.

Rnd 46: (Sc next 2 sts tog, sc in each of next 2 sts) around (18). Stuff.

Rnd 47: (Sc in next st, sc next 2 sts tog) around (12).

Rnd 48: (Sc next 2 sts tog) around, join with sl st in first sc leaving long end for sewing, fasten off. Sew opening closed.

Foot & Leg (make 2)

Rnds 1-6: Starting at **Foot,** repeat same rnds of Head & Body.

Rnd 7: Working this rnd in **back lps** only, sc in each st around.

Rnds 8-11: Sc in each st around.

Rnd 12: Sc in first 11 sts, (sc next 2 sts tog) 8 times, sc in last 9 sts (28).

Rnd 13: Sc in first 12 sts, (sc next 2 sts tog) 3 times, sc in last 10 sts (25). Stuff.

Rnd 14: Sc in first 11 sts, sc next 2 sts tog, sc in next st, sc next 2 sts tog, sc in last 9 sts (23).

Rnds 15-26: Sc in each st around. At end of last rnd, join with sl st in first sc. Leaving long end for sewing, fasten off. Stuff.

Sew Legs ½" apart to bottom of Body.

Arm (make 2)

Rnds 1-3: Repeat same rnds of Head & Body.

Rnds 4-20: Sc in each st around. At end of last rnd, join with sl st in first sc. Leaving long end for sewing, fasten off. Stuff.

Sew Arms over rnds 27-32 on sides of Body.

Ear Side (make 4)

Row 1: With brown, ch 10, sc in 2nd ch from hook, sc in each ch across, turn (9 sc).

Rows 2-7: Ch 1, sc in each st across, turn.

Row 8: Ch 1, sc first 2 sts tog, sc in each st across to last 2 sts, sc last 2 sts tog, turn (7).

Row 9: Ch 1, sc in each st across, turn.

Rows 10-13: Repeat rows 8 and 9 alternately, ending with 3 sts in last row.

Row 14: Ch 1, skip first st, sc in next st, sl st in last st, fasten off.

Holding 2 Ear Sides wrong sides together, working in ends of rows, join brown with sc in row 1, sc in each row and in each st across to opposite side of row 1, leaving long end for sewing, fasten off. Repeat with other 2 Ear Sides

Folding row 1 in half lengthwise, sew Ears to rows 6 and 7 on top of Head.

Tail

Wind brown yarn around cardboard 150 times, slide

continued on page 102

Sara Squirrel

Designed by *Barbara Anderson*

Size: 5" tall.

Materials: Worsted-weight yarn — 1½ oz. brown, small amount each white, peach, blue, orange and yellow; 12" chenille stem; scraps of black, brown and white felt; peach and black embroidery floss; comb or pet brush; craft glue or hot glue gun; polyester fiberfill; tapestry needle; E crochet hook or size needed to obtain gauge.

Gauge: 5 sc = 1"; 5 sc rows = 1".

Note: Do not join rnds unless otherwise stated. Mark first st of each rnd.

Skill Level: ☆☆ Average

FACIAL DIAGRAM

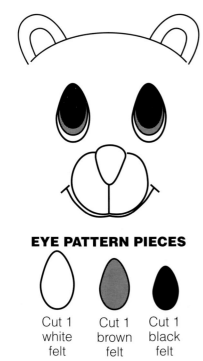

EYE PATTERN PIECES

Cut 1
white
felt

Cut 1
brown
felt

Cut 1
black
felt

SQUIRREL

Head

Rnd 1: Starting at **muzzle,** with white, ch 2, 5 sc in 2nd ch from hook (5 sc).

Rnd 2: 2 sc in first st, sc in each of next 3 sts, 2 sc in last st (7).

Rnd 3: Sc in each of first 2 sts changing to brown in last st made, 2 sc in each of next 3 sts changing to white in last st made, sc in each of last 2 sts changing to brown in last st made, fasten off white (10).

Rnd 4: 2 sc in each st around (20).

Rnd 5: Sc in each of first 3 sts, 2 sc in each of next 14 sts, sc in each of last 3 sts (34).

Rnd 6: Sc in first 4 sts; *for **cheek,** (sc next 2 sts tog) 3 times*; sc in next 14 sts; repeat between **, sc in last 4 sts, sc in first st, round now begins here (28).

Rnds 7-8: Sc in each st around.

Rnd 9: Sc in first 10 sts; for **ear opening,** ch 2, skip next 2 sts; sc in next 4 sts; for **ear opening,** ch 2, skip next 2 sts; sc in last 10 sts (24).

Rnd 10: Sc in each st and in each ch around (28).

Rnds 11-12: Sc in each st around.

Rnd 13: Sc first 2 sts tog, (sc in next st, sc next 2 sts tog) around (18). Stuff.

Rnd 14: (Sc next 2 sts tog) around (9).

Rnd 15: Sc in each st around, join with sl st in first sc leaving long end for sewing, fasten off. Stuff. Sew opening closed.

Ears

Rnd 1: With back of Head facing you, join brown with sc in 2nd ch of rnd 9, 2 sc between rnds 9 and 8, sc in each of next 2 sts on rnd 8, 2 sc between rnds 8 and 9, sc in last ch (8 sc).

Rnd 2: Sc in each st around.

Rnd 3: (Sc next 2 sts tog) around, join with sl st in first sc, fasten off. Sew opening closed. With white, using Satin Stitch (see page 158) embroider 4 sts in center of Ear according to diagram.

Repeat in other Ear opening.

Facial Features

For **nose,** with peach floss, using Satin Stitch, embroider over rnds 1 and 2 according to diagram.

For **mouthlines,** with black floss, using Outline Stitch (see page 158), embroider over rnd 3 according to diagram.

For **eye** (make 2), from felt cut eye pieces according to pattern pieces. Glue black to brown, brown to white, glue over rnds 3-5 above muzzle. For **eye outline,** with black floss, using Outline Stitch, embroider around each eye.

Body

Rnd 1: With brown, ch 10, sl st in first ch to form ring, ch 1, sc in each ch around (10 sc).

Rnd 2: Sc in each st around.

Rnd 3: 2 sc in first st, (sc in each of next 2 sts, 2 sc in next st) around (14).

Rnd 4: Sc in each st around. Sc in first st.

Rnd 5: Sc in each st around.

Rnd 6: Sc in first 4 sts; for **tummy,** 2 sc in each of next 6 sts; sc in last 4 sts (20).

Rnds 7-11: Sc in each st around.

Rnd 12: Sc first 2 sts tog, (sc in next st, sc next 2 sts tog) around (13).

Rnd 13: Sc in first st, (sc next 2 sts tog) around, join with sl st in first sc, leaving long end for sewing, fasten off. Stuff. Sew opening closed.

Sew rnds 7-11 of Head over rnd 1 of Body.

Bottom Leg (make 2)

Rnd 1: With brown, ch 2, 6 sc in 2nd ch from hook (6 sc).

Rnd 2: 2 sc in each st around (12).

Rnd 3: Sc in first 4 sts, 2 sc in each of next 4 sts, sc in last 4 sts (16).

Rnd 4: Sc in each st around. Sc in first st.

Rnd 5: Sc in each st around.

Rnd 6: Sc in each st around. Sc in first st.

Rnd 7: Sc in first 4 sts, (sc next 2 sts tog) 4 times, sc in last 4 sts (12).

continued on page 102

Rnd 8: Sc in each of first 2 sts, (sc next 2 sts tog) 4 times, sc in each of last 2 sts (8). Stuff lightly.

Rnd 9: Sc in each st around.

Rnd 10: Sc in each of first 2 sts, 2 sc in each of next 4 sts, sc in each of last 2 sts (12).

Rnd 11: Sc in each st around.

Rnd 12: (Sc next 2 sts tog) around, join with sl st in first sc, leaving long end for sewing, fasten off. Stuff. Sew opening closed.

Sew rnds 1-8 to sides of Body over rnds 8-13.

Top Leg (make 2)

Rnd 1: Starting at **paws,** with brown, ch 2, 8 sc in 2nd ch from hook (8 sc).

Rnds 2-5: Sc in each st around.

Rnds 6-7: Sc first 2 sts tog, sc in each st around (7, 6).

Rnd 8: Sc in each st around. Stuff.

Rnd 9: 2 sc in first st, sc in each st around (7).

Rnd 10: Sc in each st around. Stuff.

Rnd 11: (Sc next 2 sts tog) 3 times, join with sl st in first sc, leaving long end for sewing, fasten off. Stuff. Sew opening closed.

Sew rnds 1-4 to sides of Body over rnds 2-5. Tack rnd 1 of paws together.

Tail

For **each fringe,** cut 2 strands brown each 4" long. Holding both strands together, fold in half; lay folded strands over chenille stem, draw loose ends through fold going around stem, tighten.

Leaving ¼" unworked on each end, fringe close together covering chenille stem. Fold stem in half, twist uncovered ends together. Comb or brush strands.

Push twisted ends of stem into bottom of Body in back, sew in place.

Tack center of Tail to back of Body. Curve end of Tail downward.

FLOWER (make 1 each peach, orange and blue)

Ch 3, sl st in first ch to form ring, (ch 2, sl st) 5 times in ring leaving long end, fasten off. With yellow, using French Knot (see page 158), embroider center of Flower.

Holding Flowers together, make knot with all loose ends close to bottom of all Flowers. Sew to center. ✂

loops off, tie separate strand brown tightly around middle of all loops. Cut loops, trim and shape to 1½". Sew to rnd 41 at back of Body.

DRESS
Yoke Front

Row 1: With white, ch 22, sc in 2nd ch from hook, sc in each ch across, turn (21 sc).

Rows 2-8: Ch 1, sc in each st across, turn.

Row 9: For **shoulder,** ch 1, sc in each of first 2 sts leaving remaining sts unworked, turn (2).

Row 10: Ch 1, sc in each st across, fasten off.

Yoke Back (make 2)

Row 1: With white, ch 12, sc in 2nd ch from hook, sc in each ch across, turn (11 sc).

Rows 2-8: Ch 1, sc in each st across, turn.

Row 9: For **first shoulder,** ch 1, sc in each of first 2 sts leaving remaining sts unworked, turn (2).

Row 10: Ch 1, sc in each st across, fasten off. Sew shoulder seams.

Skirt

Rnd 1: Working in starting ch on opposite side of row 1 on Yokes, join pink with sl st in first ch of right Yoke Back, ch 3, 3 dc in each of next 10 chs; for **armhole,** ch 10; 3 dc in each ch across Yoke Front; for **armhole,** ch 10; 3 dc in each ch across Yoke Back, join with sl st in top of ch-3 (129 dc, 20 chs).

Rnd 2: Ch 3, dc in each st and in each ch around, join (149).

Rnds 3-10: Ch 3, dc in each st around, join. At end of last rnd, fasten off.

Rnd 11: Join white with sc in first st, ch 3, skip next st, (sc in next st, ch 3, skip next st) around, join with sl st in first sc, fasten off.

Neck Trim

Row 1: Join white with sl st in first st on right Yoke Back, ch 4, skip next st, dc in next st, (ch 1, skip next st, dc in next st) across, turn.

Row 2: Ch 1, sc in first dc, (ch 2, sc in next dc) across, fasten off.

For **tie,** with pink, ch 90, fasten off. Weave through sts of row 1, tie ends into a bow.

Sleeves

Rnd 1: Working around one armhole, join pink with sl st in any st, ch 3, evenly space 45 dc around, join with sl st in top of ch-3 (46 dc).

Rnds 2-5: Ch 3, dc in each st around, join.

Rnd 6: Ch 3, (skip next st, dc in next st) around, join (23).

Rnd 7: Ch 3, 2 dc in same st, 2 dc in each st around, join, fasten off (47).

Rnd 8: Join white with sc in first st, ch 3, skip next st, (sc in next st, ch 3, skip next st) around, join with sl st in first sc, fasten off.

For **tie** (make 2), with white, ch 60, fasten off. Weave through sts of rnd 6, tie ends into a bow.

Repeat on other Sleeve.

PANTIES

Rnd 1: With white, ch 60, sl st in first ch to form ring, ch 3, dc in each ch around, join with sl st in top of ch-3 (60 dc).

Rnd 2: Ch 3, dc in each st around, join.

Rnds 3-4: Ch 3; working in **back lps,** dc in next 29 sts; working in **both lps,** dc in each st around, join.

Rnd 5: Ch 3, dc in **back lps** of next 12 sts; for **tail opening,** ch 4, skip next 4 sts; dc in **back lps** of next 13 sts; working in **both lps,** dc in each st around, join.

Rnd 6: Ch 3, dc in **back lps** of next 12 sts, dc in next 4 chs, dc in **back lps** of next 13 sts; working in **both lps,** dc in each st around, join.

Rnd 7: Ch 3, dc in each st around, join.

Rnd 8: For **leg opening,** ch 3, dc in same st, dc in next 29 sts, skip last 30 sts, join (31).

Rnd 9: Ch 3, dc in each st around, join, fasten off.

Rnd 10: Join pink with sc in first st, ch 3, skip next st, (sc in next st, ch 3, skip next st) around, join with sl st in first sc, fasten off.

Rnd 8: For **leg opening,** join white with sl st in first unworked st on rnd 7, ch 3, dc in same st, dc in each st around, join (31).

Rnd 9: Ch 3, dc in each st around, join, fasten off.

Rnd 10: Join pink with sc in first st, ch 3, skip next st, (sc in next st, ch 3, skip next st) around, join with sl st in first sc, fasten off.

Sew opening at crotch closed.

Ruffles

Working in **front lps** of rnd 2 on Panties, join pink with sc in first st, (ch 2, sc) in each st across, fasten off.

Repeat Ruffles on rnds 3-5.

For **waist tie,** with pink, ch 90, fasten off. Weave through sts of rnd 1, tie ends into a bow.

For **leg ties** (make 2), with white, ch 60, fasten off. Weave through sts of rnd 10 on each leg.

BONNET

Rnd 1: With pink, ch 4, sl st in first ch to form ring, ch 3, 15 dc in ring, join (16 dc).

Rnd 2: Ch 3, dc in next st, 2 dc in each st around, join (30).

Rnd 3: Ch 3, dc in next st, (2 dc in next st, dc in next st) around, join (44).

Rnd 4: Ch 3, dc in next st, (2 dc in next st, dc in each of next 2 sts) around, join (58).

Rnd 5: Ch 3, dc in next st, (2 dc in next st, dc in each of next 3 sts) around, join (72).

Rnd 6: Ch 3, dc in next st, (2 dc in next st, dc in next 4 sts) around, join (86).

Rnd 7: Ch 3, dc in next st, (2 dc in next st, dc in next 5 sts) around, join (100).

Rnd 8: Ch 3, dc in next st, (2 dc in next st, dc in next 6 sts) around, join (114).

Rnd 9: Ch 3, dc in next st, (2 dc in next st, dc in next 7 sts) around, join (128).

Rnd 10: Ch 3, dc in next st, (2 dc in next st, dc in next 8 sts) around, join (142).

Rnd 11: Ch 3, skip next st, (dc next 2 sts tog) around, join (71).

Rnd 12: Ch 3, (dc next 2 sts tog) around, join, fasten off (36).

Rnd 13: For **brim,** skip first 4 sts, join white with sc in next st, hdc in same st, 3 dc in each of next 5 sts; (for **ear opening,** ch 10, skip next 5 sts); 3 dc in each of next 6 sts; repeat between ( ), 3 dc in each of next 5 sts, (hdc, sc) in next st leaving last 4 sts unworked, turn (52 sts, 20 chs).

Row 14: Working in rows, ch 1, sc in first st, hdc in next st, dc in each st and in each ch across to last 2 sts, hdc in next st, sc in last st, turn (72).

Row 15: Ch 1, skip first st, sc in next st, hdc in next st, dc in each st across to last 3 sts, hdc in next st, sc in next st, sl st in last st, turn (70).

Row 16: Repeat row 14, fasten off.

Row 17: Join pink with sc in first st, (ch 2, sc in next st) across, fasten off.

Cut ribbon in half; sew each end of ribbon to each end of brim, trim ends at an angle. ✂

Forever Friends

Designed by *Barbara Anderson*

Precious Puppy

Size: 8" sitting.

Materials: Chunky yarn — 3 oz. off-white and 1 oz. brown; black embroidery floss; 22" gray ½" satin ribbon; 2 brown 15-mm animal eyes with washers; tapestry needle; polyester fiberfill; H crochet hook or size needed to obtain gauge.

Gauge: 3 sc = 1"; 3 sc rows = 1".

Note: Do not join rnds unless otherwise stated. Mark first st of each rnd.

Skill Level: ☆☆ Average

HEAD

Rnd 1: Starting at **nose,** with off-white, ch 2, 8 sc in 2nd ch from hook (8 sc).

Rnd 2: 2 sc in each st around (16).

Rnd 3: Sc in each of first 3 sts, 2 sc in each of next 10 sts, sc in each of last 3 sts (26).

Rnd 4: Sc in each of first 3 sts, (sc next 2 sts tog) 4 times; for **center front of Head,** sc in next 4 sts; (sc next 2 sts tog) 4 times, sc in each of last 3 sts (18).

Rnd 5: Sc in each of first 3 sts, (sc next 2 sts tog) 2 times, 2 sc in each of next 4 sts, (sc next 2 sts tog) 2 times, sc in each of last 3 sts (18).

NOTE: To move first st, sc in first st.

Rnd 6: Sc in each st around.

Rnd 7: Sc in each of first 3 sts, 2 sc in each of next 12 sts, sc in each of last 3 sts (30).

Rnd 8: Sc in first 10 sts, (2 sc in next st, sc in next st) 5 times, sc in last 10 sts (35).

Rnds 9-11: Sc in each st around.

Attach eyes with washers over rnds 6 and 7 on Head.

Rnd 12: Sc first 2 sts tog, (sc in next st, sc next 2 sts tog) around (23).

Rnds 13-15: Sc in each st around. Stuff.

Rnd 16: Repeat rnd 12 (15).

Rnd 17: Sc in first st, (sc next 2 sts tog) around (8). Stuff.

Rnd 18: (Sc next 2 sts tog) around, join with sl st in first sc. Leaving long end for sewing, fasten off. Stuff. Sew opening closed.

With 6 strands floss, using Satin Stitch (see page 158), embroider nose as shown in photo; using small Straight Stitches (see page 158), embroider mouth lines as shown.

SMALL EYE PIECE

With brown, ch 6, sl st in 2nd ch from hook, 2 sc in next ch, 2 hdc in next ch, 2 sc in next ch, sl st in last ch leaving long end for sewing, fasten off.

Sew above left Eye leaving starting ch unsewn.

LARGE EYE PIECE

Row 1: With brown, ch 6, sl st in 2nd ch from hook, 2 sc in next ch, 2 hdc in next ch, 2 sc in next ch, sl st in last ch, turn.

Row 2: Skip first sl st, sl st in next st, 2 sc in each of next 4 sts, skip next st, sl st in last sl st, turn.

Row 3: Skip first sl st, sl st in next st, 2 sc in each of next 6 sts, skip next st, sl st in last sl st leaving long end for sewing, fasten off.

Sew above right Eye leaving starting ch unsewn.

EAR (make 2)

Row 1: With brown, ch 12, sc in 2nd ch from hook, sc in each of next 2 chs, hdc in each of next 2 chs, dc in next 5 chs, 7 dc in end ch; working on opposite side of ch, dc in next 5 chs, hdc in each of next 2 chs, sc in each of last 3 chs, turn (27 sts).

Row 2: Ch 1, sc in each of first 3 sts, hdc in next 9 sts, 2 hdc in each of next 3 sts, hdc in next 9 sts, sc in each of last 3 sts leaving long end for sewing, fasten off (30).

Sew Ears 3½" apart over rnds 11-14 of Head. Sew 4 sts of each Ear to back of Head.

NECK & BODY

Rnd 1: With off-white, ch 20, sl st in first ch to form ring, ch 1, sc in each ch around (20).

Rnds 2-4: Sc in each st around.

Rnd 5: Sc in first 7 sts, 2 sc in each of next 6 sts, sc in last 7 sts (26).

Rnds 6-7: Sc in each st around.

Rnd 8: 2 sc in first st, sc in next st, 2 sc in next st, sc in last 23 sts (28).

Rnds 9-15: Sc in each st around. Stuff.

Rnd 16: Sc in first st; for **Tail opening,** ch 5, skip next 4 sts; sc in last 23 sts.

Rnd 17: Sc in each st and in each ch around (29).

Rnd 18: Sc first 2 sts tog, (sc in next st, sc next 2 sts tog) around (19).

Rnd 19: Sc in first st, (sc next 2 sts tog) around (10). Stuff.

Rnd 20: (Sc next 2 sts tog) around, join with sl st in first sc. Leaving long end for sewing, fasten off. Sew opening closed.

Sew rnds 7-14 on bottom of Head to rnd 1 of Neck.

TAIL

Rnd 1: Working around Tail opening, join off-white with sc in any st, evenly space 9 sts around (10 sc).

Rnds 2-5: Sc in each st around.

Rnd 6: Sc in first st, (sc next 2 sts tog) 2 times, sc in last 5 sts (8).

Rnds 7-8: Sc in each st around. Stuff.

Rnd 9: Sc in each of first 2 sts, (sc next 2 sts tog) 2 times, sc in each of last 2 sts (6).

Rnds 10-11: Sc in each st around.

Rnd 12: Sc in first st, (sc next 2 sts tog) 2 times, sl st in last st. Leaving long end for sewing, fasten off. Sew opening closed.

BACK LEG (make 2)

Rnd 1: Starting at **top,** with off-white, ch 2, 8 sc in 2nd ch from hook (8 sc).

Rnd 2: 2 sc in each st around (16).

Rnd 3: (2 sc in next st, sc in each of next 2 sts) 5 times, 2 sc in last st (22).

continued on page 106

Rnds 4-5: Sc in each st around.

Rnd 6: Sc in first 4 sts, sc next 2 sts tog, (sc in next st, sc next 2 sts tog) 4 times, sc in last 4 sts (17).

Rnd 7: Sc in first 5 sts, (sc next 2 sts tog) 3 times, sc in last 6 sts (14).

Rnd 8: Sc in each st around. Sc in first st.

Rnd 9: Sc in each of first 3 sts, (sc next 2 sts tog) 4 times, sc in each of last 3 sts (10). Stuff lightly.

Rnd 10: Sc in each st around, join with sl st in first sc.

Rnd 11: Ch 3, dc in same st, dc in next st, sc in next st, sl st in next 5 sts, sc in next st, 2 dc in last st, join with sl st in top of ch-3 (12).

Rnd 12: Ch 3, dc next 2 sts tog, sc in next st, sl st in next 5 sts, sc in next st, dc next 2 sts tog, join (10).

Rnd 13: Ch 1, sc in each st around, **do not** join.

Rnds 14-15: Repeat rnd 8.

Rnd 16: Sc in each of first 3 sts, 2 sc in each of next 4 sts, sc in each of last 3 sts (14).

Rnd 17: Repeat rnd 8.

Rnd 18: Sc in each of first 3 sts, (sc next 2 sts tog) 4 times, sc in each of last 3 sts (10). Stuff.

Rnd 19: (Sc next 2 sts tog) around, join with sl st in first sc. Leaving long end for sewing, fasten off. Sew opening closed.

Working over rnds 16-19, with brown, using Satin Stitch, embroider Paw Pads on bottom of each Leg according to diagram.

PUPPY PAW PAD DIAGRAM

Sew rnds 1-8 of Legs at angle over rnds 10-16 on Body 2½" apart across back.

FRONT LEG (make 2)

Rnd 1: Starting at **top,** with off-white, ch 2, 7 sc in 2nd ch from hook (7 sc).

Rnd 2: 2 sc in each st around (14).

Rnds 3-5: Sc in each st around. Stuff lightly.

Rnd 6: Sc first 2 sts tog, (sc in each of next 2 sts, sc next 2 sts tog) around (10).

Rnds 7-15: Sc in each st around.

Rnds 16-19: Repeat same rnds of Back Leg above.

Using smaller sts, embroider Paw Pads over rnds 18 and 19 in same manner as Back Legs.

Sew rnds 1-7 of Legs ½" apart across bottom of Body over rnds 4-11.

Tie ribbon ends into a bow around Neck.

Cuddly Kitten

Size: 9½" long.

Materials: Fuzzy worsted-weight yarn — 2 oz. gray; pink embroidery floss; 18" pink ¼" satin ribbon; 2 blue 12-mm cat eyes with washers; tapestry and soft-sculpture needles; polyester fiberfill; G crochet hook or size needed to obtain gauge.

Gauge: 4 sc = 1"; 4 sc rows = 1".

Note: Do not join rnds unless otherwise stated. Mark first st of each rnd.

Skill Level: ☆☆ Average

HEAD

Rnd 1: Starting at **nose,** ch 2, 6 sc in 2nd ch from hook (6 sc).

Rnd 2: Sc in each st around.

Rnd 3: Sc in first st, 2 sc in each of next 4 sts, sc in last st (10).

Rnd 4: Sc in each of first 2 sts, 2 sc in each of next 6 sts, sc in each of last 2 sts (16).

NOTE: To move first st, sc in first st.

Rnd 5: Sc in each of first 2 sts, 2 sc in each of next 4 sts; for **center front of Head,** sc in next 4 sts; 2 sc in each of next 4 sts, sc in each of last 2 sts (24).

Rnd 6: Sc in each of first 3 sts, 2 sc in each of next 18 sts, sc in each of last 3 sts, sc in first st; rnds now begin here (42).

Rnd 7: Sc in first 4 sts, (sc next 2 sts tog) 6 times, sc in next 10 sts, (sc next 2 sts tog) 6 times, sc in last 4 sts (30).

Attach eyes with washers over rnd 5 on center front of Head.

Rnd 8: Sc in first 4 sts, (sc next 2 sts tog) 3 times, sc in next 10 sts, (sc next 2 sts tog) 3 times, sc in last 4 sts (24).

Rnd 9: Sc in first 4 sts, (sc next 2 sts tog) 2 times, sc in next 8 sts, (sc next 2 sts tog) 2 times, sc in last 4 sts (20).

Rnds 10-11: Sc in each st around. Stuff.

Rnd 12: (Sc next 2 sts tog, sc in next st) 6 times, sc last 2 sts tog (13). Stuff.

Rnd 13: Sc in first st, (sc next 2 sts tog) 6 times, join with sl st in first st. Leaving long end for sewing, fasten off. Sew opening closed.

With 6 strands floss, using Satin Stitch (see page 158), embroider nose as shown in photo; embroider mouth lines with 3 strands floss using small Straight Stitches. Using soft-sculpture needle and gray, make slight indent above each eye.

EAR (make 2)

Ch 5, dc in 3rd ch from hook, hdc in next ch, (sc, ch 2,

sc) in end ch; working on opposite side of ch, hdc in next ch, 2 dc in last ch leaving long end for sewing, fasten off.

Sew Ears slightly cupped 1" apart over rnds 7 and 8 on Head.

Cut 4 strands yarn each 3" long. Tie 2 strands to center sts of each Ear. Brush strands.

NECK & BODY

Rnd 1: Ch 18, sl st in first ch to form ring, ch 1, sc in first 4 chs, hdc in next ch, dc in next 8 chs, hdc in next ch, sc in last 4 chs (18).

Rnds 2-3: Sc in first 4 sts, hdc in next st, dc in next 8 sts, hdc in next st, sc in last 4 sts.

Rnd 4: 2 sc in each of first 3 sts, hdc in next st, dc in next 10 sts, hdc in next st, 2 sc in each of last 3 sts (24).

Rnd 5: 2 sc in each of first 4 sts, hdc in next st, (dc next 2 sts tog) 7 times, hdc in next st, 2 sc in each of last 4 sts (25).

Rnds 6-7: Sc in first 6 sts, hdc in next st, dc in next 11 sts, hdc in next st, sc in last 6 sts.

Rnds 8-13: Sc in each st around. Stuff.

Rnd 14: Sc in first st; for **Tail opening,** ch 4, skip next 4 sts; sc in last 20 sts (21).

Rnd 15: Sc in each st and in each ch around (25).

Rnd 16: (Sc next 2 sts tog) 2 times, (sc in next st, sc next 2 sts tog) around (16). Stuff.

Rnds 17-18: (Sc next 2 sts tog) around (8, 4). At end of last rnd, join with sl st in first sc leaving long end for sewing, fasten off. Sew opening closed.

Sew rnds 5-10 on bottom of Head to rnd 1 of Neck with front of Head facing sideways.

TAIL

Rnd 1: Working around Tail opening, join with sc in any st, evenly sp 9 sc around (10 sc).

Rnds 2-7: Sc in each st around. Stuff.

Rnd 8: Sc in each of first 2 sts, sc next 2 sts tog, sc in each st around (9).

Rnds 9-13: Repeat rnds 2 and 8 alternately, ending with 7 sts in last rnd.

Rnd 14: Sc in first st, (sc next 2 sts tog) 2 times, sc in each of last 2 sts (5). Stuff.

Rnd 15: Sc in first st, sc next 2 sts tog, sc in each of last 2 sts, join with sl st in first sc. Leaving long end for sewing, fasten off. Sew opening closed.

BACK LEG (make 2)

Rnd 1: Starting at **top of hip,** ch 2, 7 sc in 2nd ch from hook (7 sc).

Rnd 2: 2 sc in each st around (14).

Rnd 3: (2 sc in next st, sc in next st) around (21).

Rnds 4-6: Sc in each st around.

Rnd 7: Sc in first 4 sts, sc next 2 sts tog, (sc in next st, sc next 2 sts tog) 4 times, sc in each of last 3 sts (16).

Rnd 8: Sc in each of first 3 sts, (sc next 2 sts tog) 5 times, sc in each of last 3 sts (11).

Rnd 9: Sc in each st around, sc in first st; rnds now begin here. Stuff lightly.

Rnds 10-11: Sc in each of first 3 sts, sl st in next 5 sts, sc in each of last 3 sts.

Rnd 12: Sl st in first st, ch 3, dc in same st, dc in next st, sc in next st, sl st in next 6 sts, sc in next st, 2 dc in last st, join with sl st in top of ch-3 (13).

Rnd 13: Ch 3, dc next 2 sts tog, sc in next st, sl st in next 6 sts, sc in next st, dc last 2 sts tog, join (11).

Rnd 14: Ch 1, sc first 2 sts tog, sc in each of next 2 sts, sl st in next 4 sts, sc in each of last 3 sts (10).

Rnds 15-19: Sc in each st around. Stuff.

Rnd 20: (Sc next 2 sts tog) around, join with sl st in first sc leaving long end for sewing, fasten off. Sew opening closed.

Working over rnds 17-19, with 6 strands floss, using Satin Stitch, embroider Paw Pads on bottom of each Leg according to diagram.

Sew rnds 1-9 of Legs at angle over rnds 9-17 on Body 1" apart at back.

KITTEN PAW PAD DIAGRAM

FRONT LEG (make 2)

Rnds 1-2: Repeat same rnds of Back Leg.

Rnds 3-4: Sc in each st around.

Rnds 5-10: Sc first 2 sts tog, sc in each st around, ending with 8 sts in last rnd.

Rnds 11-13: Sc in each st around. Stuff lightly.

Rnd 14: (2 sc in next st, sc in each of next 3 sts) around (10).

Rnds 15-16: Sc in each st around. Stuff.

Rnd 17: (Sc next 2 sts tog) around, join with sl st in first sc. Leaving long end for sewing, fasten off. Sew opening closed.

Working over rnds 14-16, with 6 strands floss, using small Satin Stitches, embroider Paw Pads on bottom of each Leg according to diagram.

Sew rnds 1-4 of Legs at angle 1½" apart across bottom of Body over rnds 2-5.

Tie ribbon ends into a bow around neck. ✄

Charlie Chimp

Designed by *Barbara Anderson*

Size: 9" tall, sitting.

Materials: Worsted-weight yarn — 4 oz. brown, 1 oz. each peach, turquoise and yellow, small amount off-white; 2 black 12-mm animal eyes with washers; 12" chenille stem; black embroidery floss; ½" x 1" strip Velcro; polyester fiberfill; sewing thread; sewing and tapestry needles; F crochet hook or size needed to obtain gauge.

Gauge: 9 sc = 2"; 9 sc rows = 2".

Note: Do not join rnds unless otherwise stated. Mark first st of each rnd.

Skill Level: ☆☆ Average

CHIMP
Head

Rnd 1: Starting at **muzzle,** with peach, ch 4, 2 sc in 2nd ch from hook, 2 sc in next ch, 4 sc in end ch; working on opposite side of ch; for **center bottom,** 2 sc in each of last 2 chs (12 sc).

Rnd 2: (2 sc in next st, sc in next st) around (18).

NOTE: To move first st, sc in first st.

Rnd 3: Sc in first 14 sts leaving remaining sts unworked, move marker.

Rnd 4: Sc in first 4 sts, 2 sc in each of next 10 sts, sc in last 4 sts, join with sl st in first sc, fasten off (28).

NOTE: When changing colors (see page 158), always drop yarn to wrong side of work. Use a separate skein or ball of yarn for each color section. **Do not** *carry yarn across from one section to another. Fasten off colors at end of each color section.*

Rnd 5: Join brown with sl st in first st, ch 2, hdc in next 10 sts changing to peach (see page 158) in last st made, 2 hdc in each of next 6 sts changing to brown in last st made, hdc in last 11 sts, join with sl st in top of ch-2 (34 hdc).

Rnd 6: Ch 2, hdc in next 4 sts, 2 hdc in each of next 5 sts, 2 hdc in next st changing to peach in last st made, hdc in next 4 sts, hdc in next st changing to brown, hdc in each of next 2 sts changing to peach in last st made, hdc in next 4 sts, hdc in next st changing to brown, 2 hdc in each of next 6 sts, hdc in last 5 sts, join, fasten off peach (46).

Rnd 7: Ch 2, hdc in next 17 sts, (2 hdc in next st, hdc in next st) 5 times, 2 hdc in next st, hdc in last 17 sts, join (52).

Rnd 8: Ch 2, hdc in each st around, join. Sl st in next st.

Rnd 9: Ch 2, (hdc next 2 sts tog) 4 times, hdc in next 35 sts, (hdc next 2 sts tog) 4 times, join (44).

Attach eyes with washers 1¾" apart over rnd 6.

Rnd 10: Ch 2, hdc in each st around, join. Sl st in next st.

Rnd 11: Ch 2, hdc in each st around, join.

Rnd 12: Ch 2, hdc in each st around, join. Sl st in next st.

Rnd 13: Ch 2, hdc in each of next 3 sts, hdc next 2 sts tog, (hdc in next 4 sts, hdc next 2 sts tog) 5 times, hdc in next 6 sts, hdc last 2 sts tog, join (37).

Rnd 14: Ch 2, hdc in each st around, join. Sl st in next st. Stuff.

Rnd 15: Ch 2, (hdc next 2 sts tog, hdc in next st) around, join (25).

Rnd 16: Ch 2, hdc in each st around, join. Sl st in next st.

Rnd 17: Ch 2, (hdc next 2 sts tog) 12 times, join (13). Stuff.

Rnd 18: Ch 2, (hdc next 2 sts tog) 6 times, join, leaving long end for sewing, fasten off. Sew opening closed.

Nose & Mouth

With black floss, embroider 2 Lazy Daisy Stitches (see page 158) on rnd 2 for **nostrils** and embroider **mouth line** in Outline Stitch (see page 158) between rnds 2 and 3 stitching over rnd 3 on edges as shown in photo.

Brow

With 2 strands peach held together, ch 20, leaving long end for sewing, fasten off. Position ch around each eye section. Sew **back lps** of ch to Head, sew **front lps** between eyes to Head. Sew **front lps** of 3 chs to inside under each eye.

Ear (make 2)

Row 1: With 2 strands peach held together, ch 3, 6 hdc in 3rd ch from hook, turn (7 hdc).

Row 2: Ch 1, 2 sc in each st across, fasten off (12 sc). Sew Ears to rnd 8 on Head 3½" apart across top of Head.

Body

Rnd 1: Starting at **neck,** with brown, ch 24, sl st in first ch to form ring, ch 1, sc in each ch around, join with sl st in first sc (24 sc).

Rnd 2: Ch 2, hdc in each st around, join.

Rnd 3: Ch 2, hdc in each st around, join. Sl st in next st.

Rnds 4-6: Repeat rnds 2 and 3 alternately, ending with rnd 2.

Rnd 7: Ch 2, hdc in next 6 sts, (2 hdc in next st, hdc in next st) 5 times, 2 hdc in next st, hdc in last 6 sts, join (30 hdc).

Rnds 8-9: Repeat rnd 3 and 2.

Rnd 10: Ch 2, (2 hdc in next st, hdc in next st) 2 times, 2 hdc in next st, hdc in next 19 sts, (2 hdc in next st, hdc in next st) 2 times, 2 hdc in last st, join (36). Sl st in next st.

Rnds 11-16: Repeat rnds 2 and 3 alternately.

Rnd 17: Ch 2, hdc in next st, hdc next 2 sts tog, (hdc in each of next 2 sts, hdc next 2 sts tog) around, join (27).

Rnd 18: Ch 2, hdc next 2 sts tog, (hdc in next st, hdc next 2 sts tog) around, join (18).

Rnd 19: Ch 2, (hdc next 2 sts tog) 8 times, hdc in last st, join, leaving long end for sewing, fasten off. Stuff. Sew opening closed.

Sew bottom of rnds 8-13 of Head to rnd 1 on Body.

Bottom Leg (make 2)

Rnd 1: Starting at **hip,** with brown, ch 2, 8 sc in 2nd

continued on page 112

Clara Cow

Designed by *Michele Wilcox*

Size: 10" tall.

Materials: Worsted-weight yarn — 3½ oz. white, small amount each black, pink, beige and red; 2" square piece cardboard; polyester fiberfill; F crochet hook or size needed to obtain gauge.

Gauge: 5 sc = 1"; 5 sc rows = 1".

Note: **Do not** join rnds unless otherwise stated. Mark first st of each rnd.

Skill Level: ☆☆ Average

HEAD & BODY

Rnd 1: Starting at **top of Head,** with white, ch 2, 6 sc in 2nd ch from hook (6 sc).

Rnd 2: 2 sc in each st around (12).

Rnd 3: Sc in each st around.

Rnd 4: (Sc in next st, 2 sc in next st) around (18).

Rnd 5: (Sc in each of next 2 sts, 2 sc in next st) around (24).

Rnd 6: (Sc in each of next 3 sts, 2 sc in next st) around (30).

Rnd 7: (Sc in next 4 sts, 2 sc in next st) around (36).

Rnds 8-9: Sc in each st around.

Rnd 10: (Sc in next 5 sts, 2 sc in next st) around (42).

Rnds 11-19: Sc in each st around.

Rnd 20: (Sc in next 5 sts, sc next 2 sts tog) around (36).

Rnd 21: (Sc in next 4 sts, sc next 2 sts tog) around (30).

Rnd 22: (Sc in each of next 3 sts, sc next 2 sts tog) around (24).

Rnd 23: (Sc in each of next 2 sts, sc next 2 sts tog) around (18).

Rnd 24: Sc in each st around.

Rnds 25-27: Repeat rnds 5-7, ending with 36 sts in last rnd.

Rnd 28: Sc in each st around.

Rnd 29: Repeat rnd 10 (42).

Rnds 30-36: Sc in each st around.

Rnd 37: (Sc in each of next 2 sts, 2 sc in next st) 6 times, sc in last 24 sts (48).

Rnd 38: (Sc in each of next 3 sts, 2 sc in next st) 6 times, sc in last 24 sts (54).

Rnds 39-48: Sc in each st around.

Rnd 49: (Sc in next 7 sts, sc next 2 sts tog) around (48).

Rnd 50: (Sc in next 6 sts, sc next 2 sts tog) around (42).

Rnds 51-54: Repeat rnds 20-23, ending with 18 sts in last rnd. Stuff.

Rnd 55: (Sc in next st, sc next 2 sts tog) around, join with sl st in first sc, leaving long end for sewing, fasten off. Stuff. Sew opening closed.

NOSE

Rnd 1: With beige, ch 6, sc in 2nd ch from hook, sc in each of next 3 chs, 3 sc in end ch; working on opposite side of ch, sc in each of next 3 chs, 2 sc in last ch (12 sc).

Rnd 2: 2 sc in first st, sc in each of next 3 sts, 2 sc in each of next 3 sts, sc in each of next 3 sts, 2 sc in each of last 2 sts (18).

Rnd 3: (Sc in each of next 2 sts, 2 sc in next st) around (24).

Rnd 4: (Sc in each of next 3 sts, 2 sc in next st) around (30).

Rnd 5: (Sc in next 4 sts, 2 sc in next st) around (36).

Rnds 6-8: Sc in each st around.

Rnd 9: (Sc next 2 sts tog) around, join with sl st in first sc, fasten off. Stuff. Sew over rnds 13-20 of Head.

FACIAL FEATURES

With black, using Lazy Daisy Stitch (see page 159), embroider nostrils ¾" apart.

With red, using Straight (see page 159), and Fly Stitch (see illustration), embroider mouth as shown in photo.

With black, using Satin Stitch (see page 159), embroider eyes 1" apart over rnds 10 and 11 of Head.

For **hair,** working in rnd 1, with tapestry needle and beige, secure yarn in top of Head, *wrap yarn around finger, insert needle in next st, draw yarn through st, insert needle in same st, draw yarn through st, drop loop from finger; repeat from * 5 more times, secure yarn and fasten off.

FLY STITCH

HORN (make 2)

Rnd 1: With beige, ch 2, 6 sc in 2nd ch from hook (6 sc).

Rnd 2: 2 sc in first st, sc in each st around (7).

Rnd 3: Sc in each st around.

Rnds 4-8: Repeat rnds 2 and 3 alternately, ending with rnd 2 and 10 sts. At end of last rnd, join with sl st in first sc, fasten off. Stuff.

Sew Horns 2" apart on each side of Head.

EAR (make 2)

Rnd 1: With white, ch 2, 6 sc in 2nd ch from hook (6 sc).

Rnd 2: 2 sc in each st around (12).

Rnd 3: Sc in each st around.

Rnd 4: (Sc in next st, 2 sc in next st) around (18).

Rnds 5-9: Sc in each st around.

Rnd 10: (Sc next 2 sts tog) around, join with sl st in first sc, fasten off (9). **Do not** stuff. Flatten last rnd, fold in half forming cup. Sew under each Horn.

FRONT LEG (make 2)

Rnd 1: With white, ch 2, 6 sc in 2nd ch from hook (6 sc).

Rnd 2: 2 sc in each st around (12).

Rnd 3: (Sc in next st, 2 sc in next st) around (18).

Rnd 4: (Sc in each of next 2 sts, 2 sc in next st) around (24).

Rnds 5-8: Sc in each st around.

Rnd 9: (Sc next 2 sts tog) around (12).

Rnds 10-14: Sc in each st around.

Rnd 15: 2 sc in each st around (24).

Rnds 16-17: Sc in each st around.

Rnd 18: (Sc next 2 sts tog) around (12).

Rnds 19-25: Sc in each st around, join with sl st in first sc, fasten off. Stuff. Flatten last rnd, sew Legs on left side of Body 1" apart over rnd 31.

continued on page 112

Clara Cow

continued from page 111

HIND LEG (make 2)

Rnds 1-19: Repeat same rnds of Front Leg on page 111 (12 sc).

Rnd 20: 2 sc in each st around (24).

Rnds 21-25: Sc in each st around.

Rnd 26: (Sc in each of next 2 sts, sc next 2 sts tog) around (18).

Rnd 27: (Sc in next st, sc next 2 sts tog) around (12).

Rnd 28: (Sc next 2 sts tog) around, join with sl st in first sc, leaving long end for sewing, fasten off. Stuff. Sew opening closed. Sew rnds 20-28 over rnds 41-48 on each side of Body.

TAIL

Rnd 1: With white, ch 2, 6 sc in 2nd ch from hook. (6 sc).

Rnds 2-8: Sc in each st around. At end of last rnd, join with sl st in first sc, fasten off.

For **tassel,** wind beige yarn around cardboard 20 times, slide loops off cardboard, tie separate strand tightly around middle of all loops. Cut loops, trim. Tie 6" strand ¾" from top of tassel. Trim ends. Attach tassel to rnd 1 at end of Tail.

Sew Tail over rnds 45 and 46 at back of Body.

UDDER

Rnd 1: With pink, ch 2, 6 sc in 2nd ch from hook (6 sc).

Rnd 2: 2 sc in each st around (12).

Rnd 3: (Sc in next st, 2 sc in next st) around (18).

Rnd 4: (Sc in each of next 2 sts, 2 sc in next st) around (24).

Rnd 5: (Sc in each of next 3 sts, 2 sc in next st) around (30).

Rnds 6-7: Sc in each st around. At end of last rnd, join with sl st in first sc, fasten off. Stuff.

Sew Udder over rnds 40-51 at front of Body.

NIPPLE (make 4)

Rnd 1: With pink, ch 2, 6 sc in 2nd ch from hook (6 sc).

Rnd 2: Sc in each st around, join with sl st in first sc, fasten off.

Sew Nipples over rnds 3 and 4 of Udder.

LARGE SPOT

Rnd 1: With black, ch 2, 6 sc in 2nd ch from hook (6 sc).

Rnd 2: 2 sc in each st around (12).

Rnd 3: (Sc in next st, 2 sc in next st) around (18).

Rnd 4: Sc in first st, *(hdc, dc) in next st, (dc, hdc) in next st, sl st in next st*, (sc, hdc) in next st, (hdc, sc) in next st, sl st in next st, sc in next st, 2 sc in next st, sc in next st; repeat between **, sc in each of next 2 sts, 2 sc in next st, 2 hdc in next st, sc in last st, join with sl st in first sc, fasten off.

Sew Spot over rnds 32-44 st center back of Body.

SMALL SPOT (make 2)

Rnd 1: With black, ch 2, 6 sc in 2nd ch from hook (6 sc).

Rnd 2: 2 sc in each st around (12).

Rnd 3: (Hdc, dc) in next st, (hdc, sl st in next st, sc in next st, 2 sc in next st, (hdc, dc) in next st, (dc, hdc) in next st, sc in next st, sl st in next st, 2 hdc in each of next 2 sts, sl st in each of last 2 sts, join with sl st in top of first hdc, fasten off.

Sew Spots on each side of Body. ✂

Charlie Chimp

continued from page 109

ch from hook, join with sl st in first sc (8 sc).

Rnd 2: Ch 2, hdc in same st, 2 hdc in each st around, join with sl st in top of ch-2 (16 hdc).

Rnd 3: Ch 2, (2 hdc in next st, hdc in each of next 2 sts) around, join (21).

Rnd 4: Ch 2, hdc in each st around, join. Sl st in next st.

Rnd 5: Ch 2, hdc in each st around, join.

Rnds 6-7: Repeat rnds 4 and 5.

Rnd 8: Ch 2, hdc next 2 sts tog, hdc in next 16 sts, hdc last 2 sts tog, join (19).

Rnd 9: Repeat rnd 4.

Rnd 10: Ch 2, (hdc next 2 sts tog) 2 times, hdc in next 4 sts, 2 hdc in each of next 2 sts, hdc in next 4 sts, (hdc next 2 sts tog) 2 times, join (17). Stuff lightly.

Rnd 11: Ch 2, hdc next 2 sts tog, hdc in next 5 sts, 2

hdc in each of next 2 sts, hdc in next 5 sts, hdc last 2 sts tog, join (17). Sl st in next st.

Rnd 12: Ch 2, hdc next 2 sts tog, hdc in next 5 sts, 2 hdc in each of next 2 sts, hdc in next 5 sts, hdc last 2 sts tog, join.

Rnd 13: Repeat rnd 4.

Rnd 14: Ch 2, hdc in same st, 2 hdc in next st, hdc in next 4 sts, (hdc next 2 sts tog) 3 times, hdc in next 4 sts, 2 hdc in last st, join.

Rnds 15-16: Repeat rnds 4 and 5. At end of last rnd, fasten off.

Rnd 17: For **foot,** skip first st, join peach with sc in next st, sc in each st around (17 sc).

Rnd 18: Sc in first 6 sts, 2 sc in each of next 5 sts, sc in last 6 sts (22).

Rnd 19: Sc in first 8 sts, 2 sc in each of next 6 sts, sc in last 8 sts (28). Sc in first st.

*NOTE: For **cluster (cl),** yo, insert hook in next st, yo, draw lp through, yo, draw through 2 lps on hook, (yo, insert hook in same st, yo, draw lp through, yo, draw through 2 lps on hook) 2 times, yo, draw through all 4 lps on hook.*

Rnd 20: Sc in each st around. Sc in first st.

Rnd 21: Sc in first 10 sts, (cl, ch 1, sc in next st) 4 times, sc in last 10 sts.

Rnd 22: (Sc next 2 sts tog) 2 times, sc in next 6 sts, (sc in next ch, sc in next st) 4 times, sc in next 6 sts, (sc next 2 sts tog) 2 times (24).

Rnd 23: (Sc next 2 sts tog) around (12).

Rnd 24: Sc in each st around, join with sl st in first sc leaving long end for sewing, fasten off. Stuff. Sew opening closed lengthwise.

Sew rnds 1-8 of Legs to sides of Body 1" apart across back over rnds 11-16.

Bottom Leg Large Toe (make 2)

Rnd 1: With peach, ch 4, sc in 2nd ch from hook, sc in next ch, 2 sc in end ch; working on opposite side of ch, sc in each of last 2 chs (6 sc).

Rnd 2: Sc in each of first 3 sts, ch 3 leaving last 3 sts unworked, join with sl st in first sc (3 sc, 3 chs).

Rnd 3: Ch 1, sc in each st and in each ch around (6).

Rnd 4: Sc in first 4 sts, sc last 2 sts tog (5).

Rnd 5: Sc in each st around, fasten off. Stuff. Sew opening closed. Sew unworked sts of rnd 2 to inside of Leg over rnds 20-21.

Top Leg (make 2)

Rnd 1: Starting at **shoulder,** with brown, ch 2, 6 sc in 2nd ch from hook, join with sl st in first sc (6 sc).

Rnd 2: Ch 2, hdc in same st, 2 hdc in each st around, join with sl st in top of ch-2 (12 hdc).

Rnd 3: Ch 2, hdc in same st, hdc in next st, (2 hdc in next st, hdc in next st) around, join (18).

Rnd 4: Ch 2, hdc in each st around, join. Sl st in next st.

Rnd 5: Ch 2, hdc in each st around, join.

Rnds 6-7: Repeat rnds 4 and 5.

Rnd 8: Ch 2, hdc next 2 sts tog, hdc in next 13 sts, hdc last 2 sts tog, join (16).

Rnd 9: Ch 2, hdc next 2 sts tog, hdc in last 13 sts, join (15). Sl st in next st.

Rnds 10-11: Ch 2, hdc next 2 sts tog, hdc in next 4 sts, 2 hdc in each of next 2 sts, hdc in next 4 sts, hdc last 2 sts tog, join (15). At end of last rnd, sl st in next st. **Do not** stuff.

Rnds 12-13: Repeat rnds 10 and 11.

Rnd 14: Ch 2, hdc in each st around, join, fasten off.

Rnd 15: Join peach with sc in first st, sc in each st around (15 sc).

Rnd 16: Sc in each st around. Sc in first st.

Rnd 17: Sc in each st around.

Rnds 18-19: Repeat rnds 16 and 17.

Rnd 20: Repeat rnd 17. For **left Leg only,** join with sl st in first sc, fasten off.

Cut chenille stem in half. Fold one end under ½", insert in Leg with folded end even with rnd 20, stuff around stem.

Row 21: Working in rows, through both thicknesses, for **right Leg,** (cl in next st, sc in next st) 4 times, leaving long end for sewing, fasten off.

Row 21: Working in rows, through both thicknesses, for **left Leg,** join peach with sl st in 7th st on rnd 20, (cl in next st, sc in next st) 4 times, leaving long end for sewing, fasten off.

Sew chs on ends of cl and sc sts to sts on rnd 20.

Top Leg Large Toe (make 2)

Rnds 1-5: Repeat same rnds as Bottom Leg Large Toe. Sew unworked sts of rnd 2 to inside of Leg over rnds 13-15.

Flatten rnds 1-3 of Leg, sew slightly cupped over rnds 2-4 on sides of Body 1¾" apart across back.

SHIRT

Row 1: Starting at **neckline,** with turquoise, ch 35, sc in 2nd ch from hook, sc in each ch across, turn (34 sc).

Row 2: Working this row in **front lps** only, ch 3, dc in next 4 sts, 2 dc in each of next 6 sts, dc in next 12 sts, 2 dc in each of next 6 sts, dc in last 5 sts, turn (46 dc).

Row 3: Ch 3, dc in same st, dc in next 4 sts; (for **armhole,** ch 10, skip next 12 sts); dc in next 12 sts; repeat between ( ), dc in next 4 sts, 2 dc in last st, turn (24 sts, 20 chs).

continued on page 115

Bashful Bear

Designed by *Michele Wilcox*

Size: 9½" tall.

Materials: Fuzzy sport-weight yarn — 2 oz. beige, small amount black; two 6-mm animal eyes with washers; 12-mm animal nose with washer; small bouquet artificial flowers; 18" each ecru and pink ¼" satin ribbon; polyester fiberfill; F crochet hook or size needed to obtain gauge.

Gauge: 5 sc = 1"; 5 sc rows = 1".

Note: Do not join rnds unless otherwise stated. Mark first st of each rnd.

Skill Level: ☆☆ Average

HEAD

Rnd 1: Starting at **nose,** with beige, ch 2, 6 sc in 2nd ch from hook (6 sc).

Rnd 2: (Sc in each of next 2 sts, 2 sc in next st) around (8).

Rnd 3: Sc in each st around.

Rnd 4: (Sc in next st, 2 sc in next st) around (12).

Rnd 5: Sc in each st around.

Rnd 6: Repeat rnd 4 (18).

Rnd 7: 2 sc in each of first 12 sts, sc in last 6 sts (30).

Rnds 8-16: Sc in each st around.

Attach nose with washers over rnds 1 and 2.

Attach eyes with washers 1½" apart over rnds 6 and 7.

Rnd 17: (Sc in each of next 3 sts, sc next 2 sts tog) around (24). Stuff.

Rnd 18: (Sc in each of next 2 sts, sc next 2 sts tog) around (18).

Rnd 19: (Sc in next st, sc next 2 sts tog) around (12).

Rnd 20: (Sc next 2 sts tog) around, join with sl st in first sc leaving long end for sewing, fasten off. Stuff. Sew opening closed.

EAR (make 2)

Rnd 1: With beige, ch 2, 6 sc in 2nd ch from hook (6 sc).

Rnd 2: 2 sc in each st around (12).

Rnd 3: (Sc in next st, 2 sc in next st) around (18).

Rnds 4-5: Sc in each st around.

Rnd 6: (Sc next 2 sts tog) around leaving long end for sewing, fasten off (9).

Flatten rnd 6 on Ears and sew 2" apart over rnds 13 and 14 of Head.

BODY

Rnd 1: Starting at **neck,** with beige, ch 18, sl st in first ch to form ring, ch 1, sc in each ch around (18 sc).

Rnd 2: (Sc in each of next 2 sts, 2 sc in next st) around (24).

Rnds 3-4: Sc in each st around.

Rnd 5: (Sc in each of next 3 sts, 2 sc in next st) around (30).

Rnd 6: Sc in each st around.

Rnd 7: (Sc in next 4 sts, 2 sc in next st) around (36).

Rnd 8: Sc in each st around.

Rnd 9: (Sc in each of next 2 sts, 2 sc in next st) 6 times, sc in last 18 sts (42).

Rnds 10-17: Sc in each st around.

Rnd 18: (Sc in each of next 2 sts, sc next 2 sts tog) 6 times, sc in last 18 sts (36).

Rnd 19: Sc in each st around. **Do not** stuff.

Rnd 20: For **first leg,** sc in first 6 sts, skip next 18 sts, sc in last 12 sts (18).

Rnds 21-29: Sc in each st around.

Rnd 30: 2 sc in each of first 6 sts, sc in last 12 sts (24).

Rnds 31-34: Sc in each st around.

Rnd 35: (Sc in each of next 2 sts, sc next 2 sts tog) around (18).

Rnd 36: (Sc in next st, sc next 2 sts tog) around leaving long end for sewing, fasten off. Sew opening closed.

Rnd 20: For **2nd leg,** join beige with sc in first unworked st on rnd 19, sc in each st around (18).

Rnds 21-29: Sc in each st around.

Rnd 30: Sc in each of first 2 sts, 2 sc in each of next 6 sts, sc in last 10 sts (24).

Rnds 31-36: Repeat same rnds of first leg.

Stuff legs and Body. Sew rnds 7-15 of Head over neck.

ARM (make 2)

Rnds 1-2: Repeat same rnds of Ear (12 sc).

Rnd 3: (Sc in each of next 3 sts, 2 sc in next st) around (15).

Rnds 4-19: Sc in each st around.

Rnd 20: (Sc in each of next 3 sts, sc next 2 sts tog) around, leaving long end for sewing, fasten off. Stuff.

Flatten rnd 20, sew 3½" apart across front of Body over rnds 3-7.

Pull Arms behind Body, tack rnd 3 of Arms together. Tie ribbon around bouquet, tack to end of Arms. ✂

Row 4: Ch 3, dc in each st and in each ch across, turn (44).

Row 5: Ch 3, dc in next 12 sts, (2 dc in next st, dc in next st) 9 times, dc in last 13 sts, turn (53).

Row 6: Ch 3, dc in each st across, turn, fasten off.

Row 7: Join turquoise with sc in end of row 1, 2 sc in end of next 5 rows; working in **back lps,** 2 sc in first st on row 6, sc in next 51 sts, 2 sc in last st, 2 sc in end of next 5 rows, sc in end of row 1, fasten off.

Sleeves

Rnd 1: Join turquoise with sl st in 5th ch on row 3, ch 3, dc in next 5 chs, 2 dc in end of row 3, dc in next 12 sts, 2 dc in end of row 3, dc in last 4 chs, join (26 dc).

Rnd 2: Ch 3, dc in each st around, join.

Rnd 3: Working this rnd in **back lps** only, ch 1, sc in each st around, join, fasten off.

Repeat in other Armhole.

Sew Velcro on back of Shirt.

BANANA

Rnd 1: With off-white, ch 2, 6 sc in 2nd ch from hook (6 sc).

Rnd 2: 2 sc in each st around (12).

Rnds 3-10: Sc in each st around. Stuff.

Rnd 11: Sc in first st, 2 sc in each of next 3 sts, sc in each of next 2 sts, (sc next 2 sts tog) 3 times (12).

Rnds 12-21: Sc in each st around.

Rnd 22: (Sc next 2 sts tog) around, join with sl st in first sc, leaving long end for sewing, fasten off. Stuff. Sew opening closed.

Peel

Rnd 1: With yellow, ch 2, 6 sc in 2nd ch from hook (6 sc).

Rnd 2: Working this rnd in **back lps** only, sc in each st around.

Rnd 3: 2 sc in each st around (12).

Rnd 4: For **sections,** (sl st in next st, ch 23, sc in 2nd ch from hook, hdc in next ch, dc in next ch, tr in next 19 chs, skip next st on rnd 3) 6 times, sl st in last st, fasten off.

Sew ends of rows on 2 Peel sections together forming one piece; repeat with remaining sections for a total of 3 pieces. Sew long edges of Peel pieces together halfway up as shown in photo.

Place Banana inside Peel. ✂

Christmas Splendor

Deck the halls, the walls and any other area in your home with festive crochet designs gleaming with colorful holiday appeal. From glittery snowflakes to brilliant poinsettias, these glorious yuletide designs will embellish the atmosphere with wonderful wintertime charm. Home for the holidays is the place everyone will want to be when you add exquisite crocheted Christmas accessories to the celebration.

Poinsettia Garden

Designed by *Jacqueline Jewett*

Size: 43" x 59".

Materials: Worsted-weight yarn — 25 oz. off-white, 21 oz. red, 8 oz. green and 4 oz. gold; tapestry needle; G crochet hook or size needed to obtain gauge.

Gauge: 4 dc = 1"; 9 dc rows = 4". Each Square is 7½" square.

Skill Level: ☆☆ Average

SQUARE (make 20 off-white with red poinsettias, 15 red with off-white poinsettia)

*NOTES: When changing colors (see page 158), always drop all colors to same side of work. **Do not** carry dropped color across to next section of same color. Use a separate ball of yarn for each color section. Fasten off colors when no longer needed.*

Each square on graph equals 1 dc.

Work odd-numbered rows on graph from right to left; work even-numbered rows from left to right.

*For **cluster (cl)**, yo 2 times, insert hook in next st, yo, draw lp through, (yo, draw through 2 lps on hook) 2 times, *yo 2 times, insert hook in same st, yo, draw lp through, (yo, draw through 2 lps on hook) 2 times; repeat from * 2 more times, yo, draw through all 5 lps on hook.*

Row 1: Ch 33, dc in 4th ch from hook, dc in each ch across, turn (31 dc).

Rows 2-17: Ch 3, dc in each st across changing colors according to graph and placing cls where indicated, turn. At end of last row, **do not** turn.

Row 18: Working in ends of rows, ch 1, 2 sc in each row across, fasten off. Joining with sc in first st, repeat on opposite side of Square.

Holding red Squares right sides together, matching sts, with red, sew together in 3 rows of 5 Squares each; sew off-white Squares together around outer edge of red Squares as shown in photo.

BORDER

Long Edge

Row 1: Working across one long edge of Afghan, join green with sl st in first st, ch 3, dc in each st and in each seam across, turn.

Rows 2-3: Ch 3, dc in each st across, turn. At end of last row, fasten off.

Repeat on opposite edge of Afghan.

Short End

Row 1: Working across one short end of Afghan and in ends of rows on Long Edge, join red with sl st in row 3 of Long Edge, ch 3, dc in same row, 2 dc in each of next 2 rows changing to green in last st made, dc in each st and in each seam across to next Long Edge changing to red in last st made, 2 dc in each of next 3 rows, turn.

Rows 2-3: Working in established color pattern, ch 3, dc in each st across, turn. At end of last row, fasten off.

Rnd 4: Working around entire outer edge of Afghan, changing colors as needed to match piece, join red with sc in any corner; working left to right, **reverse sc** (see page 158) in each st and 2 reverse sc in end of each dc row around, join with sl st in first sc, fasten off. ✄

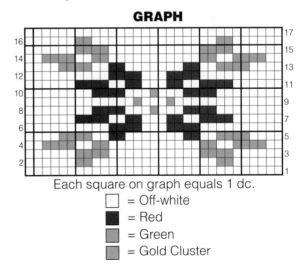

GRAPH

Each square on graph equals 1 dc.

☐ = Off-white
■ = Red
▨ = Green
▩ = Gold Cluster

Poinsettia Decor

Designed by *Hazel Henry*

Sizes: Doily is 13" across. Card Box is 3" x 4¼" x 9½".

Materials For Doily: Size-10 metallic bedspread cotton — 125 yds. gold and 50 yds. red/green; tapestry needle; No. 8 steel crochet hook or size needed to obtain gauge.

Materials For Card Box: Size-10 metallic bed-spread cotton — 300 yds. gold and 100 yds. red/green; 3" tall x 4¾" wide x 9½" long tissue box; aluminum foil; fabric stiffener; (optional: 12" x 18" piece 7-count plastic canvas; small amount red or gold 4-ply yarn); tapestry needle; No. 8 steel crochet hook or size needed to obtain gauge.

Gauge: Poinsettia Center is 1" across. 8 dc = 1"; 4 dc rows = 1".

Note: Doily may ruffle until blocked.

Skill Level: ☆☆ Average

Doily

POINSETTIA

Center

Rnd 1: With gold, ch 5, sl st in first ch to form ring, ch 1, 10 sc in ring, join with sl st in first sc (10 sc).

Rnd 2: Working this rnd in **front lps**, ch 4, (sl st in next st, ch 4) around, join with sl st in joining sl st of last rnd (10 ch lps).

Rnd 3: Working behind rnd 2, in **back lps** of rnd 1, repeat rnd 2, fasten off.

Petals

NOTES: Ch-3 at beginning of each row counts as first dc.

To dc next 3 sts tog, (yo, insert hook in next st, yo, draw lp through, yo, draw through 2 lps on hook) 3 times, yo, draw through all 4 lps on hook.

Rnd 1: Working behind rnds 2 and 3 of Center, join red/green with sl st around post of any sc on rnd 1 of Center, ch 4, (sl st around post of next st, ch 4) around, join with sl st in first sl st (10 ch sps).

Row 2: Working in rows, for **first petal**, sl st in first ch sp, ch 3, 3 dc in same sp leaving remaining ch sps unworked, turn (4 dc).

Rows 3-5: Ch 3, dc in same st, dc in each st across to last st, 2 dc in last st, turn (6, 8, 10).

Rows 6-7: Ch 3, dc in each st across, turn.

Rows 8-9: Ch 3, dc next 2 sts tog, dc in each st across to last 3 sts, dc next 2 sts tog, dc in last st, turn (8, 6).

Row 10: Ch 3, (dc next 2 sts tog) 2 times, dc in last st, turn (4).

Row 11: Ch 3, dc last 3 sts tog, fasten off (2).

Row 2: For **next petal,** join red/green with sl st in next ch sp, ch 3, 3 dc in same sp leaving remaining ch sps unworked, turn (4).

Rows 3-11: Repeat same rows of first petal. Repeat next petal 8 more times for a total of 10 petals.

EDGING

*NOTE: To **tr next 3 sts tog,** *yo 2 times, insert hook in next st, yo, draw lp through, (yo, draw through 2 lps on hook) 2 times; repeat from * 2 more times, yo, draw through all 4 lps on hook.*

Rnd 1: Join gold with sc in tip of any petal, ch 17, (sc in tip of next petal, ch 17) around, join with sl st in first sc (10 ch-17 lps).

Rnd 2: Ch 1, sc in first st, 17 sc in next ch-17 lp, (sc in next sc, 17 sc in next ch-17 lp) around, join (180 sc).

Rnd 3: Sl st in each of next 2 sts, ch 3, dc in next 14 sts, ch 5, skip next 3 sts, (dc in next 15 sts, ch 5, skip next 3 sts) around, join with sl st in top of ch-3 (150 dc, 10 ch-5 sps).

Rnd 4: Sl st in each of next 2 sts, ch 3, dc in next 10 sts, *ch 5, skip next 2 sts, dc in 3rd ch of next ch-5, ch 5, skip next 2 sts*, [dc in next 11 sts; repeat between **]; repeat between [ ] around, join (120 dc, 20 ch-5 sps).

Rnd 5: Sl st in each of next 2 sts, ch 3, dc in next 6 sts, *ch 5, skip next 2 sts, skip next ch-5 sp, (3 tr, ch 3, 3 tr) in next dc, ch 5, skip next ch-5 sp, skip next 2 sts*, [dc in next 7 sts; repeat between **]; repeat between [ ] around, join (70 dc, 60 tr, 20 ch-5 sps, 10 ch-3 sps).

Rnd 6: Sl st in each of next 2 dc, ch 3, dc in each of next 2 dc, *ch 6, skip next 2 dc, skip next ch-5 sp, tr in each of next 3 tr, ch 3, tr in 2nd ch of next ch-3, ch 3, tr in each of next 3 tr, ch 6, skip next ch-5 sp, skip next 2 dc*, [dc in each of next 3 dc; repeat between **]; repeat between [ ] around, join (70 tr, 30 dc, 20 ch-6 sps, 20 ch-3 sps).

NOTE: (Ch 2, dc next 2 dc tog) counts as dc first 3 dc tog.

Rnd 7: Ch 2, dc next 2 dc tog, *ch 6, skip next ch-6 sp, tr in each of next 3 tr, ch 5, skip next ch-3 sp, 3 tr in next tr, ch 5, skip next ch-3 sp, tr in each of next 3 tr, ch 6, skip next ch-6 sp*, [dc next 3 dc tog; repeat between

**]; repeat between [ ] around, join with sl st in top of first dc (90 tr, 20 ch-6 sps, 20 ch-5 sps, 10 dc).

Rnd 8: Ch 10, *skip next ch-6 sp, dc in next tr, ch 2, skip next tr, dc in next tr, 5 dc in next ch-5 sp, dc in each of next 3 tr, 5 dc in next ch-5 sp, dc in next tr, ch 2, skip next tr, dc in next tr, ch 6, skip next ch-6 sp*, [tr in next dc, ch 6; repeat between **]; repeat between [ ] around, join with sl st in 4th ch of ch-10.

Rnd 9: Ch 4, (2 tr, ch 3, 3 tr) in same st, *ch 5, skip

next ch-6 sp, skip next dc, skip next ch-2 sp, dc in next dc, ch 2, skip next dc, dc in next 11 dc, ch 2, skip next dc, dc in next dc, ch 5, skip next ch-2 sp, skip next dc, skip next ch-6 sp*, [(3 tr, ch 3, 3 tr) in next tr; repeat between **]; repeat between [ ] around, join with sl st in top of ch-4.

Rnd 10: Ch 4, tr in each of next 2 tr, *ch 3, tr in 2nd ch of next ch-3, ch 3, tr in each of next 3 tr, ch 6, skip next

continued on page 125

Holly Afghan

Designed by *Melody MacDuffee*

Size: 57" x 60".

Materials: Worsted-weight yarn — 38 oz. off-white, 8 oz. burgundy and 4 oz. green; H crochet hook or size needed to obtain gauge.

Gauge: 1 slanted shell = 1"; 3 slanted shell rows = 2".

Skill Level: ☆☆☆☆ Challenging

HOLLY LEAF CLUSTER
(make 18)

Rnd 1: For **first leaf,** with green, ch 14, sl st in 2nd ch from hook, (sc in next ch, hdc in next ch, dc in next ch, hdc in next ch, sc in next ch, sl st in next ch) 2 times, ch 2, sl st in same ch as last sl st; working on opposite side of ch; repeat between ( ) 2 times, **do not** join.

*NOTE: For **picot,** ch 3, sl st in top of last st made.*

Rnd 2: Working this rnd in **back lps** only, picot, *sl st in next 4 sts, picot, sl st in next 6 sts, picot, sl st in each of next 3 sts*, (sl st, ch 3, sl st) in next ch-2 sp; repeat between **; working behind first picot, join with sl st in first sl st.

Rnd 3: For **2nd leaf,** ch 18, sl st in 2nd ch from hook, (sc in next ch, hdc in next ch, dc in next ch, hdc in next ch, sc in next ch, sl st in next ch) 2 times leaving last 4 chs unworked, ch 2, sl st in same ch as last sl st; working on opposite side of ch; repeat between ( ) 2 times, **do not** join.

Rnd 4: Repeat rnd 2, fasten off.

For **berries,** with wrong side facing you, join burgundy with sl st in picot on one side of ch-4 at center of Leaves, *(yo, insert hook in same ch sp, yo, pull up long lp) 5 times, yo, draw through all lps on hook, ch 1, sl st in same ch sp; repeat from *, fasten off.

Repeat in ch-3 sp on opposite side of center ch-4.

Rnd 5: With right side facing you, join off-white with sl st around ch-4 at center of Leaves, ch 8, sl st in 2nd st after next set of berries, *ch 8, sl st in 3rd st after next picot, ch 8, sl st in 2nd st after next picot, ch 8, sl st in 2nd st after next ch-3, ch 8, sl st in 3rd st after next picot, ch 8, sl st in 2nd st after next picot*, ch 2, skip both sets of berries, sl st in 2nd st after berries on next Leaf; repeat between **, ch 8, join with sl st in first sl st, fasten off (12 ch-8 sps, 1 ch-2 sp).

AFGHAN

Row 1: With off-white, ch 124, dc in 4th ch from hook, ch 2, sc in same ch, *skip next 2 chs, dc in next ch, (dc, ch 2, sc) in next ch; repeat from * across, turn (31 ch-2 sps).

*NOTE: For **slanted shell,** (2 dc, ch 2, sc) in next ch sp.*

Rows 2-71: Ch 2, (dc, ch 2, sc) in first ch sp, slanted shell in each ch-2 sp across, turn (31 slanted shells). At end of last row, **do not** turn.

Rnd 72: Working around outer edge, in ends of rows and in sts, (ch 5, skip next row, sc in next row) 35 times, ch 7, sc in same row as last sc; working in starting ch on opposite side of row 1, ch 5, skip first 4 chs, sc in next ch, (ch 5, skip next 3 chs, sc in next ch) across, ch 7, sc in same ch as last sc, ch 5, skip first 2 rows, sc in next row, (ch 5, skip next row, sc in next row) 33 times, ch 5, (sc, ch 7, sc) in ch sp of next slanted shell, (ch 5, sc in ch sp of next slanted shell) across, ch 7, sc in same slanted shell as last sc, join with sl st in first ch of first ch-5, fasten off (35 ch-5 sps on each side, 30 ch-5 sps on each end, 1 ch-7 sp at each corner).

Rnd 73: Join burgundy with sl st in any corner ch-7 sp, (ch 2, 2 hdc, picot, 34 hdc) in same sp, 4 hdc in each ch-5 sp around with (3 hdc, picot, 3 hdc) in each corner ch-7 sp, join with sl st in top of ch-2, fasten off (146 hdc on each side, 126 hdc on each end, 4 picots).

Rnd 74: Join off-white with sc in first picot on one long edge, ch 6, sc in same picot, *[ch 4; working in sps between sts, sc in sp between corner hdc group and first 4-hdc group, (ch 4, sc in next sp between 4-hdc groups) across to 4-hdc group before next corner, ch 4, sc in sp between last 4-hdc group and corner hdc group, ch 4], (sc, ch 6, sc) in next picot; repeat from * 2 more times; repeat between [ ], join with sl st in first sc.

Rnd 75: Sl st in each of first 2 chs of next ch-6, ch 1, (sc, ch 4, sc) in same sp, *(ch 4, sc in next ch sp) across to next corner ch sp, ch 4, (sc, ch 4, sc) in next corner ch sp; repeat from * 2 more times, (ch 4, sc in next ch sp across, ch 4, join.

Rnd 76: Sl st in each of first 2 chs of next ch-4, ch 1, sc in same ch sp, ch 4, (sc in next ch sp, ch 4) around, join (146 ch sps).

Rnd 77: Ch 1, 4 hdc in first st, 4 hdc in each ch-4 sp around with 4 hdc in each corner sc, join with sl st in first hdc (600 hdc).

Rnd 78: Ch 1, sc in next st, (ch 6, skip next 5 sts, sc in next st, ch 6, skip next 4 sts, sc in next st, ch 3, sl st in ch-8 sp below first set of berries on one Leaf Cluster, ch 3, skip next 4 sts on Afghan, sc in next st, ch 3, sl st in next ch-8 sp on Leaf Cluster, ch 3, skip next 4 sts on Afghan, sc in next st, ch 6, skip next 4 sts, sc in next st, ch 6, skip next 5 sts, sc in next st) 5 times, [ch 6, skip next 5 sts, sc in next st, ch 6, skip next 5 sts, sc in next st, ch 3, sl st in ch-8 sp below first set of berries on one Leaf Cluster, ch 3, skip next 4 sts on Afghan, sc in next st, ch 3, sl st in next ch-8 sp on Leaf Cluster, ch 3, skip next 4 sts on Afghan, sc in next st, ch 6, skip next 5 sts, sc in next st, ch 6, skip next 5 sts, sc in next st], *ch 6, skip next 5 sts, sc in next st, ch 6, skip next 5 sts, sc in next st, ch 3, sl st in ch-8 sp below first set of berries on one Leaf cluster, ch 3, skip next 5 sts on Afghan, sc in next st, ch 3, sl st in

continued on page 124

next ch-8 sp on Leaf Cluster, ch 3, skip next 5 sts on Afghan, sc in next st, ch 6, skip next 5 sts, sc in next st, ch 6, skip next 5 sts, sc in next st*; repeat between **; repeat between [ ]; repeat between ( ) 5 times; repeat between [ ]; repeat between ** 2 times; repeat between [ ] omitting last sc, join with sl st in first sc.

Rnd 79: Sl st in each of next 3 chs of first ch-6, ch 1, sc in same ch sp, ch 6, sc in next ch sp; working around Leaf Cluster, *[ch 3, sl st in next free ch sp on Leaf Cluster, (ch 8, sl st in next ch sp) 2 times, ch 8, sl st in same ch sp as last sl st, (ch 8, sl st in next ch sp) 2 times, ch 4, skip next ch-2 sp, sl st in next ch sp, (ch 8, sl st in next ch sp) 2 times, ch 8, sl st in same ch sp as last sl st, (ch 8, sl st in next ch sp) 2 times, ch 3, sc in next ch sp on last rnd of Afghan], (ch 6, sc in next ch sp) 3 times; repeat from * 16 more times; repeat between [ ], ch 6, sc in next ch sp, ch 6, join.

Rnd 80: Sl st in each of first 2 chs of next ch-6, ch 1, sc in same sp, ◊*[ch 3, skip next ch-3 sp, sl st in next ch-8 sp, (ch 8, sl st in next ch sp) 10 times, ch 3, skip next ch-3 sp, sc in next ch-6 sp], (ch 6, sc in next ch sp) 2 times*; repeat between ** 3 more times; repeat between [ ]; for **corner,** ch 6, (sc, ch 8, sc) in next ch sp, ch 6, sc in next ch sp; repeat between ** 3 more times; repeat between [ ]◊, corner; repeat between ◊◊, ch 6, (sc, ch 3, sc) in next ch sp, ch 6, join, fasten off.

Rnd 81: Join off-white with sc in corner ch sp before one long edge, ch 6, sc in next ch sp, •◊ch 2, skip next ch-3 sp, sl st in next ch-8 sp, (ch 8, sl st in next ch sp) 3 times, ch 8, dc in next ch sp, ch 4, dc in next ch sp, (ch 8, sl st in next ch sp) 4 times, ch 2, skip next ch-3 sp, dc in next ch sp, ch 4, dc in next ch sp◊, *[ch 2, skip next ch ch-3 sp, sl st in next ch-8 sp; to **join,** ch 3, sl st back into last ch-8 sp made on this rnd, ch 5, sl st in next ch sp on last rnd, ch 3, sl st back into next to last ch-8 sp made on this rnd, ch 5, sl st in next ch sp on last rnd; ch 8, sl st in next ch sp, ch 8, dc in next ch sp, ch 4, dc in next ch sp, (ch 8, sl st in next ch sp) 4 times], ch 2, skip next ch-3 sp, dc in next ch sp, ch 4, dc in next ch sp*; repeat between ** 2 more times; repeat between [ ], ch 3, skip next ch-3 sp, sl st in next ch sp, (ch 6, sc in next ch sp) 2 times; repeat between ◊◊; repeat between ** 2 more times; repeat between [ ], ch 3, skip next ch-3 sp, sl st in next ch sp•, (ch 6, sc in next ch sp) 2 times; repeat between ••, ch 6, sc in next ch sp, ch 6, join.

Rnd 82: Sl st in each of first 2 chs of next ch-6, ch 1, 2 hdc in same ch sp, hdc in next ch-2 sp, 6 hdc in next ch sp, 10 hdc in next ch sp, ◊(6 hdc in each of next 5 ch sps, 2 hdc in each of next 2 ch sps) 4 times, 6 hdc in each of next 5 ch sps, [10 hdc in next ch sp, 6 hdc in next ch sp, hdc in next ch sp◊, 2 hdc in each of next 2 ch sps, hdc in next ch sp, 6 hdc in next ch sp, 10 hdc in next ch sp]; repeat between ( ) 3 times, 6 hdc in each of next 5 ch sps◊; repeat between [ ]; repeat between ◊◊, 10 hdc in next ch sp, 6 hdc in next ch sp, hdc in next ch sp, 2 hdc in last ch sp, join with sl st in top of first hdc.

Rnd 83: Ch 1, sc in first st, ch 4, skip next 4 sts, sc in next st, ch 4, skip next 3 sts, sc in next st, *(ch 4, skip next st, sc in next st) 5 times, (ch 4, skip next 3 sts, sc in next st) 41 times, (ch 4, skip next 2 sts, sc in next st, ch 4, skip next st, sc in next st) 2 times, ch 4, skip next st, sc in next st, ch 4, skip next 3 sts, sc in next st, (ch 4, skip next 4 sts, sc in next st) 2 times, ch 4, skip next 3 sts, sc in next st, (ch 4, skip next st, sc in next st) 5 times, (ch 4, skip next 3 sts, sc in next st) 33 times, (ch 4, skip next st, sc in next st) 5 times, ch 4, skip next 3 sts, sc in next st*, (ch 4, skip next 4 sts, sc in next st) 2 times, ch 4, skip next 3 sts, sc in next st; repeat between **, ch 4, skip next 4 sts, join with sl st in first sc.

Rnd 84: Sl st in each of first 2 chs of next ch-4, ch 1, sc in same ch sp, ch 4, (sc in next ch sp, ch 4) around, join.

Rnd 85: Sl st in each of first 2 chs of next ch-4, ch 1, sc in same ch sp, ch 4, (sc in next ch sp, ch 4) around skipping each center corner ch sp, join, fasten off.

Rnd 86: Join burgundy with sl st in any ch sp, ch 1, 4 hdc in same sp, 4 hdc in each ch sp around skipping each center corner ch sp, join with sl st in first hdc, fasten off.

Rnd 87: Join off-white with sc between 4-hdc groups above skipped corner ch sp before one short end of Afghan, ch 4; working in sps between 4-hdc groups, (sc in next sp, ch 4) around, join.

Rnd 88: (Sl st, ch 1, sc) in next ch sp, *[ch 4, (sc, ch 5, sc) in next ch sp, ch 4, sc in next ch sp*; repeat between ** 3 more times, (ch 4, sc in next ch sp) 28 times; repeat between ** 4 more times, sc in next ch sp; repeat between ** 4 more times, (ch 4, sc in next ch sp) 36 times; repeat between ** 4 more times], sc in next ch sp; repeat between [ ], join.

Rnd 89: Sl st in each of first 2 chs of next ch-4, ch 1, sc in same ch sp, ch 4, (sc in next ch sp, ch 4) around, join.

Rnd 90: Sl st in next ch sp, ch 1, 4 hdc in each ch sp around skipping each center corner ch sp, join with sl st in first hdc, fasten off. ✀

ch-5 sp, skip next dc, skip next ch-2 sp, dc in next dc, ch 2, skip next dc, dc in next 7 dc, ch 2, skip next dc, dc in next dc, ch 6, skip next ch-2 sp, skip next dc, skip next ch-5 sp*, [tr in each of next 3 tr; repeat between **]; repeat between [ ] around, join.

Rnd 11: Ch 4, tr in each of next 2 tr, *ch 3, skip next ch-3 sp, 3 tr in next tr, ch 3, skip next ch-3 sp, tr in each of next 3 tr, ch 7, skip next ch-6 sp, skip next dc, skip next ch-2 sp, dc in next dc, ch 2, skip next dc, dc in each of next 3 dc, ch 2, skip next dc, dc in next dc, ch 7, skip next ch-2 sp, skip next dc, skip next ch-6 sp*, [tr in each of next 3 tr; repeat between **]; repeat between [ ] around, join with sl st in top of ch-4.

NOTE: (Ch 3, tr next 2 tr tog) counts as tr first 3 sts tog.

Rnd 12: Ch 3, tr next 2 tr tog, *(ch 7, tr next 3 tr tog) 2 times, ch 10, skip next ch-7 sp, skip next dc, skip next ch-2 sp, tr next 3 dc tog, ch 10, skip next ch-2 sp, skip next dc, skip next ch-7 sp*, [tr next 3 tr tog; repeat between **]; repeat between [ ] around, join with sl st in top of first tr.

Rnd 13: Ch 1, sc in first st, *(ch 5, sc in next ch-7 sp, ch 5, sc in top of next tr) 2 times, (ch 5, sc) 2 times in next ch-10 lp, ch 5, sc in top of next tr, (ch 5, sc) 2 times in next ch-10 lp, ch 5*, [sc in top of next tr; repeat between **]; repeat between [ ] around, join with sl st in first sc, fasten off.

Card Box

SIDES

*NOTES: For **dc front post (fp**—see page 159), yo, insert hook from front to back around post of next st on row before last, yo, draw lp through, (yo, draw through 2 lps on hook) 3 times, skip next st on last rnd.*

*For **dc back post (bp)**, yo, insert hook from back to front around post of next st on row before last, yo, draw lp through, (yo, draw through 2 lps on hook) 3 times, skip next st on last rnd.*

Ch-2 at beginning of each row counts as first st.

Front of row 2 is right side of work.

Row 1: With gold, ch 202, dc in 4th ch from hook, dc in each ch across, turn (200 dc).

Rows 2-3: Ch 2, fp around each of next 3 sts, bp around next 4 sts, *fp around next 4 sts, bp around next 4 sts; repeat from * across (99 fp, 100 bp).

Rows 4-6: Ch 2, bp around each of next 3 sts, fp around next 4 sts, *bp around next 4 sts, fp around next 4 sts; repeat from * across, turn.

Rows 7-9: Repeat row 2.

Rows 10-15: Repeat rows 4-9. At end of last row, **do not** turn, fasten off.

Row 16: Join red/green with sc in first st, sc in each st across, turn.

Row 17: Ch 1, sc in each st across, turn, fasten off.

Row 18: Join gold with sl st in first st, ch 3, dc in each st across, turn.

Rows 19-20: Repeat row 2. At end of last row, fasten off.

Rows 21-23: Repeat rows 16-18.

Rows 24-25: Repeat row 2.

Row 26: Ch 1, sc in first st, (ch 5, skip next 3 sts, sc in next st) across to last 3 sts, ch 5, skip next 2 sts, sc in last st, fasten off.

With gold, sew ends of rows together.

BASE

Row 1: With gold, ch 78, dc in 4th ch from hook, dc in each ch across, turn (76 dc).

Rows 2-12: Ch 3, dc in each st across, turn. At end of last row, fasten off.

To **join,** holding Base against row 1 of Sides, working through both thicknesses, join gold with sc in any st, sc in each st around with 2 sc in end of each dc row on Base, join with sl st in first sc, fasten off.

POINSETTIA

Work same as Doily Poinsettia on page 120. With gold, sew center of Poinsettia over rows 16 and 17 on one side of Box.

FINISHING

Apply fabric stiffener to Box and Poinsettia according to manufacturer's instructions. Cover tissue box with foil. Shape crocheted box over side of tissue box. Let dry completely.

For **extra support (optional),** cut plastic canvas as follows: For **long sides,** cut two pieces each 23 x 61 holes. For **ends,** cut two pieces each 18 x 23 holes. For **base,** cut one piece 18 x 61 holes.

WHIPSTITCH

With tapestry needle and 4-ply yarn, Whipstitch (see illustration) long sides and ends together. Whipstitch base around bottom to form box. Place inside Card Box. ✂

Christmas Tree Pillow

Designed by *Michele Wilcox*

Size: 9" x 15".

Materials: Worsted-weight yarn — 3½ oz. green, 1 oz. each brown and gold, small amount each blue, red and white; polyester fiberfill; tapestry needle; H crochet hook or size needed to obtain gauge.

Gauge: 7 hdc = 2"; 5 hdc rows = 2".

Skill Level: ☆ Easy

TREE SIDE (make 2)

NOTE: Ch-2 at beginning of each row counts as first st.

Row 1: With green, ch 37, hdc in 3rd ch from hook, hdc in each ch across, turn (36 hdc).

Rows 2-5: Ch 2, hdc in each st across, turn.

Row 6: Ch 2, hdc next 2 sts tog, hdc in each st across to last 3 sts, hdc next 2 sts tog, hdc in last st, turn (34).

Rows 7-8: Ch 2, hdc in each st across, turn.

Row 9: Repeat row 6 (32).

Rows 10-11: Repeat row 7.

Row 12: Repeat row 6 (30).

Rows 13-14: Repeat row 7.

Rows 15-20: Repeat rows 6 and 7 alternately, ending with 24 sts in last row.

Rows 21-27: Repeat row 6, ending with 10 sts in last row. At end of last row, fasten off.

Sew Tree Sides together leaving center 15 sts of row 1 across bottom unsewn for Trunk opening. Stuff.

TRUNK SIDE (make 2)

Row 1: With brown, ch 16, sc in 2nd ch from hook, sc in each ch across, turn (15 sc).

Rows 2-9: Ch 1, sc in each st across, turn. At end of last row, fasten off.

Sew Trunk Sides together around 3 sides leaving top unsewn. Stuff. With brown, sew Trunk to Trunk opening.

LARGE STAR SIDE (make 2)

*NOTE: **Do not** join rnds unless otherwise stated. Mark first st of each rnd.*

Rnd 1: With gold, ch 2, 5 sc in 2nd ch from hook (5 sc).

Rnd 2: 2 sc in each st around (10).

Rnd 3: (Sc in next st, 2 sc in next st) around (15).

Rnd 4: (Sc in each of next 2 sts, 2 sc in next st) around, join with sl st in first sc (20).

Rnd 5: For **points**, sl st in next st, *(ch 4, sc in 2nd ch from hook, hdc in next ch, dc in last ch, skip next 2 sts), sl st in next 2 sts; repeat from * around to last 2 sts; repeat between ( ), join with sl st in joining sl st of last rnd, fasten off (5 points).

Sew Large Star Sides together stuffing before closing. Sew to top of Tree.

SMALL STAR (make 8)

Rnd 1: With gold, ch 2, 5 sc in 2nd ch from hook (5 sc).

Rnd 2: For **points**, ch 2, sc in 2nd ch from hook, (sl st in next st, ch 2, sc in 2nd ch from hook) around, join with sl st in first ch of first ch-2, fasten off.

Sew Small Stars to front of Tree as shown in photo.

BALL (make 4 blue, 4 white, 3 red)

Rnd 1: Ch 2, 6 sc in 2nd ch from hook (6 sc).

Rnd 2: 2 sc in each st around, join with sl st in first sc, fasten off.

Sew Balls to front of Tree as shown. ✂

Mistletoe Stocking

Designed by *Katherine Eng*

Size: 13½" long not including hanger.

Materials: Worsted-weight yarn — 3 oz. burgundy/green/beige variegated and 1 oz. burgundy; 32" burgundy ⅞" satin ribbon; tapestry needle; G crochet hook or size needed to obtain gauge.

Gauge: 4 dc = 1"; 1 sc row and 1 dc row = 1".

Skill Level: ☆☆ Average

FRONT

NOTE: Front of row 1 is wrong side of work.

Row 1: With variegated, ch 40, sc in 2nd ch from hook, (ch 1, skip next ch, sc in next ch) across, turn (20 sc, 19 ch sps).

Row 2: Ch 3, dc in same st, dc in each ch sp and in each st across, turn (40 dc).

Row 3: Ch 1, sc in first st, (ch 1, skip next st, sc in next st) across to last st, ch 1, sc in last st, turn (21 sc, 20 ch sps).

Row 4: Ch 3, dc in each ch sp and in each st across, turn (41 dc).

Row 5: Ch 1, sc in first st, (ch 1, skip next st, sc in next st) across, turn.

Rows 6-11: Repeat rows 2-5 consecutively, ending with row 3 and 23 sc and 22 ch sps.

Row 12: For **toe,** ch 3, dc in next ch sp, (dc in next st, dc in next ch sp) 6 times leaving remaining sts unworked, turn (14 dc).

Row 13: Ch 1, skip first st, sc in next st, (ch 1, skip next st, sc in next st) across, turn (7 sc, 6 ch sps).

Row 14: Repeat row 4 (13 dc).

Row 15: Ch 1, sc in first st, (ch 1, skip next st, sc in next st) across, turn.

Row 16: Ch 3, dc in next ch sp, (dc in next st, dc in next ch sp) across leaving last st unworked, turn (12 dc).

Row 17: Repeat row 13 (6 sc, 5 ch sps).

Row 18: Repeat row 16 (10 dc).

Row 19: Ch 1, skip first st, sc in next st, ch 1, skip next st, (sc in next st, ch 1, skip next st) 2 times, sc next 2 sts tog leaving last st unworked, fasten off.

Edging

With right side facing you, working in starting ch on opposite side of row 1, join variegated with sl st in first ch, ch 3, dc in next 11 chs, hdc in next 12 chs, sc in each of next 3 chs; for **heel shaping,** hdc in each of next 3 chs, dc in next 4 chs, 2 dc in next ch, hdc in each of next 3 chs, 2 sc in last ch; working in ends of rows across bottom, sc in each sc row and 2 sc in each dc row across to row 19; for **toe shaping,** working in sts across row 19, 2 sc in first st, hdc in next ch sp, hdc in next st, 3 dc in next ch sp, hdc in next st, hdc in next ch sp, 2 sc in last st; working in ends of rows across top, 2 sc in each dc row and sc in each sc row across to row 12; working in unworked sts across row 11, 2 sc in first st, (sc in next ch sp, sc in next st) 4 times, (hdc in next ch sp, hdc in next st) 5 times, (dc in next ch sp, dc in next st) 6 times, **do not** turn, fasten off.

Row 2: Join burgundy with sc in first st, sc in each st across, fasten off.

BACK

Rows 1-11: Repeat same rows of Front. At end of last row, fasten off.

Row 12: Join variegated with sl st in 16th ch sp, ch 3, dc in each st and in each ch sp across, turn (14 dc).

Row 13: Ch 1, sc in first st, (ch 1, skip next st, sc in next st) across leaving last st unworked, turn (7 sc, 6 ch sps).

Row 14: Ch 3, dc in each st and in each ch sp across, turn (13 dc).

Row 15: Ch 1, sc in first st, (ch 1, skip next st, sc in next st) across, turn (7 sc, 6 ch sps).

Row 16: Sl st in next ch sp, ch 3, dc in each st and in each ch sp across, turn (12 dc).

Row 17: Ch 1, sc in first st, (ch 1, skip next st, sc in next st) across leaving last st unworked, turn (6 sc, 5 ch sps).

Row 18: Repeat row 16 (10 dc).

Row 19: Ch 1, skip first st, sc next 2 sts tog, (ch 1, skip next st, sc in next st) 3 times leaving last st unworked, fasten off.

Edging

Row 1: Working in remaining sts on row 11, join variegated with sl st in first st at top, ch 3, dc in next ch sp, (dc in next st, dc in next ch sp) 5 times, (hdc in next st, hdc in next ch sp) 5 times, (sc in next st, sc in next ch sp) 4 times, 2 sc in last st; working in ends of rows across top, 2 sc in each dc row and sc in each sc row across to row 19; for **toe shaping,** working in sts across row 19, 2 sc in first st, hdc in next ch sp, hdc in next st, 3 dc in next ch sp, hdc in next st, hdc in next ch sp, 2 sc in last st; working in ends of rows across bottom, sc in each sc row and 2 sc in each dc row across to row 1; working in starting ch on opposite side of row 1; for **heel shaping,** 2 sc in first ch, hdc in each of next 3 chs, 2 dc in next ch, dc in next 4 chs, hdc in each of next 3 chs; sc in each of next 3 chs, hdc in next 12 chs, dc in last 12 chs, **do not** turn, fasten off.

Row 2: Join burgundy with sc in first st, sc in each st across, fasten off.

Holding Front and Back wrong sides together, matching sts of row 2 on Edging, with burgundy, sew Front and Back together leaving top open.

TOP TRIM

Rnd 1: Working around top opening, join burgundy with sc in center back seam, sc in end of each row, in center front seam and 2 sc in end of each dc row around, join with sl st in first sc (46 sc).

Rnd 2: Ch 1, sc in first st, ch 2, skip next st, (sc in next st, ch 2, skip next st) around, join (23 ch sps).

Row 3: Ch 1; for **hanger,** (sc, ch 16, sc) in first st; (sc, ch 3, sc) in each ch sp around, join, fasten off.

Tie ribbon into a bow around st on Stocking Front in upper left corner as shown in photo. ✂

Dimensional Snowflakes

Designed by *Jo Ann Maxwell*

General Instructions

Stiffening and Finishing Materials: Liquid fabric stiffener; stainless steel pins; corrugated cardboard or blocking board; plastic wrap; craft glue or hot glue gun; iridescent glitter; clear craft beading filament or clear monofilament.

1: With tapestry needle, weave in all loose ends to prevent unraveling during use.

2: Apply liquid fabric stiffener to Center and Sides following manufacturer stiffening instructions.

3: Cover cardboard or blocking board with plastic wrap. Pin crochet pieces to board, using photo of each Snowflake as a guide when shaping. When almost dry, bend Sides. Let Center dry flat.

4: With Center held between Sides, glue all 3 pieces together through the middle so that outer edges of Side pieces lift out and away from Center.

5: Apply glue to Snowflake over picots, middle and any other areas you wish to accent. Sprinkle with glitter and shake off excess.

6: For **hanging loop,** tie small piece of beading filament or monofilament to one point.

Crown Jewels

Size: 6" across.

Materials: Size-10 bedspread cotton — 100 yds. white; (see General Instructions for stiffening and finishing materials); tapestry needle; No. 5 steel crochet hook or size needed to obtain gauge.

Gauge: Rnd 1 of Center = 1" across; 7 sc = 1".

Note: Please read General Instructions before starting.

Skill Level: ☆☆ Average

CENTER

Rnd 1: Ch 5, dc in 5th ch from hook, ch 1, (dc in same ch, ch 1) 10 times, join with sl st in 3rd ch of ch-5 (12 dc, 12 ch-1 sps).

Rnd 2: Ch 1, (sc, ch 23, sc) in same st, ch 1, sc in next dc, ch 1, *(sc, ch 23, sc) in next dc, ch 1, sc in next dc, ch 1; repeat from * around, join with sl st in first sc (6 ch-23 lps).

Rnd 3: *Sc in first ch of next ch-23, (ch 1, sc in next ch) 9 times, ch 3, dc in next ch, ch 5, (tr, ch 5, tr) in next ch, ch 5, dc in next ch, ch 3, sc in next ch, (ch 1, sc in next ch) 9 times, sl st in next sc, ch 1, sc in next sc, ch 1*, [sl st in next sc; repeat between **]; repeat between [ ] around, join with sl st in joining sl st of last rnd, fasten off.

SIDE (make 2)

Rnd 1: Ch 5, dc in 5th ch from hook, ch 1, (dc in same ch, ch 1) 10 times, join with sl st in 3rd ch of ch-5 (12 dc, 12 ch-1 sps).

Rnd 2: Ch 1, (sc, ch 15, sc) in same st, ch 1, sc in next dc, ch 1, *(sc, ch 15, sc) in next dc, ch 1, sc in next dc, ch 1; repeat from * around, join with sl st in first sc (6 ch-15 lps).

Rnd 3: *Sc in first ch of next ch-15 lp, (ch 1, sc in next ch) 5 times, ch 3, dc in next ch, ch 5, (tr, ch 7, tr) in next ch, ch 5, dc in next ch, ch 3, sc in next ch, (ch 1, sc in next ch) 5 times, sl st in next sc, ch 1, sc in next sc, ch 1*, [sl st in next sc; repeat between **]; repeat between [ ] around, join with sl st in joining sl st of last rnd, fasten off.

Stiffen and finish according to General Instructions.

Love Knots

Materials: Size-10 bedspread cotton — 110 yds. white; (see General Instructions for stiffening and finishing materials); tapestry needle; No. 5 steel crochet hook or size needed to obtain gauge.

Gauge: Rnd 1 of Center = 1½" across; 7 sc = 1".

Note: Please read General Instructions before starting.

Skill Level: ☆☆ Average

CENTER

Rnd 1: Ch 5, sl st in first ch to form ring, ch 6, (tr in ring, ch 2) 11 times, join with sl st in 4th ch of ch-6 (12 tr, 12 ch-2 sps).

NOTES: *For **shell**, (2 dc, ch 2, 2 dc) in next st or sp.*

*For **picot**, ch 4, sl st in top of last st made.*

Rnd 2: Beg shell, ch 2, (sc, picot) in next tr, ch 2, *shell in next tr, ch 2, (sc, picot) in next tr, ch 2; repeat from *

continued on page 132

Crown Jewels

Love Knots

Royal Crest

Prince Charming

Noble Lace

Oblique Monarch

around, join with sl st in top of ch-3 (6 shells, 12 ch-2 sps).

Rnd 3: Sl st in next dc, sl st in next ch-2 sp, ch 6, (tr, ch 2, tr, ch 2, tr, ch 2, tr) in same sp, ch 3, *tr in ch sp of next shell, (ch 2, tr in same sp) 4 times, ch 3; repeat from * around, join with sl st in 4th ch of ch-6 (30 tr, 24 ch-2 sps, 6 ch-3 sps).

NOTE: For love knot (lk—see illustration), draw up long lp on hook, yo, draw lp through, sc in back strand of long lp.

Rnd 4: Ch 1, sc in first st, *ch 1, lk, sc in next tr, ch 1, lk, (dc, ch 3, dc) in next tr, ch 1, lk, sc in next tr, ch 1, lk, sc in next tr, sc in each of next 3 chs*, [sc in next tr; repeat between **]; repeat between [ ] around, join with sl st in first sc, **turn.**

Rnd 5: Sl st in each of next 2 sc, **turn,** ch 1, (sc, picot) in same st, *ch 5, skip next lk, sc in next sc, ch 5, skip next lk, skip next dc, (dc, ch 6, sl st in 4th ch from hook, ch 2, dc) in 2nd ch of next ch-3, ch 5, skip next dc, skip next lk, sc in next sc, ch 5, skip next lk, skip next 2 sc*, [(sc, picot) in next sc; repeat between **]; repeat between [ ] around, join, fasten off.

SIDE (make 2)

Rnd 1: Ch 5, sl st in first ch to form ring, ch 6, (tr in ring, ch 2) 11 times, join with sl st in 4th ch of ch-6 (12 tr, 12 ch-2 sps).

Rnd 2: Ch 1, sc in first st, ch 1, lk, (dc, ch 3, dc) in next tr, ch 1, lk, *sc in next tr, ch 1, lk, (dc, ch 3, dc) in next tr, ch 1, lk; repeat from * around, join with sl st in first sc (6 sc, 6 ch-3 sps).

Rnd 3: Ch 1, (sc, picot) in first st, *ch 5, skip next lk, skip next dc, (dc, ch 6, sl st in 4th ch from hook, ch 2, dc) in 2nd ch of next ch-3, ch 5, skip next dc, skip next lk*, [(sc, picot) in next sc; repeat between **]; repeat between [ ] around, join, fasten off.

Stiffen and finish according to General Instructions.

LOVE KNOT ILLUSTRATION

Step 1:

Step 2:

Completed Love Knot

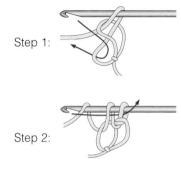

Prince Charming

Size: 5¾" across.

Materials: Size-10 bedspread cotton — 80 yds. white; (see General Instructions on page 130 for stiffening and finishing materials); tapestry needle; No. 5 steel crochet hook or size needed to obtain gauge.

Gauge: Rnd 1 of Center = 1" across; 7 sc = 1".

Note: Please read General Instructions before starting.

Skill Level: ☆☆ Average

CENTER

Rnd 1: Ch 5, sl st in first ch to form ring, ch 5, (dc in ring, ch 2) 11 times, join with sl st in 3rd ch of ch-5 (12 dc, 12 ch-2 sps).

Rnd 2: Ch 8, (tr in next dc, ch 4) around, join with sl st in 4th ch of ch-8 (12 tr).

NOTE: For picot, ch 4, sl st in top of last st made.

Rnd 3: Ch 8, sl st in 4th ch from hook, ch 10, sl st in 4th ch from hook, ch 6, (tr, picot) in same st as beg ch-8, ch 5, (sc, picot) in next tr, ch 5, *(tr, picot, ch 10, sl st in 4th ch from hook, ch 6, tr, picot) in next tr, ch 5, (sc, picot) in next tr, ch 5; repeat from * around, join with sl st in 4th ch of ch-8, fasten off.

SIDE (make 2)

Rnd 1: Ch 5, sl st in first ch to form ring, ch 5, (dc in ring, ch 2) 11 times, join with sl st in 3rd ch of ch-5 (12 dc, 12 ch-2 sps).

Rnd 2: Ch 7, sl st in 4th ch from hook, ch 9, sl st in 4th ch from hook, ch 5, (dc, picot) in same st as beg ch-7, ch 3, sc in next dc, ch 3, *(dc, picot, ch 9, sl st in 4th ch from hook, ch 5, dc, picot) in next dc, ch 3, sc in next dc, ch 3; repeat from * around, join with sl st in 3rd ch of beg ch-7, fasten off.

Stiffen and finish according to General Instructions.

Royal Crest

Size: 5¾" across.

Materials: Size-10 bedspread cotton — 110 yds. white; (see General Instructions on page 130 for stiffening and finishing materials); tapestry needle; No. 5 steel crochet hook or size needed to obtain gauge.

Gauge: Rnd 1 of Center = ¾" across; 7 sc = 1".

Note: Please read General Instructions before starting.
Skill Level: ☆☆ Average

CENTER

Rnd 1: Ch 4, sl st in first ch to form ring, ch 3, 15 dc in ring, join with sl st in top of ch-3 (16 dc).

Rnd 2: Ch 1, *sc in next st, ch 23, sl st in top of last sc made, ch 3, skip next st; repeat from * around, join with sl st in first sc (8 ch-23 lps, 8 ch-3 sps).

Rnd 3: *Sc in first ch of next ch-23, (2 sc in next ch, sc in next ch) 5 times, sc in next ch, (ch 5, sl st, ch 7, sl st, ch 5, sl st) in top of last sc made, sc in next ch, (2 sc in next ch, sc in next ch) 5 times, sl st in same sc of ch-23, ch 1, sl st in next ch-3 sp, ch 1*, [sl st in same sc of ch-23; repeat between **]; repeat between [ ] around, join with sl st in joining sl st of last rnd, fasten off.

SIDE (make 2)

Rnd 1: Ch 4, sl st in first ch to form ring, ch 3, 15 dc in ring, join with sl st in top of ch-3 (16 dc).

Rnd 2: Ch 1, *sc in next st, ch 11, sl st in top of last sc made, ch 2, skip next st; repeat from * around, join with sl st in first sc (8 ch-11 lps, 8 ch-2 sps).

Rnd 3: *Sc in first ch of next ch-11, (2 sc in next ch, sc in next ch) 2 times, sc in next ch, (ch 5, sl st, ch 7, sl st, ch 5, sl st) in top of last sc made, sc in next ch, (2 sc in next ch, sc in next ch) 2 times, sl st in same sc of ch-11, ch 1, sl st in next ch-2 sp, ch 1*, [sl st in next sc of ch-11; repeat between **]; repeat between [ ] around, join with sl st in joining sl st of last rnd, fasten off.

Stiffen and finish according to General Instructions.

Noble Lace

Size: 5¾" across.
Materials: Size-10 bedspread cotton — 100 yds. white; (see General Instructions on page 130 for stiffening and finishing materials); tapestry needle; No. 5 steel crochet hook or size needed to obtain gauge.
Gauge: Rnd 1 of Center = 1¼" across; 7 sc = 1".
Note: Please read General Instructions before starting.
Skill Level: ☆☆ Average

CENTER

Rnd 1: Ch 5, sl st in first ch to form ring, ch 6, (tr in ring,

ch 2) 11 times, join with sl st in 4th ch of ch-6 (12 tr, 12 ch-2 sps).

Rnd 2: Ch 5, dc in same st, dc in each of next 2 chs, *(dc, ch 2, dc) in next tr, dc in each of next 2 chs; repeat from * around, join with sl st in 3rd ch of ch-5 (48 tr, 12 ch-2 sps).

NOTE: For picot, ch 4, sl st in top of last st made.

Rnd 3: Sl st in first ch-2 sp, ch 5, dc in same sp, ch 4, (sc, picot) in next ch-2 sp, ch 4, *(dc, ch 2, dc) in next ch-2 sp, ch 4, (sc, picot) in next ch-2 sp, ch 4; repeat from * around, join with sl st in 3rd ch of ch-5 (12 ch-4 sps, 6 ch-2 sps).

Rnd 4: Sl st in first ch-2 sp, ch 1, sc in same sp, *(ch 6, sl st in 4th ch from hook) 4 times, ch 8, sl st in 8th ch from hook, ch 4, sl st in same ch, (ch 6, sl st in 4th ch from hook) 3 times, ch 2*, [sc in next ch-2 sp; repeat between **]; repeat between [ ] around, join with sl st in first sc, fasten off.

SIDE (make 2)

Rnd 1: Ch 5, sl st in first ch to form ring, ch 6, (tr in ring, ch 2) 11 times, join with sl st in 4th ch of ch-6 (12 tr, 12 ch-2 sps).

Rnd 2: Ch 5, dc in same st, dc in each of next 2 chs, (dc, picot, dc) in next tr, dc in each of next 2 chs, *(dc, ch 2, dc) in next ch-2 sp, dc in each of next 2 chs, (dc, picot, dc) in next tr, dc in each of next 2 chs; repeat from * around, join with sl st in 3rd ch of ch-5 (48 dc, 6 ch-2 sps).

Rnd 3: Sl st in first ch-2 sp, ch 1, sc in same sp, *ch 9, sl st in 5th ch from hook, ch 8, sl st in 8th ch from hook, ch 4, sl st in same ch, ch 5*, [sc in next ch-2 sp; repeat between **]; repeat between [ ] around, join with sl st in first sc, fasten off.

Stiffen and finish according to General Instructions.

Oblique Monarch

Size: 6½" across.
Materials: Size-10 bedspread cotton — 120 yds. white; (see General Instructions on page 130 for stiffening and finishing materials); tapestry needle; No. 5 steel crochet hook or size needed to obtain gauge.
Gauge: Rnd 1 of Center = 1" across; 7 sc = 1".
Note: Please read General Instructions before starting.
Skill Level: ☆☆ Average

CENTER

Rnd 1: Ch 5, sl st in first ch to form ring, ch 3, 4 dc in

continued on page 135

Rose Wreath

Designed by *Elizabeth A. White*

Size: 20½" across.

Materials: Worsted-weight yarn — 7 oz. off-white, 2 oz. red and small amount green; 12" Styrofoam® wreath; tapestry needle; H crochet hook or size needed to obtain gauge.

Gauge: 7 dc = 2"; 2 dc rows = 1".

Skill Level: ☆☆ Average

WREATH

Row 1: With off-white, ch 25, dc in 4th ch from hook, dc in each of next 3 chs, ch 5, skip next 3 chs, dc in last 15 chs, turn (20 dc, 1 ch-5 sp).

Row 2: Ch 3, dc in next 14 sts, ch 3, skip next ch sp, dc in last 5 sts, turn.

Row 3: Ch 3, dc in next 4 sts, ch 2, sc around both chs of last 2 rows at same time, ch 2, dc in last 15 sts, turn.

Row 4: Ch 3, dc in next 14 sts, ch 3, skip next 2 ch sps and sc, dc in last 5 sts, turn.

Row 5: Ch 3, dc in next 4 sts, ch 5, skip next ch sp, dc in last 15 sts, turn.

Rows 6-55: Repeat rows 2-5 consecutively, ending with row 3.

Row 56: Holding first and last rows together, matching sts, working through both thicknesses, sl st in first 15 sts, ch 3, sl st in last 5 sts, fasten off.

Ruffle

Rnd 1: With off-white, join with sl st around beginning ch-3 on row 1, ch 5, dc around same st; working in ends of rows, (dc, ch 2, dc) in end of each row around, join with sl st in 3rd ch of ch-5.

*NOTES: For **beginning shell (beg shell)**, (sl st, ch 3, dc, ch 2, 2 dc) in next ch sp.*

*For **shell**, (2 dc, ch 2, 2 dc) in next ch sp.*

*For **picot**, ch 3, sc in 3rd ch from hook.*

*For **front post (fp** — see page 158), yo, insert hook from front to back around post of next st on rnd before last, yo, draw lp through, (yo, draw through 2 lps on hook) 3 times, skip next st on last rnd.*

Rnd 2: Beg shell, shell in each ch sp around, join with sl st in top of ch-3.

Rnd 3: Sl st in next st, beg shell, dc in sp between last worked shell and next shell, (shell in ch sp of next shell, dc in sp between last worked shell and next shell) around, join.

Rnd 4: Sl st in next st, beg shell, fp around next dc, (shell in next shell, fp around next dc) around, join.

Rnd 5: Sl st in next st, (sl st, ch 3, 2 dc, picot, 3 dc) in next ch sp, fp around next fp, *(3 dc, picot, 3 dc) in next shell, fp around next fp; repeat from * around, join, fasten off.

Place Wreath around foam wreath, sew ends of rows together leaving Ruffle free. Turn so ch sps are at center front of Wreath.

For **hanging loop,** with off-white, ch 12, fasten off. Sew to back of Wreath.

RIBBON

Row 1: With red, ch 6, dc in 4th ch from hook, dc in each of last 2 chs, turn (4 dc).

Rows 2-55: Ch 3, dc in each st across, turn. At end of last row, fasten off.

Weave ribbon through Wreath, going under groups of 3 chs and over single chs. Tack ends to secure.

ROSE (make 3)

Row 1: With red, ch 48, sc in 8th ch from hook, (ch 3, skip next 2 chs, sc in next ch) 10 times, (ch 2, skip next ch, sc in next ch) across, turn (16 ch sps).

Row 2: For **petals,** ch 1, (sc, ch 1, 3 dc, ch 1, sc) in each of first 5 ch sps, (sc, ch 1, 5 dc, ch 1, sc) in each of next 5 ch sps, (sc, ch 1, 3 dc, tr, 3 dc, ch 1, sc) in each of last 6 ch sps, fasten off.

Roll petals into flower shape with larger petals on outside, tack in place to secure.

LEAF (make 8)

With green, ch 9, sc in 2nd ch from hook, (hdc in next ch, dc in next ch, tr in each of next 2 chs, dc in next ch, hdc in next ch), 3 sc in last ch; working on opposite side of ch; repeat between ( ), 2 sc in last ch, join with sl st in first sc, fasten off.

Sew Roses and Leaves to Wreath as shown. ✂

Dimensional Snowflakes

continued from page 133

ring, ch 7, (5 dc in ring, ch 7) 3 times, join with sl st in top of ch-3 (20 dc, 4 ch-7 sps).

Rnd 2: Sl st in next 4 dc, sl st in next ch, ch 5, *skip next ch, dc in next ch, ch 2, (dc, ch 7, dc) in next ch, ch 2, dc in next ch, ch 2, skip next ch*, [skipping next 5 dc, dc next 2 chs tog, ch 2; repeat between **]; repeat between [ ] 2 more times, dc in last ch leaving last 2 lps on hook, insert hook in 3rd ch of ch-5, yo, draw through all 3 lps on hook (20 dc, 16 ch-2 sps, 4 ch-7 sps).

*NOTE: For **shell**, (2 dc, ch 2, 2 dc) in next st or sp.*

Rnd 3: Ch 1, sc in same st, ch 9, skip next 2 dc, shell in 4th ch of next ch-7, ch 9, skip next 2 dc, *sc in next dc, ch 9, skip next 2 dc, shell in 4th ch of next ch-7, ch 9, skip next 2 dc; repeat from * around, join with sl st in first sc (8 ch-9 lps, 4 shells).

NOTE: Joining (ch 1, sc) on next rnd counts as ch-2 sp.

Rnd 4: Sl st in each of next 3 chs, ch 5, skip next ch, dc in next ch, (ch 2, skip next ch, dc in next ch) 2 times, *ch 2, shell in ch sp of next shell, ch 2, skip next 2 dc of same shell, dc in next ch, (ch 2, skip next ch, dc in next ch) 3 times*, [ch 2, skip next 2 chs, skip next sc, skip next 2 chs, dc in next ch, (ch 2, skip next ch, dc in next ch) 3 times; repeat between **]; repeat between [ ] around; to **join,** ch 1, sc in 3rd ch of ch-5 (36 ch-2 sps, 4 shells).

Rnd 5: Ch 1, sc around joining sc just made, *ch 14, skip next 4 ch-2 sps, (2 dc, ch 7, sl st in 5th ch from hook, ch 2, 2 dc) in next shell, ch 14, skip next 4 ch-2 sps*, [sc in next ch-2 sp; repeat between **]; repeat between [ ] around, join with sl st in first sc, fasten off.

SIDE (make 2)

Rnd 1: Ch 5, sl st in first ch to form ring, ch 3, 4 dc in ring, ch 7, (5 dc in ring, ch 7) 3 times, join with sl st in top of ch-3 (20 dc, 4 ch-7 sps).

Rnd 2: Sl st in next 4 dc, sl st in next ch, ch 5, *skip next ch, dc in next ch, ch 2, (dc, ch 7, dc) in next ch, ch 2, dc in next ch, ch 2*, [skipping next 5 dc, dc next 2 chs tog, ch 2; repeat between **]; repeat between [ ] around, join with sl st in 3rd ch of ch-5 (20 dc, 16 ch-2 sps, 4 ch-7 sps).

Rnd 3: Ch 1, sc in same st, *ch 9, skip next 2 dc, (2 dc, ch 7, sl st in 5th ch from hook, ch 2, 2 dc) in 4th ch of next ch-7, ch 9, skip next 2 dc*, [sc in next dc; repeat between **]; repeat between [ ] around, join with sl st in first sc, fasten off.

Stiffen and finish according to General Instructions. ✂

Gifts & Goodies

Lavish the important people in your life with a heartfelt offering of pretty and practical crocheted treasures that express their individuality and style. Perfect for celebrating special occasions or just to say "I care," beautiful hand-made accessories are lasting reminders of the place someone holds in your heart. Make any day a holiday when you favor a loved-one with something created by you, especially for them.

Simply Sarah

Designed by *Rosemarie Walter*

Size: Dress fits 13" porcelain-look doll.

Materials: Sport yarn — 4 oz. rose; size-10 bedspread cotton — 120 yds. white; 13" porcelain-look doll; 20" piece of ¼" elastic; 12" white ¼" satin picot ribbon; pink ¼" satin ribbon rosebud with leaves; 2 round 6-mm white beads; medium sized safety pin; white sewing thread; sewing and tapestry needles; No. 1 steel and D crochet hooks or size needed to obtain gauge.

Gauge: With **D hook and sport yarn,** 5 dc = 1"; 5 dc rows = 2".

Note: Use D hook and sport yarn unless otherwise stated.

Skill Level: ☆☆ Average

DRESS

Skirt Center Panel

Row 1: Ch 14, dc in 4th ch from hook, dc in each ch across, turn (12 dc).

Rows 2-14: Ch 3, dc in each st across, turn. At end of last row, fasten off.

Skirt Side Panels

Row 1: For **first side,** working in ends of row across one long edge of Center Panel, join with sc in first row, sc in same row, 2 sc in each row across, turn (28 sc).

Row 2: Working this row in **front lps** only, ch 3, dc in each st across, turn.

Rows 3-19: Ch 3, dc in each st across, turn. At end of last row, fasten off.

For **trim,** using No. 1 steel hook and bedspread cotton, working in **back lps** of row 1, join with sc in first st, ch 2, sc in same st, (sc, ch 2, sc) in each st across, fasten off.

For **2nd side,** repeat on opposite long edge of Center Panel.

Bodice

Row 1: Starting at **neckline,** ch 22, sc in 2nd ch from hook, sc in each ch across, turn (21 sc).

Row 2: Ch 1, 2 sc in each st across, turn (42).

Rows 3-7: Ch 1, sc in each st across, turn.

Row 8: Working this row in **front lps** only, ch 1, sc in first 6 sts; for **armhole,** ch 9, skip next 9 sts; sc in next 12 sts; for **armhole,** ch 9, skip next 9 sts, sc in last 6 sts, turn.

Row 9: Ch 1, sc in each st and in each ch across, turn.

Row 10: To **join Bodice and Skirt,** holding pieces right sides together, working through both thicknesses, sl st in each st and in end of each row across easing Center Panel to fit, fasten off.

Sleeves

Rnd 1: Working around one armhole opening, join with sl st in center ch of ch-9, ch 3, dc in next 4 chs, dc in end of next row, 2 dc in **back lp** of each of next 9 sts, dc in end of next row, dc in last 4 chs, join with sl st in top of ch-3 (29 dc).

Rnds 2-8: Ch 3, dc in each st around, join.

NOTE: Using medium-sized safety pin, pin edges of 4½" elastic piece together to form ring.

Rnd 9: Working this rnd over elastic ring (see page 158), ch 1, sc in each st around leaving pinned ends of elastic free, join with sl st in first sc.

Rnd 10: Ch 3, dc in each st around, join with sl st in top of ch-3, fasten off.

Pull both ends of elastic tightly to gather making sure this will fit over hand and snug to arm; overlap ends and sew to secure. Trim ends close to stitching.

Repeat on other armhole.

Sleeve Ruffles

Rnd 1: With No. 1 steel hook and bedspread cotton, join with sl st in any st on rnd 10, ch 4, (dc in next st, ch 1) around, join with sl st in 3rd ch of ch-4.

Rnd 2: Sl st in first ch sp, ch 1, (sc, ch 2, sc) in each ch sp around, join with sl st in first sc, fasten off.

Repeat on other Sleeve.

Bodice Ruffle

Row 1: Working in **remaining lps** of row 7 on Bodice, with right side facing you, with No. 1 steel hook and bedspread cotton, join with sl st in first st, ch 4, dc in same st, *ch 1, (dc, ch 1, dc) in next st; repeat from * across, turn.

Row 2: Sl st in first ch sp, ch 1, (sc, ch 2, sc) in each ch sp across, fasten off.

For **neck trim,** working in starting ch on opposite side of row 1, with wrong side facing you, with No. 1 steel hook and bedspread cotton, join with sc in first st, ch 2, sc in same st, (sc, ch 2, sc) in each st across, fasten off.

Fold ribbon in half, sew to center front of Bodice over row 5. Sew rosebud over fold of ribbon.

For **center back seam,** with tapestry needle and sport yarn, sew lower 18 sts of Skirt Side Panels together.

For **buttonhole placket,** join with sl st in bottom of left back opening, sc in next 9 sts of Skirt, sc in end of next sc row on Bodice; for **buttonhole,** ch 3; sc in end of next 7 rows; for **buttonhole,** ch 3; sl st in end of last row, fasten off.

With sewing needle and thread, sew beads to opposite side of Bodice corresponding to buttonholes.

continued on page 141

Lacy Tissue Cover

Designed by _Michele Wilcox_

Size: Fits standard boutique-style tissue box.

Materials: Worsted-weight yarn — 3½ oz. blue, ½ oz. white and small amount lt. pink; size-3 pearl cotton — small amount each green, dk. pink and yellow; 1 yd. pink ¼" satin ribbon; embroidery and tapestry needles; F crochet hook or size needed to obtain gauge.

Gauge: 9 sc = 2"; 9 sc rows = 2".

Note: Row 1 is wrong side of work.

Skill Level: ☆☆ Average

COVER SIDE (make 4)

Row 1: With blue, ch 19, sc in 2nd ch from hook, sc in each ch across, turn (18 sc).

Rows 2-25: Ch 1, sc in each st across, turn. At end of last row, fasten off.

TOP

Row 1: With blue, ch 19, sc in 2nd ch from hook, sc in each ch across, turn (18 sc).

Rows 2-9: Ch 1, sc in each st across, turn.

Row 10: Ch 1, sc in first 4 sts; for **opening,** ch 10, skip next 10 sts; sc in last 4 sts, turn.

Row 11: Ch 1, sc in each sc and in each ch across, turn.

Rows 12-18: Ch 1, sc in each st across, turn. At end of last row, fasten off.

To **assemble,** matching sts, with blue, sc Sides and Top together forming box. For **trim,** join white with sc in any st, (ch 3, sc in next st) around bottom, Sides and Top.

HEART

Row 1: With pink, ch 2, 3 sc in 2nd ch from hook, turn (3 sc).

Row 2: Ch 1, 2 sc in first st, sc in each st across with 2 sc in last st, turn (5).

Row 3: Ch 1, sc in each st across, turn.

Rows 4-5: Repeat row 2 (7, 9).

Row 6: Repeat row 3.

Row 7: Repeat row 2 (11).

Rows 8-9: Repeat row 3.

Row 10: For **first side,** ch 1, sc in first 5 sts leaving remaining sts unworked, turn (5).

Row 11: Ch 1, sc first 2 sts tog, sc in next st, sc last 2 sts tog, turn, fasten off (3).

Row 10: For **2nd side,** skip next st on row 9, join pink with sc in next st, sc in last 4 sts, turn (5).

Row 11: Repeat same row of first side, **do not** fasten off.

Rnd 12: Working around outer edge, ch 1, sc in each st and in end of each row around with 2 sc in upper corners and 3 sc in tip of heart, join with sl st in first sc, fasten off (34).

For **trim,** join white with sl st in center top st of Heart, (sc, hdc, ch 2, hdc, sc) in next st, *sl st in next st, (sc, hdc, ch 2, hdc, sc) in next st; repeat from * around, join with sl st in first sl st, fasten off.

With dk. pink and yellow, using French Knot (see page 159), embroider flowers according to Embroidery Diagram. With green, using Straight and Lazy Daisy Stitches (see page 159), embroider leaves and stems according to diagram. Sew Heart to one side of box.

EMBROIDERY DIAGRAM

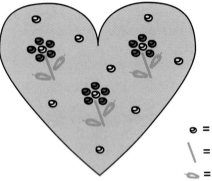

Starting in corner above Heart, weave ribbon through ch sps around top of Cover; tie into a bow on corner. ✄

◉ = **French Knot**

╲ = **Straight Stitch**

◞ = **Lazy Daisy Stitch**

Simply Sarah

continued from page 139

Skirt Ruffle

Rnd 1: Working around bottom of skirt, join with sc in center back seam, 2 sc in end of each row and sc in each st around, join with sl st in first sc.

Rnd 2: Working this rnd in **back lps** only, ch 3, dc in same st, 2 dc in each st around, join with sl st in top of ch-3, fasten off.

Rnd 3: With No. 1 steel hook and bedspread cotton, join with sl st in first st, ch 4, (dc in next st, ch 1) around, join with sl st in 3rd ch of ch-4.

Rnd 4: Sl st in first ch sp, ch 1, (sc, ch 2, sc) in each ch sp around, join with sl st in first sc, fasten off.

For **trim,** working in **front lps** of rnd 1, with No. 1 steel hook and bedspread cotton, join with sc in first st, ch 2, sc in same st, (sc, ch 2, sc) in each ch sp around, join with sl st in first sc, fasten off.

HAT

Rnd 1: Ch 4, 14 dc in 4th ch from hook, join with sl st in top of ch-3 (15 dc).

Rnds 2-3: Ch 3, dc in same st, 2 dc in each st around, join (30, 60).

Rnd 4: Ch 3, dc in each st around, join.

Rnd 5: Repeat rnd 2 (120).

Rnds 6-7: Ch 3, dc in each st around, join.

NOTE: With remaining 11" piece of elastic, overlap ends 1" and sew together to form circle.

Rnd 8: Working over elastic circle (see page 158), ch 1, sc in each st around, join with sl st in first sc.

Rnd 9: Ch 3, dc in each st around, join with sl st in top of ch-3, fasten off.

Ruffle

Rnd 1: With No. 1 steel hook and bedspread cotton, join with sl st in any st, ch 4, (dc in next st, ch 1) around, join with sl st in 3rd ch of ch-4.

Rnd 2: Sl st in first ch sp, ch 1, (sc, ch 2, sc) in each ch sp around, join with sl st in first sc, fasten off. ✄

Hidden Warmth

Designed by *Patricia Hall*

Size: Fits over 11¾" x 14¾" heating pad.

Materials: Worsted-weight yarn — 11 oz. white, 1 oz. red, small amount each green and lt. orange; 3 yds. green ⅜" satin ribbon; tapestry needle; F and G crochet hooks or sizes needed to obtain gauges.

Gauges: With **F hook,** Flower is 2" across. Leaf is 1½" across. With **G hook,** 17 sc = 4"; 4 sc rows = 1".

Skill Level: ☆☆ Average

COVER FRONT

Row 1: With G hook and white, ch 49, 2 sc in 3rd ch from hook, (skip next ch, 2 sc in next ch) across, turn (48 sc).

Rows 2-57: Ch 1, skip first st, 2 sc in next st, (skip next st, 2 sc in next st) across, turn. At end of last row, **do not** turn or fasten off.

Rnd 58: Working in ends of rows and in sts around outer edge, ch 1, sc in side of same st, sc in each row across to last row, skip last row; working in starting ch on opposite side of row 1, 3 sc in first ch, sc in each ch across to last ch, 3 sc in last ch; working in ends of rows, skip first row, sc in each row across to last row, skip last row, 3 sc in next st, sc in each st across to last st, 2 sc in last st, join with sl st in first sc (214 sc).

Rnd 59: Ch 3, *skip next st, (hdc in next st, ch 1, skip next st) across to next 3 corner sts*, [(hdc in next st, ch 1) 3 times; repeat between **]; repeat between [ ] 3 more times, (hdc in next st, ch 1) 2 times, join with sl st in 2nd ch of ch-3.

Rnd 60: Sl st in first ch sp, ch 3, 2 dc in same sp, ch 1, (3 dc in next ch sp, ch 1) around, join with sl st in top of ch-3.

Rnd 61: Ch 3, dc in each of next 2 sts, 2 dc in next ch sp, (dc in each of next 3 sts, 2 dc in next ch sp) around, join, fasten off.

Rnd 62: Join red with sc in any st, sc in each st around, join, fasten off.

COVER BACK

Rows/Rnds 1-59: Work same rows/rnds of Cover Front. At end of last rnd, fasten off.

FLOWER (make 4)

Rnd 1: With F hook and lt. orange, ch 4, sl st in first ch to form ring, ch 1, 10 sc in ring, join with sl st in first sc, fasten off (10 sc).

Rnd 2: Working this rnd in **front lps** only, join red with sc in first st, ch 4, sc in same st, (sc, ch 4, sc) in each st around, join, fasten off.

Rnd 3: Working in **back lps** of rnd 1, join red with sc in first st, ch 5, sc in same st, (sc, ch 5, sc) in each st around, join, fasten off.

LEAF (make 10)

With F hook and green, ch 7, sc in 2nd ch from hook, hdc in next ch, dc in each of next 2 chs, hdc in next ch, 3 sc in end ch; working on opposite side of ch, hdc in next ch, dc in each of next 2 chs, hdc in next ch, sc in last ch, leaving long end for sewing, fasten off.

For **long stem,** with F hook and green, ch 40, sl st in 2nd ch from hook, sl st in each ch across, leaving long end for sewing, fasten off.

For **medium stem** (make 3), with F hook and green, ch 13, sl st in 2nd ch from hook, sl st in each ch across, leaving long end for sewing, fasten off.

For **short stem,** with F hook and green, ch 7, sl st in 2nd ch from hook, sl st in each ch across, leaving long end for sewing, fasten off.

With short stems at bottom and medium stems at top, sew Flowers, Leaves and stems to Front Cover as shown in photo.

Holding Cover Front and Back wrong sides together, with heating pad between, starting at bottom corner and working over heating pad cord, weave ribbon through ch sps of rnd 59; tie ends into a bow. ✄

Ring Bearer's Pillow

continued from page 142

sc) in next st, ch 3, skip next st, sc in next st, (ch 3, sc in next ch sp) 2 times, *ch 3, sc in next st, ch 3, skip next st, (sc, ch 3, sc) in next st, ch 3, skip next st, sc in next st, (ch 3, sc in next ch sp) 2 times; repeat from * around; to **join,** ch 1, hdc in first sc (48 sc, 48 ch sps).

Rnd 7: Ch 1, sc around joining hdc, ch 3, sc in next ch sp, ch 3, (sc, ch 3, sc, ch 5, sc, ch 3, sc) in next ch sp, ch 3, (sc in next ch sp, ch 3) 2 times, (sc, ch 5, sc) in next ch sp, ch 3, *(sc in next ch sp, ch 3) 2 times, (sc, ch 3, sc, ch 5, sc, ch 3, sc) in next ch sp, ch 3, (sc in next ch sp, ch 3) 2 times, (sc, ch 5, sc) in next ch sp, ch 3; repeat from * around, join with sl st in first sc, fasten off.

Sew rnds 1-4 to center of Front.

FINISHING

1: Holding Front and Back wrong sides together, with worsted-weight yarn, sew rnd 33 together, stuffing before closing.

2: Sew stems of 2 ribbon roses to center of Motif.

3: Cut 1/8" ribbon in half. Tie one piece into 2 1/2" bow. Using ends of same bow, tie into another 2 1/2" bow. Repeat with other pieces. Glue or sew each bow to each side of ribbon roses.

4: Cut 1/4" ribbon into 4 pieces each 16" long. Tie each piece into a 3" bow around stem of each remaining ribbon rose, glue in place. Sew each ribbon rose to each corner of Front Border. ✄

Pink Confection

Designed by *Sandra Smith*

Size: 22½" x 69½".

Materials: Pompadour baby yarn — 10 oz. white and 4 oz. pink; adjustable hairpin loom; tapestry needle; C crochet hook or size needed to obtain gauge.

Gauge: 1 shell and 1 sc = 1"; 1 shell row = ½".

Note: Shawl was made using 11 strips. To **make an afghan,** add strips, add length to strips and/or use 4-ply yarn.

Skill Level: ☆☆ Average

STRIP NO. 1
Center

Adjust loom to 1" width. With crochet hook, ch 1 loosely, slide loop off hook and onto right-hand prong of loom (see illustration No. 1). Holding yarn in your right hand, turn loom from right to left so that the yarn passes behind both prongs and ch-1 lp is on opposite prong (see illustration No. 2). Insert crochet hook under front and over back of ch-1 lp, yo, draw lp through, yo, draw through lp on hook (see illustration No. 3). *Turn loom from right to left and sc in next lp in same manner (see illustration No. 4); repeat from * until you have 409 lps on each side. Slide strip off loom, **do not** fasten off. If loom becomes too full, slide all loops off, then thread last 3 or 4 back onto loom and continue working (see illustration No. 5).

Border

Rnd 1: Working around outer edge and keeping one twist in each loop, (ch 3, sc in each lp across to end, ch 3), sc in center of Center on end; repeat between ( ), join with sl st in center sc on end of Center (820 sc, 4 ch-3 sps).

*NOTES: For **beginning shell (beg shell),** (ch 3, 2 dc, ch 2, 3 dc) in same st.*

*For **shell,** (3 dc, ch 2, 3 dc) in next st.*

Rnd 2: Beg shell, skip next ch-3 sp, shell, *skip next 2 sts, sc in next st, skip next 2 sts, shell in next st*; repeat between ** around to next ch-3 sp, (skip next ch-3 sp, shell in next st) 2 times; repeat between ** around to last ch-3 sp, skip last ch-3 sp, join with sl st in top of ch-3, fasten off (140 shells, 136 sc).

HAIRPIN LACE ILLUSTRATION

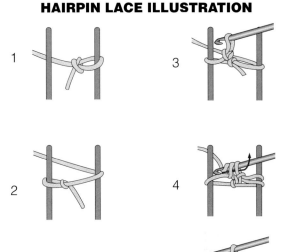

STRIP NO. 2
Center

Work same as Center on Strip No. 1.

Border

Rnd 1: Repeat same rnd of Strip No. 1 Border (820 sc, 4 ch-3 sps).

*NOTE: For **joining shell,** 3 dc in next st, ch 1, sl st in corresponding shell on last Strip made, ch 1, 3 dc in same st.*

Rnd 2: Beg shell, skip next ch-3 sp, shell in next st, (skip next 2 sts, sc in next st, skip next 2 sts, shell in next st) across to next ch-3 sp, skip next ch-3 sp, shell in next st, skip next ch-3 sp, joining shell, (skip next 2 sts, sc in next st, skip next 2 sts, joining shell) across to last ch-3 sp, skip last ch-3 sp, join with sl st in top of ch-3, fasten off.

Repeat Strip No. 2, nine more times for a total of 11 Strips.

TRIM

With wrong side of Shawl facing you, working between Strips, join pink with sl st in joining sl st of first joining shell, *3 tr in next sc between Shells of first Strip, ch 1, sl st in next sc between shells of 2nd Strip, ch 1, 3 tr in same st as first 3-tr group, sl st in joining sl st of next joining shell; repeat from * across length of Strip, fasten off. Work trim between each Strip. ✁

Quick & Easy Slippers

Designed by *Jocelyn Sass*

Size: Instructions given fit 8½" Sole. Changes for 9" and 9½" Soles are in [ ].

Materials: Worsted-weight yarn — 5 [5, 5½] oz. peach and 1 oz. cream; 1½ yds. peach ¼" satin ribbon; tapestry needle; G crochet hook or size needed to obtain gauge.

Gauge: 4 sts = 1"; 3 hdc rows = 1".

Note: Do not join rnds unless otherwise stated. Mark first st of each rnd.

Skill Level: ☆☆ Average

SLIPPER (make 2)
Sole

Rnd 1: With peach, ch 28 [30, 32], 2 sc in 2nd ch from hook, sc in next 13 [14, 15] chs, hdc in each of next 2 chs, dc in next 10 [11, 12] chs, 6 dc in end ch; working on opposite side of ch, dc in next 10 [11, 12] chs, hdc in each of next 2 chs, sc in next 13 [14, 15] chs, 2 sc in last ch (60 sts) [64 sts, 68 sts].

Rnd 2: 2 sc in each of first 2 sts, hdc in next 24 [26, 28] sts, 2 dc in each of next 8 sts, hdc in next 24 [26, 28] sts, 2 sc in each of last 2 sts (72 sts) [76 sts, 80 sts].

Rnd 3: 2 sc in each of first 3 sts, hdc in next 16 [17, 18] sts, skip next st, hdc in next 7 [8, 9] sts, skip next st, (dc in each of next 3 sts, 2 dc in next st) 2 times, 2 dc in each of next 2 sts, (dc in each of next 3 sts, 2 dc in next st) 2 times, skip next st, hdc in next 7 [8, 9] sts, skip next st, hdc in next 16 [17, 18] sts, 2 sc in last st (78) [82, 86].

Rnd 4: Working this rnd in **back lps** only, sc in each st around.

Rnd 5: Sc in each st around, join with sl st in first sc, fasten off.

Top

Rnd 1: Join peach with sl st in center back of heel on narrow end of Sole, ch 2, hdc in next 26 [28, 30] sts, (dc next 2 sts tog) 12 times, hdc in last 27 [29, 31] sts, join with sl st in top of ch-2 (66) [70, 74].

Rnd 2: Ch 2, hdc in each st around, join.

Rnd 3: Ch 2, hdc in next 18 [20, 22] sts, (dc next 2 sts tog) 13 times, hdc in last 21 [23, 25] sts, join (53) [57, 61].

Rnd 4: Ch 2, hdc in each st around, join.

Rnd 5: Ch 2, hdc in next 19 [21, 23] sts, (dc next 2 sts tog) 5 times, hdc in last 23 [25, 27] sts, join (48) [52, 56].

Rnd 6: Ch 2, hdc in each st around, join.

Rnd 7: Ch 1, sc in first st, ch 1, skip next st, (sc in next st, ch 1, skip next st) around, join with sl st in first sc (24 ch-1 sps) [26 ch-1 sps, 28 ch-1 sps].

Rnd 8: Ch 1, sc in each sc and in each ch-1 sp around, join, **turn,** fasten off.

Ruffle

Rnd 1: With wrong side of rnd 8 on Top facing you, working in **back lps** only, join cream with sl st in center back st, ch 3, skip next st, (2 dc, ch 2, 2 dc) in next st, skip next st, *dc in next st, skip next st, (2 dc, ch 2, 2 dc) in next st, skip next st; repeat from * around, join with sl st in top of ch-3.

*NOTE: For **front post** (**fp**—see page 159), yo, insert hook from front to back around post of next st on rnd before last, yo, draw lp through, (yo, draw through 2 lps on hook) 3 times, skip next st on last rnd.*

Rnd 2: Ch 1, fp around first ch-3, (3 dc, ch 2, 3 dc) in next ch sp, skip next 2 dc, *fp around next dc, (3 dc, ch 2, 3 dc) in next ch sp, skip next 2 dc; repeat from * around, join with sl st in top of first fp.

Rnd 3: Ch 1, fp around first fp, (3 dc, ch 2, 3 dc) in next ch sp, *fp around next fp, (3 dc, ch 2, 3 dc) in next ch sp; repeat from * around, join, fasten off.

For **ankle trim,** working in **front lps** of rnd 8 on Top, join peach with sl st in any st, sl st in each st around, join with sl st in first sl st, fasten off.

For **Sole trim,** with Sole facing you, working in **front lps** of rnd 3, work same as ankle trim.

Cut ribbon in half. Starting at **front of Slipper,** weave one piece through ch sps of rnd 7 on Top, bring ends up through Ruffle; tie into a bow.

Repeat on other Slipper. ✂

Elegant Accessories

Designed by *Jocelyn Sass*

Sizes: Jewelry Bag is 4" tall when closed. Sachet is 5" across. Cover fits 17" wide plastic hanger.

Materials For One Set: 100% cotton 3-ply sport yarn — 6 oz. blue and 2 oz. white; 2 yds. blue ¼" satin ribbon; ½ yd. white ⅜" satin picot ribbon; 1 yd. white 3.5-mm satin cord; ½ yd. white satin fabric; ⅔ cup potpourri; clothespins; craft glue or hot glue gun; white sewing thread; sewing and tapestry needles; E crochet hook or size needed to obtain gauge.

Gauge: 5 dc = 1"; 3 dc rnds = 1".

Notes: For **beginning shell (beg shell),** ch 3, (dc, ch 2, 2 dc) in same st or sp.

For **shell,** (2 dc, ch 2, 2 dc) in next st or sp.

For **beginning V-stitch (beg V-st),** ch 6, dc in same st or sp.

For **V-stitch (V-st),** (dc, ch 3, dc) in next st or sp.

Skill Level: ☆☆ Average

Jewelry Bag

BAG

Rnd 1: Starting at **bottom,** with blue, ch 4, 11 dc in 4th ch from hook, join with sl st in top of ch-3 (12 dc).

Rnd 2: Ch 4, (dc in next st, ch 1) around, join with sl st in 3rd ch of ch-4 (12 dc, 12 ch sps).

Rnd 3: Sl st in first ch sp, beg shell, shell in each ch sp around, join with sl st in top of ch-3.

Rnd 4: Sl st in next dc, sl st in ch sp of same shell, beg shell, shell in ch sp of each shell around, join.

Rnd 5: Sl st in next dc, sl st in ch sp of same shell, beg shell, ch 1, (shell in next shell, ch 1) around, join (12 shells, 12 ch-1 sps).

Rnd 6: Sl st in next dc, sl st in ch sp of same shell, beg shell, ch 2, skip next ch-1 sp, (shell in next shell, ch 2, skip next ch-1 sp) around, join.

Rnd 7: Sl st in next dc, sl st in ch sp of same shell, ch 3, (2 dc, ch 2, 3 dc) in same sp, ch 2, skip next ch-2 sp, *(3 dc, ch 2, 3 dc) in next shell, ch 2, skip next ch-2 sp; repeat from * around, join.

Rnd 8: Sl st in each of next 2 dc, sl st in next ch-2 sp, ch 3, (2 dc, ch 2, 3 dc) in same sp, ch 3, skip next ch-2 sp, *(3 dc, ch 2, 3 dc) in next ch-2 sp, ch 3, skip next ch-2 sp; repeat from * around, join.

Rnd 9: Sl st in each of next 2 dc, sl st in next ch-2 sp, ch 3, (2 dc, ch 2, 3 dc) in same sp, shell in next ch-3 sp, *(3 dc, ch 2, 3 dc) in next ch-2 sp, shell in next ch-3 sp; repeat from * around, join.

Rnd 10: Sl st in each of next 2 dc, sl st in next ch-2 sp, ch 3, (2 dc, ch 2, 3 dc) in same sp, ch 1, shell in next shell, ch 1, *(3 dc, ch 2, 3 dc) in next ch-2 sp, ch 1, shell in next shell, ch 1; repeat from * around, join.

Rnd 11: Sl st in each of next 2 dc, sl st in next ch-2 sp, ch 3, (2 dc, ch 2, 3 dc) in same sp, *ch 2, skip next ch-1 sp, shell in next shell, ch 2, skip next ch-1 sp*, [(3 dc, ch 2, 3 dc) in next ch-2 sp; repeat between **]; repeat between [ ] around, join.

Rnd 12: Sl st in each of next 2 dc, sl st in next ch-2 sp, ch 3, (2 dc, ch 2, 3 dc) in same sp, *ch 3, skip next ch-2 sp, shell in next shell, ch 3, skip next ch-2 sp*, [(3 dc, ch 2, 3 dc) in next ch-2 sp; repeat between **]; repeat between [ ] around, join.

Rnd 13: Sl st in each of next 2 dc, sl st in next ch-2 sp, beg shell, shell in each ch-3 sp, in each ch-2 sp and in each shell around, join (48 shells).

Rnds 14-15: Repeat rnd 5.

Rnd 16: Repeat rnd 6.

Rnd 17: Sl st in next dc, sl st in ch sp of same shell, beg shell, ch 3, skip next ch-2 sp, *shell in next shell, ch 3, skip next ch-2 sp; repeat from * around, join.

Rnd 18: Ch 3, dc in each dc, dc in each ch-2 sp and 2 dc in each ch-3 sp around, join (336).

Rnd 19: Ch 3, dc in each st around, join.

Rnd 20: Ch 1, sc in same st, ch 3, skip next 2 sts, (sc in next st, ch 3, skip next 2 sts) around, join with sl st in first sc, fasten off (112 ch sps).

Rnd 21: For **trim,** join white with sl st in any ch sp, beg V-st, ch 1, sc in next ch sp, ch 1, *V-st in next ch sp, ch 1, sc in next ch sp, ch 1; repeat from * around, join with sl st in 3rd ch of ch-6 (56 V-sts, 56 sc).

Rnd 22: Sl st in ch sp of same V-st, ch 5, (dc, ch 2) 4 times in same sp, *skip next 2 ch-1 sps, sc in ch sp of next V-st, ch 2, skip next 2 ch-1 sps*, [(dc, ch 2) 5 times in ch sp of next V-st; repeat between **]; repeat between [ ] around, join with sl st in 3rd ch of ch-5, fasten off.

For **lining,** cut two circles from satin fabric each 12¼" across. Holding both pieces right sides together, using ¼" seam, hand or machine stitch around outer edge leaving opening for turning. Turn right side out, stitch opening closed. Place lining on wrong side of Bag centered over rnds

continued on page 152

Elegant Accessories

continued from page 151

1-18. Tack in place around outer edge and to center over rnd 1. Weave satin cord through sps between shells on rnd 17.

For **rosette** (make 2), with white, ch 14, 2 dc in 4th ch from hook, 3 dc in each ch across, fasten off. Roll into shape, tack in place.

Sew one rosette to each end of cord. Pull ends to gather; tie into a bow.

Sachet

FRONT
Rnd 1: With blue, ch 6, sl st in first ch to form ring, ch 3, 23 dc in ring, join with sl st in top of ch-3 (24 dc).

Rnd 2: Ch 1, sc in same st, ch 4, skip next 2 sts, (sc in next st, ch 4, skip next 2 sts) around, join with sl st in first sc (8 ch sps).

Rnd 3: Sl st in first ch sp, beg shell, ch 2, (shell in next ch sp, ch 2) around, join.

Rnd 4: Sl st in next dc, sl st in ch sp of same shell, beg shell, ch 4, skip next ch-2 sp, (shell in next shell, ch 4, skip next ch-2 sp) around, join.

Rnd 5: Sl st in next dc, sl st in ch sp of same shell, beg shell, ch 5, skip next ch-4 sp, (shell in next shell, ch 5, skip next ch-4 sp) around, join.

Rnd 6: Ch 1, sc in same st, sc in each dc, sc in each ch-2 sp and 4 sc in each ch-5 sp around, join with sl st in first sc, fasten off (72).

Rnd 7: For **trim,** working this rnd in **front lps** only, join white with sl st in any st, beg V-st, ch 1, skip next st, sc in next st, ch 1, skip next st, *V-st in next st, ch 1, skip next st, sc in next st, ch 1, skip next st; repeat from * around, join with sl st in 3rd ch of ch-6 (18 V-sts).

Rnd 8: Repeat rnd 22 of Jewelry Bag on page 151.

BACK
*NOTE: For **liner,** cut two circles from satin fabric each 4¼" across. Holding both pieces right sides together, hand or machine stitch ¼" seam around outer edge leaving opening for turning. Turn right side out, fill with potpourri and stitch opening closed.*

Rnds 1-6: Repeat same rnds of Sachet Front. At end of last rnd, **do not** fasten off.

Rnd 7: To **join,** hold Front and Back wrong sides together, matching sts of rnd 6, working through both thicknesses, in **back lps** of Front and in **both lps** of Back, ch 1, sl st in each st around inserting liner before closing, join with sl st in first sl st, fasten off.

Hanger Cover

SIDE (make 2)
Rnd 1: With blue, ch 4, sl st in first ch to form ring, ch 3, 11 dc in ring, join with sl st in top of ch-3 (12 dc).

Rnd 2: Ch 3, dc in same st, 2 dc in each st around, join (24).

Rnds 3-8: Ch 3, dc in each st around, join.

Rnd 9: Ch 3, dc in next 6 sts, 2 dc in next st, (dc in next 7 sts, 2 dc in next st) around, join (27).

Rnds 10-11: Repeat rnd 3.

Rnd 12: Ch 3, dc in next 7 sts, 2 dc in next st, (dc in next 8 sts, 2 dc in next st) around, join (30).

Rnd 13: Beg shell, skip next 2 sts, (shell in next st, skip next 2 sts) around, join with sl st in top of ch-3 (10 shells).

Rnds 14-21: Sl st in next dc, sl st in ch sp of same shell, beg shell, shell in each shell around, join.

Rnds 22-23: Sl st in next dc, sl st in ch sp of same shell, beg shell, ch 1, (shell in next shell, ch 1) around, join.

Rnds 24-25: Sl st in next dc, sl st in ch sp of same shell, beg shell, ch 2, (shell in next shell, ch 2) around, join. At end of last rnd, leaving long end for sewing, fasten off. Wrap blue ¼" ribbon around hook of hanger, gluing as you work. Let dry. Slip Cover Sides onto hanger. Matching shells, sew together around rnd 25.

TRIM
Row 1: With white, ch 5, dc in 4th ch from hook, dc in last ch, turn (3 dc).

Rows 2-106: Ch 3, dc in each of last 2 sts, turn. At end of last row, **do not** turn.

Row 107: Working in ends of rows across one long edge, ch 1, sc in first row, (ch 3, sc in next row) across, turn (105 ch sps).

Row 108: Sl st in first ch sp, beg V-st, (ch 1, sc in next ch sp, ch 1, V-st in next ch sp) across, turn (53 V-sts).

Row 109: Sl st in ch-3 sp of beg V-st, ch 5, (dc, ch 2) 4 times in same sp, skip next 2 ch-1 sps, sc in ch-3 sp of next V-st, ch 2, *(dc, ch 2) 5 times in ch-3 sp of next V-st, skip next 2 ch-1 sps, sc in ch-3 sp of next V-st, ch 2; repeat from * across to last V-st, dc in ch-3 sp of last V-st, (ch 2, dc) 4 times in same sp, fasten off.

Glue rows 1-106 around outside of Hanger Cover on Back, easing at curves. Hold in place with clothespins until dry. Tie white picot ribbon into a bow around base of hook. ✄

Needles & Pins

Designed by *Denise Cheek*

Size: 7½" across.

Materials: Worsted-weight yarn — 2½ oz. white; 48" blue ⅛" satin ribbon; 8 small spools thread (assorted colors); polyester fiberfill; blue sewing thread; tapestry needles; G crochet hook or size needed to obtain gauge.

Gauge: 4 dc = 1"; 2 dc rows = 1".

Note: Use one strand yarn and one strand blue thread from large spool held together throughout.

Skill Level: ☆☆ Average

TOP

Rnd 1: Ch 5, sl st in first ch to form ring, ch 3, 11 dc in ring, join with sl st in top of ch-3 (12 dc).

Rnd 2: Ch 3, dc in same st, 2 dc in each st around, join (24).

Rnd 3: Ch 3, 2 dc in next st, (dc in next st, 2 dc in next st) around, join (36).

Rnd 4: Ch 3, dc in next st, 2 dc in next st, (dc in each of next 2 sts, 2 dc in next st) around, join (48).

Rnd 5: Ch 3, dc in each of next 2 sts, 2 dc in next st, (dc in each of next 3 sts, 2 dc in next st) around, join (60).

Rnd 6: Working this rnd in **back lps** only, ch 3, dc in each st around, join.

Rnds 7-8: Ch 3, dc in each st around, join. At end of last rnd, fasten off.

BOTTOM

Rnds 1-5: Repeat same rnds of Top. At end of last rnd, fasten off.

RUFFLE

Rnd 1: To **join,** holding Top and Bottom wrong sides together with top facing you, working through both thicknesses in **back lps** only, join with sc in first st, sc in each st around stuffing firmly before closing, join with sl st in first sc (60 sc).

Rnd 2: Ch 3, dc in each of next 3 sts, 2 dc in next st, (dc in next 4 sts, 2 dc in next st) around, join (72).

Rnd 3: Ch 3, dc in same st, 2 dc in each st around, join, fasten off (144).

FINISHING

1: Cut ribbon into 8 pieces each 6" long. For **each bow,** starting with first st of each rnd, [*wrap one piece of ribbon around st of rnd 3 on Ruffle and st of rnd 7 on Top; tie ends into a bow*; skip next 17 sts of rnd 3 on Ruffle and skip next 6 sts of rnd 7 on Top; repeat between ** in next st, skip next 17 sts of rnd 3 on Ruffle and skip next 7 sts of rnd 7 on Top]; repeat between [ ] around.

2: With 18" strand yarn, (pull through center of small spool, then weave behind Ruffle under bow) around, placing small spools in pockets on Ruffle between bows as shown in photo, tie into a knot to secure. Pull knot inside first small spool to hide.

3: For **center shaping,** using tapestry needle and 6" strand yarn, starting at **bottom,** (draw needle up through center to Top, secure, bring down through center) 2 times, pull tight, tie into a knot to secure. ✄

Rosebud Bed Jacket

Designed by *Ceil Cummings*

Size: Fits up to 16" neckline.

Materials: Sport-weight yarn — 6 oz. white; 6 lt. pink med. satin roses; 2 yds. lt. pink ⅜" satin ribbon; white sewing thread; sewing and tapestry needles; F crochet hook or size needed to obtain gauge.

Gauge: 5 dc = 1"; 5 dc rows = 2".

Skill Level: ☆☆ Average

JACKET

NOTE: Ch-2 is not used or counted as a stitch.

Row 1: Ch 82, dc in 4th ch from hook, dc in each ch across, turn (80 dc).

Row 2: Ch 2, dc in same st, dc in each st across, turn.

Row 3: Ch 2, dc in same st, dc in next st, (2 dc in next st, dc in next st) across, turn (119).

Row 4: Ch 2, dc in same st, (2 dc in next st, dc in next st) across with dc in last st, turn (178).

Row 5: Ch 2, dc in same st, dc next 2 sts tog, dc in each st across, turn (177).

*NOTE: For **front post (fp**—see page 159), yo, insert hook from front to back around post of next st, yo, draw lp through, complete as dc.*

Row 6: Ch 2, dc in same st, dc in next st, fp around next st, (dc in each of next 3 sts, fp around next st) 43 times, dc in each of last 2 sts, turn (44 fp, 133 dc).

Row 7: Ch 2, dc in same st, dc in next st, fp around next fp, (dc in each of next 3 sts, fp around next fp) 7 times, *[dc in next st, 2 dc in next st, dc in next st, fp around next fp]; repeat between ( ); repeat between [ ] 2 times; repeat between ( ); repeat between [ ]*; repeat between ( ) 8 more times; repeat between [ ]; repeat between ( ) 8 more times; repeat between **; repeat between ( ) 7 more times, dc in each of last 2 sts, turn (44 fp, 142 dc).

Row 8: Ch 2, dc in same st, dc in each dc and fp around each fp across, turn.

Row 9: Ch 2, dc in same st, dc in next st, fp around next fp, (dc in each of next 3 sts, fp around next fp) 7 times, *[dc in next st, 2 dc in next st, dc in each of next 2 sts, fp around next fp]; repeat between ( ); repeat between [ ] 2 times; repeat between ( ); repeat between [ ]*; repeat between ( ) 8 more times; repeat between [ ]; repeat between ( ) 8 more times; repeat between **; repeat between ( ) 7 more times, dc in each of last 2 sts, turn (44 fp, 151 dc).

Row 10: Ch 2, dc in same st, dc in each dc and fp around each fp across, turn.

Row 11: Ch 2, dc in same st, dc in next st, fp around next fp, (dc in each of next 3 sts, fp around next fp) 7 times, *[dc in each of next 2 sts, 2 dc in next st, dc in each of next 2 sts, fp around next fp]; repeat between ( ); repeat between [ ] 2 times; repeat between ( ); repeat between [ ]*; repeat between ( ) 8 more times; repeat between [ ]; repeat between ( ) 8 more times; repeat between **; repeat between ( ) 7 more times, dc in each of last 2 sts, turn (44 fp, 160 dc).

Row 12: Ch 2, dc in same st, dc in each dc and fp around each fp across, turn.

Row 13: Ch 2, dc in same st, dc in next st, fp around next fp, (dc in each of next 3 sts, fp around next fp) 7 times, *[dc in each of next 3 sts, 2 dc in next st, dc in each of next 2 sts, fp around next fp]; repeat between ( ); repeat between [ ] 2 times; repeat between ( ); repeat between [ ]*; repeat between ( ) 8 more times; repeat between [ ]; repeat between ( ) 8 more times; repeat between **; repeat between ( ) 7 more times, dc in each of last 2 sts, turn (44 fp, 169 dc).

Row 14: Ch 2, dc in same st, dc in each dc and fp around each fp across, turn.

Row 15: Ch 2, dc in same st, dc in next st, fp around next fp, (dc in each of next 3 sts, fp around next fp) 7 times, *[dc in each of next 3 sts, 2 dc in next st, dc in each of next 3 sts, fp around next fp]; repeat between ( ); repeat between [ ] 2 times; repeat between ( ); repeat between [ ]*; repeat between ( ) 8 more times; repeat between [ ]; repeat between ( ) 8 more times; repeat between **; repeat between ( ) 7 more times, dc in next st, 2 dc in last st, turn (44 fp, 179 dc).

Row 16: Ch 1, sc in first st, (ch 3, skip next 2 sts, sc in next st) across, turn (74 ch sps, 75 sc).

Row 17: Ch 1, sc in first st, ch 3, (sc in next ch sp, ch 3, 3 dc in next ch sp, ch 3) across to last st, sc in last st, turn.

Row 18: Ch 1, sc in first st, ch 3, (sc in next ch sp, ch 3) across to last st, sc in last st, turn.

Row 19: Ch 2, 3 dc in first ch sp, (ch 3, sc in next ch sp, ch 3, 3 dc in next ch sp) across, turn.

Rows 20-32: Repeat rows 18 and 19 alternately, ending with row 18. At end of last row, fasten off.

Row 33: Working in starting ch on opposite side of row 1, for **neck shaping,** join with sc in first ch, sc in each ch across, turn (80).

Row 34: Ch 1, sc in each st across, turn, fasten off.

EDGING

*NOTE: For **picot,** ch 3, sc in 2nd ch from hook, ch 1.*

Working around outer edge of Jacket, with right side facing you, starting at **neck edging,** join with sc in first st, sc in next st, picot, evenly spacing around, work pattern of (sc in each of next 2 sts or rows, skip next st or row, picot) around, join with sl st in first sc, fasten off.

FINISHING

1: Cut 20" piece of ribbon, weave through row 3 of Jacket, sew ends to Jacket to secure.

2: Weave remaining ribbon through row 2 of Jacket, leaving 12" on each end loose for ties.

3: Sew 3 roses each 1½" apart over end of each front on Jacket.

4: For **lapels,** turn back and sew each edge of neck to Jacket. ✂

Yarn & Hooks

Always use the weight of yarn specified in the pattern so you can be assured of achieving the proper gauge. It is best to purchase extra of each color needed to allow for differences in tension and dyes.

The hook size stated in the pattern is to be used as a guide. Always work a swatch of the stitch pattern with the suggested hook size. If you find your gauge is smaller or larger than what is specified, choose a different size hook.

Gauge

Gauge is measured by counting the number of rows or stitches per inch. Each of the patterns featured in this book will have a gauge listed. Gauge for some small motifs or flowers is given as an overall measurement. Proper gauge must be attained for the project to come out the size stated, and to prevent ruffling and puckering.

Make a swatch in the stitch indicated in the gauge section of the instructions. Lay the swatch flat and measure the stitches. If you have more stitches per inch than specified in the pattern, your gauge is too tight and you need a larger hook. Fewer stitches per inch indicates a gauge that is too loose. In this case, choose a smaller hook size. Next, check the number of rows. If necessary, adjust your row gauge slightly by pulling the loops down a little tighter on your hook, or by pulling the loops up slightly to extend them.

Once you've attained the proper gauge, you're ready to start your project. Remember to check your gauge periodically to avoid problems later.

Pattern Repeat Symbols

Written crochet instructions typically include symbols such as parentheses, asterisks and brackets. In some patterns a diamond or bullet (dot) may be added.

( ) Parentheses enclose instructions which are to be worked again later or the number of times indicated after the parentheses. For example, "(2 dc in next st, skip next st) 5 times" means to follow the instructions within the parentheses a total of five times. If no number appears after the parentheses, you will be instructed when to repeat further into the pattern. Parentheses may also be used to enclose a group of stitches which should be worked in one space or stitch. For example, "(2 dc, ch 2,

2 dc) in next st" means to work all the stitches within the parentheses in the next stitch.

* Asterisks may be used alone or in pairs, usually in combination with parentheses. If used in pairs, the instructions enclosed within asterisks will be followed by instructions for repeating. These repeat instructions may appear later in the pattern or immediately after the last asterisk. For example, "*Dc in next 4 sts, (2 dc, ch 2, 2 dc) in corner sp*, dc in next 4 sts; repeat between ** 2 more times" means to work through the instructions up to the word "repeat," then repeat only the instructions that are enclosed within the asterisks twice.

If used alone an asterisk marks the beginning of instructions which are to be repeated. Work through the instructions from the beginning, then repeat only the portion after the * up to the word "repeat"; then follow any remaining instructions. If a number of times is given, work through the instructions one time, repeat the number of times stated, then follow the remainder of the instructions.

[ ] Brackets, ◊ diamonds and • bullets are used in the same manner as asterisks. Follow the specific instructions given when repeating.

Finishing

Patterns that require assembly will suggest a tapestry needle in the materials. This should be a #16, #18 or #26 blunt-tipped tapestry needle. When stitching pieces together, be careful to keep the seams flat so pieces do not pucker.

Hiding loose ends is never a fun task, but if done correctly, may mean the difference between an item looking great for years or one that quickly shows signs of wear. Always leave 6-8" of yarn when beginning or ending. Thread the loose end into your tapestry needle and carefully weave through the back of several stitches. Then, weave in the opposite direction, going through different strands. Gently pull the end and clip, allowing the end to pull up under the stitches.

If your project needs blocking, a light steam pressing works well. Lay your project on a large table or on the floor, depending on the size, shaping and smoothing by hand as much as possible. Adjust your steam iron to the permanent press setting, then hold slightly above the stitches, allowing the steam to penetrate the thread. Do not rest the iron on the item. Gently pull and smooth the stitches into shape, spray lightly with starch and allow to dry completely.

Stiffening

There are many liquid products on the market made specifically for stiffening doilies and other soft items. For best results, carefully read the manufacturer's instructions on the product you select before beginning.

Forms for shaping can be many things. Styrofoam® shapes and plastic margarine tubs work well for items such as bowls and baskets. Glass or plastic drinking glasses are used for vase-type items. If you cannot find an item with the dimensions given in the pattern to use as a form, any similarly sized item can be shaped by adding layers of plastic wrap. Place the dry crochet piece over the form to check the fit, remembering that it will stretch when wet.

For shaping flat pieces, corrugated cardboard, Styrofoam® or a cutting board designed for sewing may be used. Be sure to cover all surfaces of forms or blocking board with clear plastic wrap, securing with cellophane tape.

If you have not used fabric stiffener before, you may wish to practice on a small swatch before stiffening the actual item. For proper saturation when using conventional stiffeners, work liquid thoroughly into the crochet piece and let stand for about 15 minutes. Then, squeeze out excess stiffener and blot with paper towels. Continue to blot while shaping to remove as much stiffener as possible. Stretch over form, shape and pin with rust-proof pins; allow to dry, then unpin.

Skill Level Requirements:

★ *Easy* — Requires knowledge of basic skills only; great for beginners or anyone who wants quick results.

★ ★ *Average* — Requires some experience; very comfortable for accomplished stitchers, yet suitable for beginners wishing to expand their abilities.

★ ★ ★ *Advanced* — Requires a high level of skill in all areas; average stitchers may find some areas of these patterns difficult, though still workable.

★ ★ ★ ★ *Challenging* — Requires advanced skills in both technique and comprehension, as well as a daring spirit; some areas may present difficulty for even the most accomplished stitchers.

For More Information

Sometimes even the most experienced needlecrafters can find themselves having trouble following instructions. If you have difficulty completing your project, write to:

Private Collection Editors
The Needlecraft Shop
23 Old Pecan Road
Big Sandy, Texas 75755

Our sincere thanks and appreciation go to the following for graciously providing their services in the making of the photographs for the chapter openings in this book:

Kitchen Charm: Model—Kepen Gilliam; photographed at the home of Kepen & Robin Gilliam.

Family Comforts: Models—Rush, Alexandrea, Korey & Taylor Shirley; photographed at the home of Ruth & Bill Whitaker.

Beautiful Baby: Model—Michaela Hutchins; photographed at the home of Mike & Jill Hutchins.

Sun-Kissed Gardens: Model—Susannah Ramsey; photographed at the home of Donna Robertson.

Playful Pets: Models—Blake Rohus & Jenny the Cat; photographed at the home of Fran Rohus.

Christmas Splendor: Models—Greg, Nancy, Caleb & Graham Traylor; photographed at The Needlecraft Shop Photography Studio, Big Sandy.

Gifts & Goodies: Model—Chrispen French; photographed at The Season's Best (Mineola, TX), Ruth Judge/Nell French.

Basic Stitches

Front Loop (a)/Back Loop (b)
(front lp/back lp)

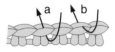

Chain (ch)
Yo, draw hook through lp.

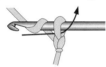

Slip Stitch (sl st)
Insert hook in st, yo, draw through st and lp on hook.

Single Crochet (sc)
Insert hook in st (a), yo, draw lp through, yo, draw through both lps on hook (b).

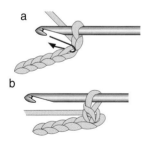

Half Double Crochet (hdc)
Yo, insert hook in st (a), yo, draw lp through (b), yo, draw through all 3 lps on hook (c).

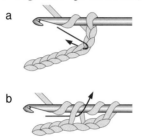

Double Crochet (dc)
Yo, insert hook in st (a), yo, draw lp through (b), (yo, draw through 2 lps on hook) 2 times (c and d).

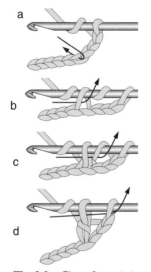

Treble Crochet (tr)
Yo 2 times, insert hook in st, yo, draw lp through, (yo, draw through 2 lps on hook) 3 times.

Final Step

Double Treble Crochet (dtr)
Yo 3 times, insert hook in st, yo, draw lp through, (yo, draw through 2 lps on hook) 4 times.

Final Step

Triple Treble Crochet (ttr)
Yo 4 times, insert hook in st, yo, draw lp through, (yo, draw through 2 lps on hook) 5 times.

Final Step

Changing Colors

Single Crochet Color Change
(sc color change)
Drop first color; yo with 2nd color, draw through last 2 lps of st.

Double Crochet Color Change (dc color change)
Drop first color; yo with 2nd color, draw through last 2 lps of st.

Standard Stitch Abbreviations

ch(s)	chain(s)
dc	double crochet
dtr	double treble crochet
hdc	half double crochet
lp(s)	loop(s)
rnd(s)	round(s)
sc	single crochet
sl st	slip stitch
sp(s)	space(s)
st(s)	stitch(es)
tog	together
tr	treble crochet
tr tr	triple treble crochet
yo	yarn over

Decreasing

Single Crochet next 2 stitches together
(sc next 2 sts tog)
Draw up lp in each of next 2 sts, yo, draw through all 3 lps on hook.

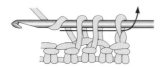

Half Double Crochet next 2 stitches together
(hdc next 2 sts tog)
(Yo, insert hook in next st, yo, draw lp through) 2 times, yo, draw through all 5 lps on hook.

Double Crochet next 2 stitches together
(dc next 2 sts tog)
(Yo, insert hook in next st, yo, draw lp through, yo, draw through 2 lps on hook) 2 times, yo, draw through all 3 lps on hook.

Special Stitches

Front Post/Back Post Stitches
(fp/bp)
Yo, insert hook from front to back (a) or back to front (b) around post of st on indicated row; complete as stated in pattern.

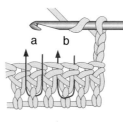

Afghan Knit Stitch

Knit #1

Knit #2

Knit #3

Knit #4

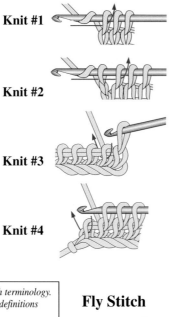

Reverse Single Crochet
(reverse sc)
Working from left to right, insert hook in next st to the right (a), yo, draw through st, complete as sc (b).

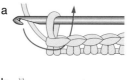

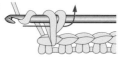

Sc Over Wire

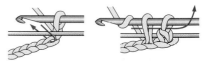

Whipstitch
is used to join two or more pieces together.

Backstitch

The patterns in this book are written using American crochet stitch terminology. For our international customers, hook sizes, stitches and yarn definitions should be converted as follows:

US		= UK
sl st (slip stitch)	=	sc (single crochet)
sc (single crochet)	=	dc (double crochet)
hdc (half double crochet)	=	htr (half treble crochet)
dc (double crochet)	=	tr (treble crochet)
tr (treble crochet)	=	dtr (double treble crochet)
dtr (double treble crochet)	=	ttr (triple treble crochet)
skip	=	miss

Thread/Yarns
Bedspread Weight	=	No.10 Cotton or Virtuoso
Sport Weight	=	4 Ply or thin DK
Worsted Weight	=	Thick DK or Aran

Measurements
1"	=	2.54 cm
1 yd.	=	.9144 m
1 oz.	=	28.35 g

Crochet Hooks	
Metric	**US**
.60mm	14
.75mm	12
1.00mm	10
1.50mm	6
1.75mm	5
2.00mm	B/1
2.50mm	C/2
3.00mm	D/3
3.50mm	E/4
4.00mm	F/5
4.50mm	G/6
5.00mm	H/8
5.50mm	I/9
6.00mm	J/10

But, as with all patterns, test your gauge (tension) to be sure.

Fly Stitch

French Knot

Lazy Daisy Stitch

Outline Stitch

Straight Stitch

Satin Stitch

Index